TOWERS FOR THE WELFARE STATE

TOWERS FOR THE WELFARE STATE

An Architectural History of British Multi-storey Housing 1945–1970

Stefan Muthesius and Miles Glendinning
Photographic consultant: Nicholas Warr

THE **SCOTTISH**
C E N T R E
FOR CONSERVATION **STUDIES**

First published 2017
by the Scottish Centre for Conservation Studies
Minto House, 20 Chambers Street, Edinburgh EH1 1JZ, Scotland

The Scottish Centre for Conservation Studies is part of the
University of Edinburgh.

British Library Cataloguing in Publication Data
A catalogue record of this book is available from the British Library
ISBN: 978-1-9999205-2-4 (pbk)

Printer: Page Bros, Norwich
Typesetter: Emily Benton
Publication co-ordinator: Ruxandra-Iulia Stoica

Distribution: S. Muthesius AMA
University of East Anglia, Norwich, NR4 7TJ
s.muthesius@uea.ac.uk

THE **SCOTTISH**
C E N T R E
FOR CONSERVATION **STUDIES**

THE UNIVERSITY *of* EDINBURGH
Edinburgh College of Art

Contents

Acknowledgements

First of all our thanks go to the University of East Anglia for making available its research facilities, above all the expertise of Dr. Nicholas Warr, Curator of the Photographic Collections of the School of Art History and World Art Studies (AMA). We are also very grateful to the University of Edinburgh for its help with financing the type-setting.

Crucial was the kindness of Emap (Architectural Press) and the *Municipal Journal,* and of many other journals, in allowing us to use their illustrations.

Our further thanks are due to the libraries, archives and local studies centres at Birmingham, Bristol, Enfield, Hackney, Leeds, Liverpool, Newcastle upon Tyne, Norwich (the Archive of the Library of the University of East Anglia, Curator Bridget Gillies, with extensive holdings on tower block history), Nottingham, Portsmouth (John Stedman), Sheffield and Southampton. Above all we are grateful to the London Metropolitan Archives, the Library of the Institute of Civil Engineers, and, of course, ever helpful, the Library of the Royal Institute of British Architects; last but not least, our thanks are due to the Art and Architecture Library of Cambridge University.

Special thanks also go to R.A. Bage, Timothy Brittain-Catlin, Philip Boyle (DOCOMOMO-UK), Katherine Breen, Barnabas Calder, Daniel Chitson, Ellen Creighton, Catherine Croft (The 20th Century Society), Hannah Garrow, Elin Jones, Hans-Curt Köster, Bianca Lee, Manfred Mückstein, Michał Murawski, Michael Wood, Dorothea Muthesius, Katarzyna Murawska-Muthesius, Alan Powers, Philip Steadman, Ruxandra-Iulia Stoica, Paul Thompson and Michael Wood.

The material in this book is extensively complemented by the free-access 'TOWER BLOCK UK' database, a project supported by the Heritage Lottery Fund and hosted at the Scottish Centre for Conservation Studies: www.towerblock.eca.ed.ac. uk This database provides information and illustrations on all post-war multi-storey public housing blocks in the UK. The data it contains is derived from the Gazetteers in our 1994 book, *Tower Block – Modern Public Housing in England, Scotland, Wales and Northern Ireland* (which can also now be downloaded free from the database). That work supplements the present book in its chapters on state and municipal patronage in Section II, as well as on aspects of planning and social policy.

Norwich | Edinburgh Autumn 2017

Preface

The starting point of this book is a basic definition of the post-Second World War Welfare State, namely the assumption that public authorities should provide what the private sector was deemed unable to provide, or not able to provide at the right standards. 'Improvement' in the post-war years was synonymous with innovation. This included the fields of town planning, architecture and construction, and especially the sphere of housing. The book begins by introducing the innovators, state and municipal, especially the latter, and their teams of experts, the architects, engineers and builders. It then goes on to discuss the new rationale for building high, with all the associated innovations in planning, construction and environmental design, whether formal-aesthetic, practical and constructional, or symbolic. Finally, the story of towers in any given place is principally the story of that particular municipality and its desire to innovate and impress.

COVER
Glasgow, Townhead, St. Mungo Drive, 1967, seen here from the City Centre.

FRONTISPIECE
London, Swedenborg Gardens, Stepney E1. Stockholm House with Shearsmith House behind, 1968–72; with 28 floors the latter is the highest of the blocks designed by the architects of the Greater London Council. Photo early 1970s (cf. p. 47).

LEFT
Birmingham, Durham Tower, Summerhill Street, 1968 (cf. p. 188).

The estate in 1962.

The vision of 1957.

A distant view towards central London in 1961.

Brawne House today.

LONDON BRANDON ESTATE

Hillingdon Street, Southwark, SE17. Planned from 1954/5, designed in 1956 and completed in late 1960, this London County Council estate represented the first major effort to clear a large area of old housing in an inner suburb (although the project became known also for the way it rehabilitated some of the larger Victorian terraces). Density 136 persons per acre. LCC architect in charge Edward Hollamby; engineers F.J. Samuely and Partners, builders Wates. The construction combines cross walls with in situ and precast framework and prefabricated panels for the external walls. Each of the 16 main floors contains four two-bedroom flats. (cf. p. 46, 83). The planned building cost of each flat, at £3,200, was more than double that of a five-roomed house. The additions on the top contain four penthouse flats. 'Fear of monotony' led to the unusual formalist division of the elevation into four zones. A contemporary summary: 'an economical fusion of structural and architectural aspects'.

PART ONE – THE PROVIDERS

1 'Power symbols of the Welfare State'

Difficult as it is to imagine today, until 1960 the skies over Britain's cities had remained almost entirely un-scraped. The London height limit was 100 feet, or 30 metres, a maximum of ten or eleven storeys. A few of the most recent offices and private blocks of flats in the capital had reached twelve storeys, or very exceptionally a few more, while the London County Council had experimented with eleven-storey tower flats, but none of these structures could be characterised as skyscrapers, as they made no real impact beyond their immediate surroundings. And even during 1960 the first real office skyscrapers, London's Vickers (now Millbank) Tower and the CIS Tower in Manchester, both just over 100 metres high, were still far from complete.

However, one might put into the race at this point the first group of major council towers, the London County Council's Brandon Estate in Southwark, planned from 1955 and completed during 1960. While their eighteen storeys reached only 52 metres (or 170 feet), the sheer number of the blocks, six of them, made an enormous impact. Hardly a year later Westminster City Council's Hide Place (or Hide Tower), 68 metres and 23 storeys high, was reaching completion. Soon London public housing landmarks of 23 storeys or more were no rarity, while by the early 1970s in exceptional cases the height of council dwellings rose to 31, with Trellick Tower in London and the Red Road development in suburban Glasgow, and to 32 storeys, in the case of the Sentinels in central Birmingham; with their height of over 90 metres, these public housing tower blocks could almost match the highest office blocks in the land.

'The Welfare State's first major addition to the new power symbols of the Metropolis' – so we read in the *Architects' Journal* about the Brandon Towers in 1961, in an extensive appraisal written, quite possibly, by the editor, London's premier architectural critic, J.M. Richards; for him the blocks were landmarks dominating the 'decaying and formless mass of south London'.[1] There was no doubt that this estate suited precisely Richards' image of a 'modern city' and in particular that of a new 'High London', which he himself had conjured up a few years before.[2] There must have been a climate of keen expectations in those years, the excitement of knowing that tall buildings were about to become a reality. Initiated mainly by the housing architects of the London County Council, the years

1956 to 1960 saw an intense debate about tall buildings of all kinds which concentrated on their overall shape, their siting and their grouping and on the impact on their surroundings – a discussion to be taken up below in Chapter Eight.

But who exactly was going to live in these Welfare State towers? The primary definition of the new 'Welfare State' in our context appears a simple one: it referred to the state and, above all, the municipalities, as providers of 'social services'. They were to supply many of those services which the private sector was deemed to have provided either badly or not at all. Crucial was the striving for Modernity in all fields. Quality service meant modernised service. Secondly, and most boldly and innovatively, with the post-1945 Welfare State there was no selection of the recipients; every citizen was entitled in like measure to receive the same services, and that, according to historian Rodney Lowe, 'at a standard well above the barest minimum'. The flagships of this new British Welfare State were the National Health Service, followed by education. Historians of the post-World War II welfare state have devoted rather less space to the history of housing and their verdict is less straightforward, even though the basics appear clear: 'The third major achievement under the classic welfare state was housing'. Through the decades, so argued Lowe, 'the quality of housing rose sharply' and 'the absolute shortage of housing was eradicated' – while market solutions, when they were tried, had been 'failures'. On the other hand, there had also been problems with public housing; the high-rise 1960s are invariably singled out as a special phase, and Lowe's conclusion at that point is: 'a vigorous housing policy did not automatically ... resolve social problems. It could, and often did, actually intensify them'.[3]

A precise characterisation of public housing as to who was to occupy it is a more complicated matter. Charitably built housing for a very limited number of lower class citizens had been known for centuries. Non-profit-making blocks of flats in towns had been built from the 1840s and 'council housing' on a large scale, that is partly state-financed house building by local authorities, had begun in 1918. The recipients aimed for were clearly those who could not afford the rents in the private market for an equivalent dwelling. But there were always problems with the precise designation of this kind of housing.

London, Lambeth Council Offices, 1970.

It was never clear to what extent public housing should serve the very poor or destitute. For the pre-1918 blocks of flats the frequently used label was 'artisans' dwellings', denoting the upper strata of the working class. Another much used term was 'working class housing', but it was less precise, as it was also used for small dwellings of any kind.[4]

From World War II onwards, several factors contributed to a far sharper rise in public concern for the 'housing problem': the extent of war destruction, especially in London; the coupling of housing issues with town planning issues; and the growing boldness of those planners and their visions of the post-war world. Echoing the Swedish concept of the 'folkhem' as universal social provision, 'housing' was now seen as an issue that should transcend class barriers. In 1949 the legislators duly took the decisive step and stripped the term housing of the designation 'working class'; in Scotland the previously universal term 'housing scheme' was increasingly frowned on as class-stigmatised. Clearly, all this can be understood as an echo of initiatives, like the health reforms, that were to benefit the whole of the population. In practice, though, problems of class stratification remained. In 1957 Margaret Willis, a sociologist employed by the LCC felt she had to admonish architects to be aware of their inevitably middle class background.[5]

In purely practical terms, in day to day decisions, the question as to whom the new 'council dwellings' were built for can be answered very precisely: they were to serve the applicants on the local authority's housing waiting list. Like the wait for a hospital place, the wait on the housing list could be a long one. But beyond that there were striking differences. Each municipality was legally obliged merely to investigate the state of housing in its town – though this would normally imply a need to build new housing. This could then be dubbed 'general needs housing'. But whereas the hospitals had to treat all comers, there was no compulsion for the Council to house everybody, or even to even give everybody a place on the waiting list. Conversely, the applicant, when offered a dwelling, did not have to accept it and could try and make a case for a more suitable one.

A most complex procedure had developed. Basically, prospective tenants had to be 'acceptable'. The Manager could decline the offer of 'a tenancy to a person or family on the grounds that they are known or likely to be bad tenants ... The applicant's suitability ... is usually judged by a visit to his present accommodation ... tidiness and cleanliness...', whereby 'trained housing assistants can distinguish between untidiness and dirt due to adverse conditions, and that which is due to poor standards of home care.' A similar attitude applied to examining the applicant's financial situation. When slum clearing increased from the mid-1950s onwards, it must have become more difficult to decide who or what was to be blamed for poor standards. A general notion was that slum dwellers simply had to be rehoused, but there was still much vagueness about it, such as in the stipulation: 'it was the authority's 'statuary duty to give reasonable preference to families living in insanitary or overcrowded conditions'.

Upper floor views in an unidentified (London?) block, 1963.

As might be expected, there was no shortage of encouraging words regarding management- tenant relationships. John P. Macey was England's most eminent housing manager, having served as chief official for both Birmingham and London County Councils; in his words 'good management may be defined as the application of skill in caring for the property ... and in developing a sound relationship between landlord and tenant, and between the tenants themselves ...' At the end of his long book *Housing Management* of 1965 it turns out that all matters discussed so far about the nature of tenant-management relationships really applied to houses and that a separate chapter had to be devoted to 'High Density Housing – Special Problems'. To begin with, 'the cost of maintenance and management for multi-storey flats ... is roughly double the figure for houses'. 'And certainly,' staffs have a good deal more supervision to do in high flats'; 'resident caretakers are most desirable'. There is a hint here that it is not all a matter of a simple getting used to the novelty of it all. 'As a background to all these physical changes, there is the change in mental environment when a family goes to live among new neighbours in entirely new surroundings'.[6]

Finally, at the same time there were notions, in the context of a comprehensive understanding of the function of the Welfare State, that local authorities should also provide dwellings at the opposite end of the scale, for the strata above the level of the 'deserving' classes, to be let at 'cost rent'. In the end, such council housing remained a rarity in Britain (cf. p. 116). Even in London, by 1962 the proportion of those dwellings was

estimated at no more than 5%,[7] by far the best known example being the City of London's Barbican Estate, a housing group that was council-built but did not serve as social housing.

'Progress' and 'modernity' were key values for a new council housing estate and for a new hospital alike. But the differences between the two provisions, again, were striking. The hospital buildings, and the therapies offered within them, having been tested extensively, were deemed to be completely trustworthy, and the cure of an illness thus marked the complete end of a process. Housing provision, by contrast, was always something ongoing. Tenants could not be expected to fit precisely into their new abodes in every case. Aware of this, the designers of dwellings constantly tried new models. A large new public hospital building always fulfilled its practical aims without controversy and thereby its purely architectural-visual qualities never played a major role; the principal visual message was simply cleanliness. Newness and cleanliness were important messages sent out by the council flats as well. But a tower could also be understood as something that goes beyond practical purpose, to appear as an architectural manifestation, in the narrower sense of that term, as well as a visual marker of a very specific kind of political aspiration.

2 Standards, numbers, costs

Modern kitchen in a Leeds council dwelling, 1964.

'The chief joy of a Post war house or flat is the bathroom and kitchen', wrote Britain's premier authority in all matters of public housing design, A.W. Cleeve Barr, in 1958.[1] The present book deals with the external qualities of the new dwellings; yet above all it was the amenities inside the flats that seemed to be the primary desire for all concerned. The 1950s was still a time when the vast majority of small older houses were devoid of modern bathing facilities, and when a proper bathroom might be lacking even in council dwellings less than two decades old.[2] Post-World War II provisions inside the dwelling aimed to go along with new technologies of all kinds and to fit out the dwellings with as many of the new, fixed, built-in furnishings as possible. 'Every thought has been put into providing maximum comforts for the tenant': such was the doubtless council-inspired comment in the *Municipal Review* in 1960, regarding a new multi-storey block in Newcastle's 15-storey Scotswood Road redevelopment.[3] A few years later the Housing Manager of Portsmouth City Council presented, as a response to criticisms of recent council housing voiced in the local newspaper, a list of fittings in a typical new municipal multi-storey block of 21 storeys, which had just been built by Wimpey, one of the foremost builders of public housing:

- underfloor heating
- double-glazed windows
- separate WC and bathroom
- fitted wardrobe in bedrooms
- fitted cupboards
- stainless steel sink
- laminated working tops in kitchens
- immersion heater
- electric drying cabinet
- car park[4]

Left page: From the *Municipal and Public Services Journal*, 1969.

Less pressing, but equally significant, were considerations of dwelling size. Local-authority councillors and designers were convinced that 'internal space standards in British municipal housing are without peer'.[5] But this was rather too simplistic a statement. The benchmark for assessing floor-space was a three-bedroomed standard suburban house. Most pre-1950 council houses measured around 1000 square feet, or 93 square metres. Rooms in flats, it was stressed, 'should be much the same as in houses'.[6] However, the years around 1949–51 brought an appreciable reduction of sizes, down to 900 square feet, or 84 square metres, for the average council dwelling. The principal reason given was financial savings, in order to accelerate overall production. But this reasoning also went along with new kinds of analyses of the standard house type, criticising the frequent inflexibility of traditional modes of use, especially the frequent underuse of some of the rooms.[7] As regards another important measure, the height of rooms, the 1950s brought a slight lowering, from 8 feet plus to 8 feet (2.44 metres) or even to a figure of slightly less than 8 feet.[8]

In 1961 the Government's comprehensively conceived booklet, *Homes for Today and Tomorrow* (also called the 'Parker Morris Report', after its parent committee's chairman, Sir Parker Morris), reduced recommended floor spaces in England and Wales even further, to 750 square feet, or 70 square metres for a four-person dwelling. The Parker Morris space standards became mandatory for all new council dwellings only from 1969 to 1980. Inevitably, laments could be registered at most times, such as in 1956: 'housing standards have steadily fallen since the war and costs have risen'.[9] Clearly, once again, all these measures were taken principally to increase output. However, to see it all simply as part of an inevitable problem of all low-rental provision, as the 'problem quantity vs. quality' (Nicholas Bullock)[10] could be simplistic.

The Report carefully explored all dwelling types with regard to suggesting more precise ways of fitting plans to use in each case; size as such was not the only issue. Crucial was another measure, that of the rate of occupancy; in 1966 this was 0.88% per habitable room in council housing, which was relatively close to the figure of 0,67% for private housing;[11] the figure at which overcrowding was held to begin was put at 1.3 persons per room.

Beyond these simple statistics one has to take account of the much increased number of the types of dwellings built by local authorities, ranging from bungalows for the aged, two-storey and three-storey houses, in themselves ranging from two to five bedrooms, to maisonettes with two bedrooms or three bedrooms, as well as flats of a wide range of shapes and sizes. The Government housing design handbook, *Flats and Houses 1958* proposed more than a dozen kinds of dwellings. The 'mixed development' formula, to be discussed in Chapter Nine, was precisely an attempt to offer an optimal selection. During the 1960s, new kinds of complex, high or medium-density 'conglomerates' of dwellings contained a vast range of combinations of houses and flats, and the number of possibilities became uncountable.

Impressive by any standards was the overall quantitative result of the mighty 'national building effort'. From 1945 to the end of 1969 over 4.1 million public dwellings were built, which comprised 59% of total housing production, thus exceeding private sector building. In the interwar period the proportion of publicly built homes had been a 'mere' 28% – although even this was a very high figure when compared with the output of most other countries. The result was that the proportion of local authority-rented dwellings among the total of homes in Britain was rising to a peak of 30 per cent.[12] Naturally, official and semi-official pronouncements in this matter almost always stressed the need to build even more. For instance, in 1962 the Minister of Housing, Sir Keith Joseph, claimed that six million new dwellings were still needed during the next twenty years.[13] By the end of that decade, however, more satisfied voices were heard, saying, for instance, that 'the crude national housing shortage should be over in five years' time',[14] or even hinting that, by 1973, there might be a surplus.[15] The great factor of uncertainty concerned the number of older dwellings that still had to be demolished.

The principal issue in the statistics of the post-World War II decades is the proportion of flats to houses, and in particular the proportion of high blocks. The total figure of council dwellings built up to 1979 was just under five million, of which well over three million were houses. A further one million were built as walk-up flats, many of them in Scotland, following the time-honoured tenement tradition. That left about 400,000 flats in blocks of six storeys and over. Excluding from these the inhabitants of the four lowest floors, amounting to perhaps 100,000, as well as the inhabitants of the maisonette type of flat, especially in London, which was claimed to preserve some of the feel of a two-storey house, the number of flats high up would total, very roughly speaking, around 300,000. Finally, of the total of 400,000 flats in all high blocks, 11%, or roughly 45,000, were situated in blocks containing 20 storeys and over, with Scotland and London showing the greatest concentration of them. The average height of the remainder of the high blocks can be estimated at around 11 storeys.[16] Thus, in the end, the number of dwellers living at what one might characterise as great height remained quite small.

All the more intense, however, were the arguments as to who should want to live in flats, who would actually prefer a flat to a house. As will be explained in Chapter 9 on the planning of flats, it was precisely those who planned the first high blocks, the LCC designers of the early 1950s, who also stressed the need for at least a small number of houses in every new estate. At no time did commentators in England depart from the maxim that families with young children ought to be allocated houses rather than flats, or, if not a flat, then at least a maisonette; and there was a strong awareness of cases where that rule was being broken. But there was also a strong faction that went further, especially within the Garden City Association, whose leader, the planner-propagandist Frederic Osborn, maintained in 1956 that only five to ten per cent of the population would opt for a flat.[17] On the opposite side, one may say, was J P Macey, Birmingham's Housing Manager, perhaps nationally the most experienced, and certainly the most respected figure in his profession, who, in 1959, put the figure of those preferring houses at 80%.[18] By 1968, during the period of the greatest adversity to high flats, the Institute of Housing Managers held that '10 per cent will live willingly in high flats'.[19] These statements were usually not specific as regards the height of the block. In the end one might venture the following very simple assessment of the building-types of public housing, namely that the total of 10 per cent of high flats actually built during those decades corresponded quite closely to what had been desired or required by the tenants.

England was an exceptional country, where flats were dearer to build than houses, a fact that many remarked on, but for which a really plausible explanation was never forthcoming.[20] Concerning the costs of tall buildings, there was even greater imprecision. In 1960, Sir Robert Matthew, an undoubted expert on all aspects of public housing and one-time principal architect at the LCC, confessed that 'singularly little is known about the cost of tall buildings'.[21] Thus more approximate estimates had to serve instead. Among English commentators, one rule-of-thumb was that if a house costs £1,500 to build, the amount needed for the equivalent flat would be nearly double that figure.[22] High blocks of maisonettes were somewhat cheaper than high flats in towers. Implicitly, so to speak, general costs were going up because high blocks contained a growing proportion of small dwellings, all of which needed the same set of expensive service installations. There was a good number of further variables. It made a great deal of difference, for instance, whether a lift served four, six or eight flats. In other cases, costs could be driven up by rising land prices. Besides, there were the high prestige or prototype cases, such as the pioneering Brandon flats that came in at around £3200 apiece; Birmingham's Sentinels had been planned to cost £4000 each, while the Greater London Council's 31-storey Trellick Tower, Westminster, marked the very top, with each dwelling costing £4654.[23]

In other words, modern housing could not come cheap. But very rarely was the issue put bluntly: 'somebody had to pay for all this'. The fact was that in the case of providing new flats for the inhabitants of the slums and older rented accommodation generally, it was the tenants' pockets that were tapped first of all. In the North of England some occupants of old properties were said to have been paying a fifteenth of their income in rent, whereas in their new council dwellings they had to part with an eighth. In Birmingham rents were said to have jumped even further, from a twentieth of income for a slum property to a sixth in new council dwellings.[24] Admonitions from government agencies regarding public expenditure on housing often sounded ambivalent. The key government design manual, *Flats and Houses 1958,* continuously oscillates: 'The basic aim is to ensure value for money, but this is by no *means* necessarily the same as lowest initial costs, for the architect will rightly aim to evolve economical designs of the highest quality out of the many possible ways of meeting the requirements ...'[25] In response to some newspaper criticisms of recent council dwellings in Portsmouth, the City's Housing Officer, whom we cited at the beginning of this chapter, summed it all up before the Housing Committee: 'This is what the public has a right to expect because Local Authority Housing is a social service as well as a large business enterprise'.[26]

3 The Welfare State providers

The Queen's visit to Wickham House, in 1962, part of the LCC's Stifford Estate, Stepney, London E1 (cf. p. 73).

The great post-war consensus

The actual building of most post-war public housing in Britain was undertaken by the municipalities, which were legally empowered and financially aided by central government to do so. These interactions, and the ways in which councils set about their massive task, will be discussed in the next chapter. But neither level of government could have acted with the fervour it did, had there not been the encouragement of the breadth and depth of the post-war Welfare State consensus. This spanned from the highest styles of rhetoric to the plethora of individual professional commitments. 'Rebuilding Britain', no less, was the aim and housing was its principal component. As the *Daily Mail Book of Post-war Homes* of 1944 declared, "HOUSING" – what an enormous field of future joint endeavour, responsibility, scientific application and hope that one simple word implies to-day'.[1] This kind of monumentally simple rhetoric continued into the 1950s, certainly at the top political level, as for instance when Harold Macmillan, the Housing Minister from 1951 to 1955, quoted his Prime Minister, Winston Churchill, with the catchphrase, 'work, food, homes'.[2] More detailed exhortations were given by Macmillan's predecessor, the socialist Minister of Health, Aneurin Bevan, who saw housing as an integral part of the new social services, and for whom the lack of good housing was 'responsible not only for a great deal of domestic infidelity but also for a great deal of neurosis in modern society'.[3] As we shall see, Bevan actually sided with the avant-garde of architects and planners, advocating high blocks of flats even in suburban surroundings. All subsequent English

housing ministers, including Duncan Sandys, Keith Joseph and Richard Crossman, together with their equivalents in Scotland, were agreed on the vast number of new dwellings still needed at each stage.

The breadth of support for this agenda was indicated in the Parker Morris Report's appendix, listing towns visited and institutions and agencies consulted, around 50 in each case. There were the central government's own research groups, such as the Building Research Station as well as the Ministry of Housing's Research and Development Group, active from 1956. But the majority of agencies were professional and voluntary organisations, such as the obvious ones, like the Society of Housing Managers. Casting the net more widely, the Report called upon the prestigious Royal Society of Health as well as lesser-known business-sponsored agencies, such as the British Refrigeration Association, or the short-lived Women's Gas Federation. Naturally, membership of these groups overlapped, and some of the principal protagonists kept moving between the numerous bodies, whether state, municipal or voluntary, such as London County Councillor Evelyn (later Baroness) Denington, or the architect A.W. Cleeve Barr. The latter was probably the most influential agent of all in the design field, having been involved with the Hertfordshire School programme, from where he joined the LCC Architects' Department, to end up as an official of central government, personifying the archetypal 'official' architect whose outlook oscillated, in Alan Powers's words, 'between mechanist and humanist philosophies, between efficiency and compassion'.[4]

In their accompanying discourses the professions were often mixing self-advertisement with self-exhortation in a very particular way, such as the *Architects' Journal* writing in a leader in 1946: '... it is clear that the architect will have to shoulder the pioneering work in establishing new codes'.[5] There was, however, also a very material reason for pursuing this particular rhetoric with regard to public housing, namely the fact that, until the mid -1950s, central government was severely restricting almost all other kinds of building projects, including private housing. A celebrated case of the architectural profession's actual fight for recognition within a local authority, the LCC, will be related in chapter Five. In any case, the prevailing common spirit resulted in a constant stream of lectures and discussions which formed the bedrock of the profession's self-understanding. The length of those perorations is almost unimaginable today. Most of them were published verbatim in the professional journals; to cite just one of the RIBA's lectures, entitled 'The Organisation of the Building Industry and the Architect's Responsibilities. Discussion on the Papers by Sir Thomas Bennett K.B.E. [F (RIBA)] and Mr. D.E. Woodbine Parish, Past President of the London Master Builders' Association' ... 'the President in the Chair ...'; the conference was printed in its entirety, taking up 13 pages in the Institute's monthly journal.[6] Any research into British public housing of the period needs to consult a seemingly unlimited number of periodicals. For architecture one must turn to over half a dozen major journals, three of them appearing weekly, with countless serials serving the more technical branches of construction. There were a number of journals entitled 'Housing', almost entirely devoted to public housing. Town planning was covered by three journals. Other periodicals were purely commercial undertakings, such as the *Surveyor* and the *Municipal Journal,* both weeklies – with only the latter still going strong, the principal organs for all matters urban. Both journals recorded new housing projects, largely based on the information given to them directly by the councils, which meant that buildings were not usually selected according to any architectural kind of ranking. Also, and importantly, unlike the architectural journals, the *Municipal Journal* and the *Surveyor* did not operate a London bias.

Town planners and sociologists

An essential underpinning of the great consensus was provided by the discourses conducted by two groups which comprised both academics and practitioners: the town planners and the sociologists. 'We must plan well' was one of the battle-cries of the later war years, conjuring up a future happy and well-ordered, indeed, a completely re-ordered, country.[7] Up to that time, 'town planning' had been understood principally as a set of restrictions, regulating what kind of building was to be allowed where. Now an act of planning was meant to set out a positive course of action.[8] To determine the nature of a site, the density and the size of a new housing project, the city or borough architect was to co-operate closely with the city or borough planner, as well as with the housing manager. Indeed, in some towns some or all of these municipal posts might have

been completely new creations, as before 1945 the physical shape of the great majority of towns had been administered through their technical and financial services, those of the borough surveyor or borough engineer and the rent collector. To begin with, a 'plan' was now visualised by means of lavishly drawn proposals, of which Abercrombie's sumptuous *County of London Plan* of 1943 was the best known example. It appeared at exactly the right moment and thus made an enormous impact, especially with its plans for multi-storey housing blocks situated in ample parkland.[9] During the same years Birmingham's City Engineer, Herbert Manzoni, produced similarly-inspired and even grander schemes for his city.

By no means all of these grand intentions stayed on paper. For their advocates, modernist planning and modernist architecture appeared to be one and the same thing. Many of the most eminent personalities in town planning theory and practice, such as Sir Patrick Abercrombie or Robert Matthew, had in fact been trained as architects. Britain's post-war New Towns developed with astonishing rapidity, especially the group around London. Already by 1950 substantial completed parts of Harlow New Town could be admired – including a tower block, all of it the work of the architect-planner Sir Frederick Gibberd. The other large-scale undertaking which involved the planners was slum-clearance. Previous campaigns of this kind had been limited to small pockets of the worst kinds of housing. With new, greatly extended powers for expropriation, local-authority planners began from the mid-1950s to deal with vast tracts of urban land, calling them Comprehensive Redevelopment Areas (CDA). The most publicised examples of Modernist slum-clearance could be found in London's East End and in Glasgow's Gorbals. What re-emerged in those areas usually bore no relationship at all to previous street layouts and building patterns, and regularly included two new elements: ample greenery and high blocks.

From the war years onwards another key word proliferated in architectural pronouncements: 'social', which, like 'planning', always entailed a promise of a better society. In fact, for a time, the two terms became almost interchangeable; 'planning is now primarily a social ... activity'.[10] One could also attach the term 'social' to the buildings themselves: 'a house group is an architectural cum social form'.[11] When Berthold Lubetkin, one of the most noted Modernist practitioners, active in Finsbury's public housing, was asked, late in his life, what he meant by 'marching shoulder to shoulder with the working classes', his simple answer was 'good architecture'.[12]

Naturally, no town or group of homes could be 'planned' without knowing in advance who was going to live there. Increasingly, the process of inquiry was called housing sociology. Sociology as a discipline had been on the rise since at least the early 1900s. Throughout the decades, it remained strongly allied to social reform. After the War the profession received a further substantial boost; it was not surprising when, in 1946, a planner claimed that the 'sociologist is universally recognised as part and parcel of the local team ... with duties not unlike those of the Medical Officer of Heath.'[13] – even though not many such appointments have become known. In 1957, Margaret Willis, 'Sociologist to the London County Council', provided a convenient summary of the ways in which she could assist the architect of new housing projects. First came demography for the initial planning stage – knowing the number, size and composition of households for any given project. Beyond that, the sociologist could inform the architect about all aspects of the future inhabitants' 'physical, mental and emotional well-being', which could help, for instance, in planning heating provision.[14] However, as with town planning, many, if not most architects believed that they were more than capable of dealing with all these issues by themselves. 'Taking up the post of City Architect in Norwich in 1955, I taught the housing manager sociology', remembered David Percival – incoming, as he was, from Coventry, one of the most renowned city planning offices at the time.[15]

Two key concepts dominated the debates of the planners and the sociology-minded designers: 'neighbourhood', used mainly by the former, and 'community', the catchword of the latter group. Both terms carried a strong social-reformist ring. Of the two, 'neighbourhood' had a more practical and administrative ring, dealing with questions of population size, the issues of allocating schools and shopping centres to a district, and all matters of traffic layout. The concept of community one may see as a complement to practical planning, relating more to the inhabitants' mental faculties, their feelings regarding togetherness, or its absence; it was usually concerned with smaller groups of dwellings, with an estate, or with sections within an estate. Again, as most housing architects saw themselves perfectly capable of dealing with the technical aspects of town planning, they likewise felt competent to respond to all demands to create a 'community feeling': it was held to stem directly from their layouts and designs in a more narrowly architectural sense: 'architecture [is] an expression (or even the expression) of community life'.[16]

Whether or not the specific terms 'community' or neighbourhood were used, these concepts were clearly derived from a long tradition of utopianist thinking. By 1950 some English housing architects, especially within the London County Council, were propagating a new formula that seemed to them to promise cohesion and contentment, a formula which they called 'mixed development'. As with all architectural utopias, this idea appeared very straightforward: every estate should allocate dwellings for a variety of occupants, from young to old, from single people to large families. But what was new was that this 'mixing' now also implied a strong diversity of dwelling types, ranging from the bungalow via the row-house

and the low block of flats to the tower block: in fact, the latter was almost a 'must' in such a context. Occasionally it was claimed that even smaller units of housing could contribute to the hoped-for sense of togetherness. According to the Central Housing Advisory Committee's report, *Living in Flats*, in 1952, 'large blocks of flats, to a greater extent than any streets of houses, may have the effect of creating some sort of community sense among the occupiers'.[17]

Undoubtedly 'planning' and 'sociology' were terms which could lend authority to any pronouncement about housing, as there seemed to be a morally-charged inevitability about them. They manifested the kinds of conviction which underpinned all new ventures in planning and design, including blocks of flats, and high blocks in particular. For the Modernist town planner these types of buildings would help greatly with the general functioning of a populous town, and they would create room for ample healthy greenery in particular. For the modern sociologist a close togetherness of people could not be anything other than a positive factor. One may thus conclude that these two groups, together with their adherents in the design professions, provided an expert, even academic underpinning for the buildings reported in this book. In the early to mid-sixties this continuing consensus was joined by another powerful panacea, that of the new technologies, including those generated by commercial building firms; all these enthusiasms, in combination, were held to be capable of propelling society forward faster than ever before. The great spate of high blocks in the 1960s can be seen as the last fruit of these convictions.

And yet, by the mid-1960s, some of those professionals had already begun to go their own ways once again. Town planners stayed largely within the technical sphere. Academic sociology, including 'housing sociology', was undergoing a profound change: instead of preaching, in the spirit of social reform, how inhabitants should live, a new more strictly empirical approach was emerging, which favoured the investigation of groups of people, and groups of dwellings, as they existed. Very soon this could result in a view that communities could be happier in a built environment that had specifically not been 'planned', technically or sociologically, that had simply grown during long periods of time, and which could, for that reason be considered visually attractive, too.[18] New understandings of 'urban' and the new term 'townscape' marked values that departed from the older values of 'town planning' or 'community'. A profound distrust of the 'new' had begun to set in. The great post-war consensus did not seem to apply any more, the unison of fervour with regard to public housing had begun to disappear.

4 Council Powers: Organising and financing post-war public housing

London, Stafford Cripps Estate, Gee Street, Old Street, EC1, 1951–53. The Labour politician Cripps died in 1952. At the time the three blocks were the highest in the country.

The British term for public housing may seem a peculiar one. However, 'council housing' pinpoints the actual authority which, in almost every case, took the decision to erect a group of dwellings. Although it was central government which initiated major campaigns of public housing through Acts of Parliament, which legitimised the local authorities in making their decisions, and supported them with advice and subsidies or loans. The term 'council housing' reminds us constantly that the actual decision making bodies were the Councils, made up of the local councillors, aldermen and bailies, who had been elected by the citizens, and who then realised the work through the support of salaried local-authority experts directly accountable to them. Indeed, in Britain, it was the municipalities who had organised their public welfare systems long before the central state's social undertakings had coalesced.

In this respect, Britain very much went its own way. In France and most other western European countries it was arms-length bodies which organised cheap housing, in the Soviet bloc it was a plethora of central state departments. In most countries there was actually a strong distrust of allowing local authorities to become the direct prime-movers in the field, with the occasional exception, such as mighty 'Red Vienna' in the 1920s. But Britain was unique in giving local municipal authorities the lead role in the national 'housing drive', allowing them to plan, build and manage large social housing stocks. Partly, this stemmed from the longstanding traditions of civic pride and municipal

power, especially in poor relief, to which, gradually, other areas, such as education, health, power infrastructure and transport had been added.[1]

Between its large-scale launch in 1919 and the start of the Second World War, the council housing system had achieved remarkable output figures, hardly matched in any other country. Across Britain as a whole, it accounted for 28% of all new housing built in 1919–39, even though all this was paralleled in England by strong government efforts to encourage mass home-ownership by lower-middle-income families. In Scotland, council housing had begun to establish an even more dominant position, which would become even more entrenched after 1945.[2]

FIRST MAN IN WAS MINISTER

Top left: Aneurin ('Nye') Bevan, Labour Minister of Health (which included housing) opens a new block in Shoreditch, London in 1950.
Top right: A rushed Richard Crossman, Labour Minister of Housing and Local Government, inspecting Bison blocks in Cumbernauld in 1965.
Left: Dame Evelyn Sharp (from 1968 Baroness Sharp) served in the Ministries of Health and Town Planning and later in the Ministry of Housing and Local Government until the 1960s.

Central government, local authorities

In terms of party politics, the dominant initial post-World War II political context was provided by the Labour government of 1945–51, which left welfare-state socialism as, in some ways, the default ethos of post-war reconstruction. But council housing, in conjunction with encouragement of home ownership, continued to burgeon thereafter under the Conservatives and Labour alike, in England and Wales. In post-war Scotland, the position was rather different. Here, council housing, and the Labour Party, became hugely dominant, with only localised pockets of homeownership.

At a local level, however, political differences were not a matter of Labour versus Conservative. Indeed, the Conservative (or, in Scotland, Unionist) Party was not generally organised at local level in most cities outside London, but instead the non-socialists took the form of ratepayer groups, under such names as Moderates, Progressives, or Independents. Labour normally

operated in a more unified and organised way, which allowed them generally to take the initiative, with the Progressives often providing support in a consensual way behind the scenes. Local political controversies were not usually concerned with policy matters such as housing output but, rather, with scandals or symbolic conflicts. More important than party politics was the competition between the different council committees, each defending and expanding its own fiefdom: in general, the Housing Committee became one of the most important committees in any large local authority in the post-war period, and its activities often took on a life of their own, setting out to defend its power against that of other, 'predator' committees, such as the planning committee.[3]

So what was the role of central government within this system? Firstly, there never was a single dedicated state authority for housing – as indicated by the fact that housing was dealt with in conjunction with health, and, for a time in England, administered under the Ministry of Housing and Local Government,

Bradford, opening ceremony at
York House multi-storey block, 1957.

a wording that is telling in itself. In Scotland, where housing was a devolved area, administered by the 'Scottish Office', it was dealt with initially under the 'health' heading, and after 1962 along with planning, as part of the 'Scottish Development Department'. In some ways, central government's housing role was rather like an imposing facade, with less than expected 'behind the scenes'. At first glance, it seemed that it played an important role in turning on and off the taps of overall encouragement of output, through the overall setting of targets. Labour was more demanding, or ambitious, in these national initiatives, but some of the most famous innovators were Tory ministers, such as Harold Macmillan in the early 1950s and Sir Keith Joseph in the early 1960s. At the end of the 1960s, into the early 1970s, the devaluation and oil crises led to the scaling back of all these 'national housing drives', and to a switch in policy towards area 'rehab'. But in any case many aspects of these overarching national campaigns consisted to a large

extent of rhetoric – as exemplified by the early and mid 1960s campaign for 'industrialised building', in which the government made largely futile attempts to persuade individual councils to form collaborative 'consortia' to commission serial contracts. But the precise role of all these central initiatives always remained unclear, not least owing to the very broad scope of macroeconomic factors such as interest rates, or the lending policies of the Public Works Loan Board.[4]

The government could try to influence municipal housing production more precisely in two ways: firstly, by attempts to directly regulate housing policy details and even the types of housing built; and secondly, through Exchequer subsidies with conditions attached. In the area of regulation, its power to direct housing production was in practice restricted by organisational incapacity in England and Wales and political weakness in Scotland. The only firmly established procedure

Right: 'A lifetime's ambition fulfilled. Mr. E.E. Woods, O.B.E., J.P. (centre) stands on the roof of Poynter House after having declared open the high-rise block on the estate that bears its name. Mr. Woods was a member of Hammersmith Council for well over 40 years and has devoted his life to improving housing conditions in the borough.'
Below: London Edward Woods Estate, St. Ann's Villas, Hammersmith, W1, 1964–68; Poynter House is the block in the distance.

Left: 'Slum kitchen in Nottingham', from the *Architects' Journal* in 1956: small old urban
dwellings could not be seen as anything other than squalid.
Right: Old vs. New: the target here was the state of an unidentified run-down larger Victorian town
house, presumably in London, though this juxtaposition of 1970 might already have been intended
to cast doubts on the validity of the blanket condemnation of 19th century urban dwellings.

was the vetting of tenders for 'loan-sanction' purposes, but this
occurred at too late a stage in the development process to affect
building policy, being concerned solely with value for money, and
it did not in any case apply to Britain's largest housing authority, the LCC. Informal initial appraisals of proposals by government architects or planners, or advisory initiatives (such as
the 'Parker Morris' report) exerted much less effect, and were
usually opposed to large-scale flat building.

In Scotland, the strength of the individual municipalities, and
the corresponding weakness of the central Scottish Office
in housing matters, was especially pronounced. The vast
new council schemes catered for the lower middle class and
working class, skilled and unskilled alike. Overall per-capita
public-housing output in Scotland from 1945 to 1970 was twice
that of England and Wales over the post-war period, and by the
early 1960s the proportion of total housing output built by public
agencies (79%) was much higher than in any other country in
Europe or North America. No central government initiative
could escape the long shadow of Glasgow and its satellites,
their housebuilding and letting fuelled by those 'warring barons',
the bailies and councillors. As one Scottish Office civil servant
recalled: 'Glasgow Corporation was the power in the land – no
Minister sitting in Edinburgh could do much about Glasgow!'
The principal attempted riposte of the Scottish Office to municipal housing power was the setting-up of the Scottish Special
Housing Association (SSHA), a nationwide programme initiated
in 1937, which accounted for up to a maximum of 10% of public
housing output, especially in new towns and planner-controlled
growth areas; it was profoundly distrusted, and obstructed, by
Glasgow and the large Labour authorities.[5]

Slum clearance, town planning and the 1960s increase in numbers and height

Internationally speaking, one of the most distinctive characteristics of mass housing in Britain was the emphasis on the demolition of housing considered as defective or backward, and labelled
as 'slums' – with the large urban municipal authorities playing the
leading role. Partly, this was because housing decay appeared
to be faster in Britain than in many other countries; and partly
it was also fuelled by the British tradition of public outcry concerning urban conditions, which went back to the middle of the
19th century. Gradually, all this was matched by greater municipal
powers to remove the decayed properties, something which other
countries did not possess. Successive Acts had given the towns
power to compulsorily purchase land and buildings, under which
the private owners were compensated only for the site value,
rather than the market value of their property.[6]

It cannot be the task here to exactly define the term 'slum', or
the reasons that motivated the repeated campaigns against
decayed areas of older small houses. Strong factors of purely
visual dislike were involved, including the distaste for Victorian
ornament, coupled, as it so often was, with the external stig-
mata of war-time neglect. Inside, the state of sanitary provision appeared shocking: in 1953 37% of all homes were without
a bathroom. Naturally, overall statistics concerning the actual
number of bad old properties varied considerably. In 1963 it was
estimated that during the following 20 years three and a half
million old houses would need replacing. Moreover, according
to Cleeve Barr in 1967, decay appeared to be on the increase, at
the rate of 100,000 houses per year.[7]

London, St. Anne's Neighbourhood Stepney RDA, E14. 'Redevelopment' often entailed the complete removal of all old houses as well as creating an almost completely new road layout. Building here began around 1955; today some of the blocks form part of Locksley Estate; a tower was not built in that spot.

The problem went even deeper than that; not only were there still many rows of the smallest and most obsolete types of houses still to be cleared, but there were also the so-called twilight areas, those better class dwellings which were considered basically sound, but were seen to be in danger of failing at an unspecifiable future time. The *Norwich Plan* of 1945 got carried away with this idea, to the point of proposing the eventual destruction of virtually all the city's areas of 19th century terraced houses. During the post-war decades, each of the major Northern and Midland cities tried to claim that their slums were the worst in England – although London every so often also asserted that it still topped the league table in that respect – while Scottish housing commentators had taken it as read, ever since the 1917 Ballantyne Housing Report, that Scottish housing conditions as a whole were worse than anything in England.[8]

The later 19th century had already seen a number of well-known clearances and rebuilding schemes in London, Liverpool, and Glasgow, small in scale at first, but greatly expanding during the interwar years. What followed were the most drastic demonstrations of municipal power, razing vast areas, often completely changing the street pattern and rebuilding the area to completely new plans, with new communal facilities of all kinds. The first major London redevelopment area using new types of buildings was a complex mosaic of sites in Stepney and Poplar (in today's Tower Hamlets) from the mid-fifties. Birmingham declared five 'RDAs', or re-development areas around the City Centre. By far the most dramatic story was that of Glasgow's Gorbals and other clearance areas, with their spectacular destruction of the blackened tenements and

erection of shiny and very high new blocks of different kinds.[9] In these post-war years, however, the general autonomy of local authorities in housing matters, including slum-clearance, did not imply a general unity of purpose regarding the overall aims and strategies of building among all the protagonists. Far from it: for the large councils were increasingly ridden by fundamental conflicts regarding the resettlement of the slum dwellers, most significantly between 'housing' and 'planning' factions concerning the relationship between council housing and land policy.

As a municipal affair, slum clearance in Britain had traditionally been the concern of municipal engineers and surveyors, and had tended to have the effect of bolstering traditional housing committee power. In some cities, such as Salford, that situation continued unabated throughout the post-war period. But increasingly, within local authorities, the expansionist town planning profession was beginning to make itself felt, trying to absorb slum-clearance within its own burgeoning 'empire'. Here the planners often worked in close alliance with housing architects, arguing that slum redevelopment should not be carried out piecemeal but according to designed 'comprehensive development areas', or CDAs, and should be set in the wider context of regional schemes, including overspill and new towns, again all comprehensively planned. The exemplars here were the County of London and Greater London plans of 1943 and 1944, or in Scotland, the Clyde Valley Regional Plan of 1946 and 1949. The principal aim of all these was to reduce density by design-based formulae, embedded within an overall plan, rather than piecemeal interventions.[10]

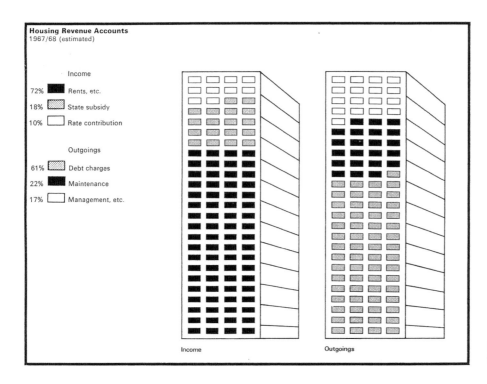

Housing Revenue Accounts
1967/68 (estimated)

Income

72% Rents, etc.

18% State subsidy

10% Rate contribution

Outgoings

61% Debt charges

22% Maintenance

17% Management, etc.

Income   Outgoings

London, Council housing
finance 1967/8.

In this area of 'regional planning' – in contrast to the relative ineffectiveness of central government in public housing policy – government planners played a significant role in helping their municipal counterparts. They helped devise a strategy under which the population displaced by the density reduction would be moved away from the cities altogether to planned New Towns or rural 'overspill reception' towns; council Housing Committees were to be prevented or impeded from accommodating the 'decanted' citizens in large-scale peripheral developments by the designation of green belts around major cities.[11] The formula of comprehensive planning also introduced a new inflexibility, from the housing committees' point of view, by deterring ad-hoc gap-site development. But for traditional 'housers' in the large cities, the key thing that made this pattern of intervention unacceptable was the fact that its reduction of density involved the loss of population and of local taxation revenue. The gradual realisation of this fact led in many cases to a split between different interests within individual local authorities, seen at its most dramatic in Glasgow, where the housing committee was pitted against the planning committee. Everyone in British housing was agreed on the necessity for slum redevelopment, with its implication of the constant whittling down of the residue of private rented housing generally, but the big disagreement was about how this was to be done. This conflict led in many cities by the 1950s to a strong perception of a 'land trap' – in the sense that planning pressures seemed (from the perspective of municipal 'housers') to be inexorably whittling away at land supply within their boundaries. This, in turn, fuelled the new policy of exploiting multi-storey blocks as a way of circumventing the reduction in land availability. Thus, paradoxically, in this respect the planners' pressure was having an opposite effect to their original intention of reducing urban densities.[12]

Eventually, by the 1960s, this powerful yet conflict-ridden 'council housing' system would help generate the uniquely variegated 'Council Tower' landscapes of mass housing, through a complex process of interaction between the entrenched power and autonomy of local authorities in British housing, and the impact of the new post-war pressures on output and land supply. In the remainder of this chapter, we will trace how the housing factions within the great cities, alarmed at the threat of population loss through the linkage of slum-clearance and overspill proposed by the council and central government planners, decided of their own volition to revive output through multi-storey building, while the housing interests within the government trailed along in their wake, opportunistically devising rules and subsidies to legitimise and assist the snowballing demand to build high flats – on which central government ministers increasingly came to depend on, for their part, so as to bolster their 'national' output figures.

In this process, there was a radical difference in approach between England and Wales on the one hand, and Scotland on the other. In the former, the Ministry of Housing and Local Government began from the mid-1950s to attempt, by administrative and subsidy changes, to scale down general council housebuilding and redirect it into slum-clearance, while in Scotland 'general needs' building continued unabated, with expanded slum-clearance seen by the Scottish Office housing administrators as an enhancement rather than a replacement. The beginning of large-scale multi-storey building across urban Britain from the mid/late 1950s seemed especially attractive in towns where land shortage coincided with continuing slum overcrowding, as this was leading to a vicious circle in the decanting of slum-dwellers. The overcrowding meant that more replacement houses would be needed than

Achievements in the (recently greatly enlarged) London Borough of Enfield in 1967. Second from the right: Anthony Greenwood, Minister of Housing.

existed already in the slum areas (a liability which became progressively heavier as clearance spread); yet the 'land trap' was all the time reducing authorities' options in the location of the replacement housing. In other words, any clearance was effectively 'ring-fenced'. For hard-pressed urban authorities, especially in London, faced with the self-compounding land loss caused by slum decanting, multi-storey blocks allowed gap sites to be exploited as and when they came up, potentially making possible a self-contained process of decanting within clearance areas. In a 'ring-fenced' slum area, there was now a new method of proceeding with decanting and clearance, which would provide the inhabitants with Modern homes as quickly as possible, without overspill. In the words of Cllr. Eric Smythe, the late 1960s Housing Committee Chairman of Enfield London Borough Council, 'Firstly, you had to create the holes to put a tower block up, which you did by pulling a couple of streets down. Then you put in the block, and commenced pulling down the rest of the area!'[13]

In turn, all this ferment, via the strong autonomy of local authorities, to the emergence of a wide variety of responses through council building programmes – at the same time as the central government began to turn on the taps for overall output in the late 50s and early 60s – years of relatively low completion figures but furious preparations for building expansion. We will trace this diversity in far greater detail in later chapters. In general, however, one extreme was represented by those cities where the planning/design alliance established a general ascendancy and succeeded in embedding tower blocks within more architecturally complex and variegated design formulae – above all in London, where the picture was, however, complicated by the two level system of the LCC/GLC and boroughs; in Manchester, where the entrenched garden city tradition led to

a plain lack of interest in mass high-density building and population retention; and in individual designer-controlled provincial cities such as Sheffield and Coventry, where the architects and planners enjoyed strong support from 'enlightened' councillors.[14] A second, opposed category was that of cities where the housing production-led ethos remained dominant, such as Liverpool or Salford. A third category was that of cities with a strong ethos of local pride and some designer input, which built large numbers of multi-storey flats but stood apart from the worst confrontations, such as Newcastle, Bristol, or above all Birmingham. Finally, there were the new towns, which were, of course, not local authorities at all, but essentially administrative bodies under central government control, and whose architectural policies tended to favour a middle-of-the-road mixed development pattern, incorporating few if any high blocks.

Financing and organising high flats in the 'sixties

In evaluating the driving-forces of the 1960s housing boom, some historians have also identified the general government 'modernisation of Britain' campaign as a central determinant of government housing policy, and have devoted much attention to the pronouncements of ministers such as Richard Crossman, or of 'establishment' reformers such as J.B. Cullingworth and D.V. Donnison.[15] Indeed, some help did come from direct ministerial involvement and encouragement, for example under the post-1964 Labour government, where junior Minister Robert Mellish acted as a highly effective 'progress-chaser' in Greater London.[16] But now, as always, the political and architectural rhetoric of 'mass production' and 'system building' remained curiously detached from the

17

day-to-day organisation of building. Arguably, the central government activity which most significantly helped the expansion of public housing in the mid-1960s was the least public of all: the continuous behind-the-scenes negotiation between spending departments and Treasury, to secure authorisation of higher output. The most tangible help, in England, was provided by a modification of the allocations system, within the four-year programmes demanded by Circular 21/65. A group of 'priority authorities' was established, covering 60% of public housing output: the dozen or so largest cities were singled out for the most favourable treatment.[17]

The way in which central government shaped its building subsidies to councils has also frequently been cited as a special driver for multi-storey blocks. Indeed, over several years in the late 1950s and early 60s, the whole system appeared tailored strongly towards high flats, and more especially (in England) if it concerned projects involving slum-clearance. In general, the effects of British government policy on subsidies were rather complex. Although subsidy changes could, over time, influence broad directions of housebuilding, they could not easily influence the level of construction of specific building types, unless these had already been backed by the larger municipalities. For although the latter were reluctant to build without subsidy, they could neutralise minor subsidy changes in the short term by pooling rents or subsidies on existing properties, or by drawing further on rate revenue (local property taxation) to support their Housing Revenue Account (the overall budget supporting any local authority's housing operations).

In the specific area of multi-storey building, the central government subsidy innovation that had most directly assisted the initial late 1950s spread of high flats across Britain was a special multi-storey subsidy introduced in 1956–57 in both England and Scotland. The main reason for its introduction, however, had stemmed from the pressure of the largest councils themselves, which had become increasingly convinced of the need to build their way out of the 'land trap' using high blocks. The prime mover was Birmingham Corporation, whose leadership bluntly applied its political muscle as early as 1953 to force MHLG to devise a 'discretional expensive site flats subsidy'. The newly-arrived City Architect, A. G. Sheppard Fidler, was amazed at this effortless exercise of municipal power: 'They said, "Look, Minister, you've got to change this! We're the City of Birmingham, not some tiddly little country town – we want these rules changed!" And he did! I was staggered – I thought it was fantastic!'[18]

From 1956–57 onwards, special multi-storey subsidies were available nationally, over and above the basic subsidy which the Government had made available since 1952 for any kind of dwelling (£26 14s. in England and Wales). In Scotland, there was a simple 'deficit subsidy' for flats of six or more storeys, covering two-thirds of any excess over 'average' dwelling costs. In England and Wales, from 1956, there was a more complicated system of fixed supplements increasing with building height, valid for all flats, not just high blocks. It meant that for a flat in a four-storey block there was a jump of 50% in subsidy

over that for a three-storey block; with a 6-storey block the jump per dwelling amounted to over 100%, and thereafter for each further floor there was a regular increase, so that flats in twenty-storey blocks attracted three times the amount for a house, which amounted to a total of about £80 per flat. From 1965–67 onwards the English incremental system was phased out, and instead a 'cost-plus' deficit subsidy for all council housing in Britain was introduced, topped up by flat-rate subsidies of £30–40 for high flats. These state subsidies were of course relatively small in relation to the overall building costs (around 2–3% of the total), but when later detractors of high blocks were looking for a scapegoat factor to 'blame' for their construction, they appeared an easy target. Furthermore, the subsidies were also tied to a system of cost limits – 'indicative costs' in Scotland, mandatory 'yardsticks' in England and Wales. Its implementation saw a fresh divergence between Scotland and England, with civil servant administrators prioritising output considerations in the former, but in the latter showing greater deference to the advice of government planners and architects, who frequently pressed for lower densities or more variegated architectural design solutions.[19]

But this shift away from high blocks would only really begin at the end of the 1960s. At the beginning of the decade, for a few fleeting years, everything seemed to have come together to favour the massed building of multi-storey blocks, not just in the large slum clearance areas but in all urban contexts, including inner-urban gap sites or locations on the edge of town. The cities' embrace of high blocks for the purpose of large-scale production, supported by the government's alterations to the subsidy structure, had produced the potential for their massed building on all available sites, as a routine policy. In land supply, the possibility now beckoned of a 'virtuous circle' which would emancipate high blocks from their initial land-shortage context. Their use in exploiting gap-sites and the way they produced a housing gain from initial sections of redevelopments had begun to create some very substantial slum-cleared areas. These, along with an increasing number of large peripheral sites such as Birmingham's Castle Bromwich Airfield or Dundee's Ardler sites, could then be developed with high blocks. To those concerned with housing production, it did not matter that multi-storey 'site cramming' in the outer suburbs might conflict with the architectural and planning orthodoxies that high blocks should be used in 'high density' inner areas, and in designer-controlled mixed developments. When output was the goal, all sites within a city's boundaries were seen on equal terms, purely on the basis of their potential yield in the number of dwellings. In the early 1960s, most 'provincial' high blocks still stood as isolated outcrops. But now they were an accepted housing pattern: soon, massive schemes could be routinely channelled through council committees almost without discussion. A major contractor's architect recalls, 'I used to joke, in Dundee's Housing Committee for instance, that there was often far lengthier discussion about rebuilding public lavatories than about doing multi-storeys!'[20]

5 Architects, engineers, builders and 'package deals'

The local authority architects assert themselves

Enter the architect. So far all new post-war dwellings were accepted to be good, practical dwellings. But did councils really provide the variety of dwellings needed by contemporary society? And were they 'modern', in the sense of being architecturally innovative? By 1950 a growing pool of architectural opinion held that, on the whole, they were not. A chorus had been building up, a group of designers and their advocates in some journals had emerged, who claimed loudly that public housing needed a radical new input by the architectural profession, or, what it really meant, by the younger practitioners, by those who deemed themselves Modernists.

To begin with, this appeared simply an extension of the 'post-war consensus', which held that no profession could remain outside it, and that everybody should strive towards the modernisation of the country. Given the post-war shortages, and the obvious need to prioritise repair of the damage caused by the war, immediate architectural spectacles could hardly be expected. Crucially for the careers of most architects of those years were the draconian state rationing measures which gravely restricted the building of anything other than utilitarian types of architecture, that was schools, factories and public housing. The official end to wartime and post-war restrictions of labour and materials only came in 1954. However strong the social reformist idealism entertained by the post-war practitioners, it was also out of sheer material necessity that so many architects had to opt for public commissions, including low-cost types of dwellings.

Hitherto, a few eminent architects had occasionally provided what were designated 'model designs' for public housing, or had acted at an elevated level as consultant town planners to local authorities. Normally, council dwellings were designed by the borough engineers or surveyors, or by minor local architects who remained virtually unknown. The two decades after 1945 marked a radical change in this position, in that virtually all ambitious younger practices in London contributed at least one or two public housing estates, as one-off commissions from the capital's various municipalities. At the same time, during the 1950s, the position of 'Architect to the Council' – i.e. chief architect of the London County Council, the LCC – was held successively by two major figures in the profession, Robert Matthew and Leslie Martin,[1] both future RIBA Gold Medal winners, whose high standing attracted a wide range of well-regarded architects to take on salaried positions within the LCC Architect's Department. Hence, in a new sense, almost everything shown in this book can be classified as 'architect-designed architecture', allowing, naturally, for a considerable gap in prestige between the best and the least known designers. This does not, however, mean that, after a lapse of 50 or 60 years, it is always possible to actually trace their names.

But the powers of the architect in this 'public' context were not as straightforward as they might have seemed. In the 'normal', commercial client-architect situation, either party is free to enter into a relationship, or to decline; the council architect, by contrast, was entirely dependent on what his or her client required. Municipal architects thus always dealt with the same body, a collective institutional client, fronted by a specialist committee of publicly elected members, usually in this case the Housing Committee. Projects normally required several stages of committee approval, bound into complex financial rules, and it was for the elected members at each stage to approve, to demand modifications, or to reject the architect's proposal. On the face of it, the council's 'housing powers', disposing of contracts amounting to sometimes millions of pounds, were very considerable indeed.

At the same time, most councillors' capabilities with regard to the more detailed architectural issues were necessarily rather limited. In all strictly technical matters, such as heating, they had to rely on the architect, just as they relied on the expertise of the municipal surveyors or engineers. Architects felt it was their bad luck when they encountered a committee that was both ignorant and articulate. The councillors' carefully regulated responsibilities were principally towards the local ratepayers and national taxpayers, as well as towards the users, so as to provide them with the best practical amenities as they could be afforded. Purely architectural considerations, in the narrower, aesthetic sense of the word, very rarely entered the councillors' deliberations, or at any rate they were not normally recorded in the minutes. Neither did meetings assess new housing when building had finished, although rare cases of wider recognition, such as the national and international praise for the LCC Roehampton Estate, were noted with some pride.

The architects' own wider world was, above all, their professional press. Here they were free from any interference from their clients. Council architects often sent advance information about their projects to the journals, sometimes even before official approval by the council, and then again after completion. The power of the collective institution of the architectural press in those years has already been alluded to. The aim of the journals was to stress their own importance and thereby that of the profession generally, by using a tone that was both admonitory and self-congratulatory: to quote once again: '... the architect will have to shoulder the pioneer's work in establishing new codes'.[2] At times, though, the two most influential journals published by the Architectural Press, the *Architectural Review* and the *Architect's Journal*, embarked on campaigns that promoted their own views specifically, at the expense of some designers' work, when they launched into condemnations of certain modes of design, sometimes even condemning those which they

Left: London, Hilldrop Estate, Dalmeny Avenue, Islington, N7, 1946–48. Designed by the LCC Housing Department under Cyril H Walker, shown in the *Architect's Journal* in 1949 as a negative example.

Right: Today's impression of the blocks and the district is rather one of suburban spaciousness and leafiness.

themselves had previously supported. A major example was the very concept of the tower block, strongly advocated by the journals in the 1950s and then condemned from the later 1960s.[3]

In 1949, the whole of the architectural issues came to the fore in an affair concerning LCC housing design, in a controversy that provoked major changes in the design processes of public housing in Britain. As a prelude to this, a few London Metropolitan Boroughs, that is, the 'second tier' of municipalities, below the LCC, had begun to employ private Modernist firms immediately after 1945. Foremost among these was Berthold Lubetkin's office (Tecton), in Finsbury. In Westminster the young team of Powell and Moya won a competition for a large development in Pimlico. In both these cases, the architects employed the most up-to-date mode of the high slab block with Modernist elevations.

The housing built immediately after 1945 by the LCC itself presented a rather different picture. On the face of it, it impressed not only through its quantity, but also with the large average size of its dwellings and its provision of modern conveniences. The issue that came to the fore, suddenly, in early 1949, was not concerned with any of these material aspects, but purely with the look of the blocks. Almost all of these LCC blocks were built in massive red brick. They were mostly of the balcony access type, in itself a controversial element (as we will see below in Chapter 11). With their boldly curved horizontal contours, often formed by the balconies, one could today label them as Art Deco; but at that time anything looking as heavy as that could not legitimately be called 'Modern'.

In March 1949 the *Architects' Journal* launched a devastating critique of these flats, branding them 'sheer bad architecture', 'crude and clumsy', of 'depressingly low standard ', with some estates also showing 'a quite terrifying density of population.' Perhaps rashly, the LCC decided to react and to invite opinions. The *Architects' Journal* printed a large number of letters which were overwhelmingly critical, some witheringly so, such as Berthold Lubetkin, writing that the estates were 'pathetically uninhibited by any consciousness of the very existence of design'. Unprecedented was also the journal's avalanche of pictures of blocks with comments pointing out their alleged defects. The LCC responded by staging an exhibition at County Hall. Appearing on the radio, the chairman of the LCC Housing Committee, C.W. Gibson, praised the dwellings as 'comfortable homes', while declining to 'discuss the aesthetic merits of individual buildings'. The architectural faction, on its part, derided arguments about comfort, claiming that those modern amenities were now 'universally' expected. Even *The Times*, in a short leader, fully endorsed the architects' stand: while recognising the pressure for numbers, it warned that 'it is by its quality that today's housing will be judged tomorrow'.[4]

For the rebel architects and their apologists, there was one principal and eminently simple reason for the perceived failure: the blocks were not designed by architects – or, at any rate, by an architect-headed department. The LCC officer in charge of public housing design was Cyril H. Walker, O.B.E., M.C., F.I.R.C.S., M.I. Mun. E., L.R. Hsg., the Council's Director of Housing and Valuer – an eminent public official, but certainly not an architect by training. Responsibility for housing design had been transferred to him in 1946 away from the Council's Architect, despite protests from the RIBA and other organisations.[5] In 1949 the Scotsman Robert Matthew took the reins as the new LCC Architect, a staunch Modernist, who was just about to begin designing what became the most admired Modern public building in Britain, the Royal Festival Hall. Matthew led the fight-back by inciting J.M Richards, the *Architectural Journal*'s editor, to launch the press campaign against Walker. Many others could be counted on the rebels' side and practically all the other architectural journals joined in, as well as all those town planners who had supported the ideas of the *County of London Plan* of 1943. The Minister of Health himself, Nye Bevan (whose department included housing), was on record as pleading to local authorities to employ architects for their housing design.[6]

The upshot of this upheaval was three-fold: firstly, it legitimised a new stress in 'advanced' public housing design, combining a strong architectural aesthetic with utopianist planning, as epitomised by the new concept of mixed development; secondly, it opened the doors of all public housing to International-Style

Modernism; and thirdly, it provided a resounding reinforcement of the power of architectural criticism as such.

The changes triggered by the controversy in the LCC Architect's Department were very considerable.[7] In 1950 there were 20 salaried architects, but by 1956 the group had grown to over 400. Important names, coming from private practices, but already known for their advanced work in the Boroughs, had joined: H J Whitfield Lewis, of the firm Norman & Dawbarn, who had been responsible for the small but heavily praised St. Pancras Way group of flats, became Chief Housing Architect; Michael Powell from the firm Powell & Moya, then near to completing the first phase of their Pimlico scheme for Westminster, became Lewis's deputy; another key figure was Colin Lucas, formerly of the firm Connell Ward & Lucas, the most avant-garde of the English interwar designers. It was Whitfield Lewis who took the decisive step straightaway in planning a mixed development with tower blocks at the Ackroydon Estate in Wandsworth. In 1953, the great organiser Robert Matthew was succeeded as LCC Architect by his deputy, Leslie Martin – a quieter figure yet widely respected for his particular academic kind of approach to planning and design. What the Department was now eager to foreground was not the power of the individual designer, but a new ethics of architectural teamwork. A new 'Technical Development and Research' group was established within the Department, concerning itself principally with all kinds of building components, aspiring to create useful tie-ups with the building industry, as well as co-operating with the many other architectural research agencies in the country.[8] Yet it was precisely that close co-operation with the diverse specialisms which was said to also lead to a 'maximum of creative ideas and initiatives',[9] or, as the architectural journalist Robert Furneaux Jordan put it in an effusive account of the Department's work in 1956, it 'freed staff ... solely for architecture'.[10] All in all, the architects of the LCC saw themselves not as just producing designs according to trusted formulae, but as innovators and idealists in every respect: all the LCC housing discussed in this book were being newly conceived.

Finally, the enthusiasm of the new generation of designers was matched by the devotedness of the new Housing Committee chairs and deputy chairs, by Reginald Stamp and Evelyn Denington, in particular. In the LCC, the world of council housing had made possible the emergence of a public authority which, armed with unprecedented financial and legal powers, could behave almost like an eighteenth century urban developer, and that on the scale of an entire metropolis. When the Ackroydon Estate received an architectural award, in 1955, the architects, in the person of Leslie Martin, showered praise on the councillors: 'it was Mr. Fiske, who, as Chairman of the Town Planning Committee took the decisions that have led to mixed development' and Mrs. Denington had been equally 'helpful'. 'I should like to say how much we valued their confidence'.[11]

In short, its admirers believed, that the LCC's department was the best architectural department in the world. Or, in a confident variation on an old popular saying about the Empire, the LCC Architect's Department was the 'great enterprise in which

H. J. Whitfield Lewis, LCC Principal Housing Architect 1950–59, seen here in 1956.

A.W. Cleeve Barr (centre) of the LCC Architect's Department meets members of the building profession to discuss new ways of architect-builder co-operation in 1955.

the concrete never sets'.[12] One may, indeed, add another superlative: of all the kinds of dwelling that had ever been built in Britain, the council tower block was now the one that was most consistently 'architecturally' designed.

Beyond the LCC, many other municipal architectural departments also began to gain in importance in those years. But in these, being much smaller in size, there was less emphasis on team work, and more on the dominating figure of the city or borough architect. The LCC 'exported' ambitious designers in all directions: Arthur Ling to Coventry, D. Jenkins to Hull, J.A. Maudsley to Birmingham, and Walter Bor to Liverpool. Closer at hand, within Greater London, Thomas North moved to West Ham and Ted Hollamby to Lambeth. The architectural prestige of many of the New Towns also ensured that they would feed this burgeoning apparatus of council architecture, with Crawley, for instance, supplying A G Sheppard Fidler, the first holder of the most noted of the newly-created City Architect posts, in Birmingham. 'Number three' in national impact among municipal architects was Ronald Bradbury of Liverpool, coming from Glasgow. By contrast, other major departments were led by widely recognised figures in post since before the war, such as J. Nelson Meredith in Bristol and R.A.H. Livett in Leeds. Whatever their backgrounds, it was public housing design that provided the foundation for the high status that the major local authority architects could now be claiming.[13]

Engineers and contractors

Any investigation of high blocks must begin with the realisation that they require completely new methods of construction. Traditionally, an architect would trust the builder, who, in turn, would trust traditional ways of building. When it came to new modes of construction, requiring a greater familiarity with physics and chemistry, neither the traditionally-minded architect nor the 'ordinary' builder would have had much of an idea. We will return to the actual methods of building in Chapter 10 below; here the issue is the ways in which the various professions attempted to come together to organise the new processes of construction.[14]

Enter the engineer. Until well into the 20th century British architects had hardly been interested in engineering issues. But now, exactly at the time when architects felt they had 'arrived', postulating that the design of a council house was theirs, and only theirs, a new phase was beginning in which architects were urged to profess their intense co-operation with all the other agents involved in the construction of 'their' dwellings. For any building above five, six or seven storeys the traditional method of walling up from the ground would simply not do any more. A number of methods of construction offered themselves, which meant, in effect, that practically for every block its construction had to be newly devised. A further factor in the equation was the demand for economy; the search was on for the optimal solution. The most straightforward method of building high would have been to use a steel framework and clad it as required, but that was a particularly expensive method; instead high blocks of housing normally used reinforced concrete, which is cheap as a material but the erection and cladding of which presents endless problems. Coupled with the usually complex planning tasks, mixing flats of different sizes, the building of a council block was becoming a demanding task.[15]

London, Picton Street, Camberwell, SE5, 1954–56; 'experimental maisonette blocks' by LCC Architects (A.W. Cleeve Barr); engineers: Arup, helped by the Government's Building Research Station; contractor: Laing (cf. pp. 68, 83).

An early model of architect-contractor co-operation was that between Berthold Lubetkin and Ove Arup, an up-and-coming, architecturally-orientated young engineer, which had already begun before the war. For Lubetkin's Finsbury blocks Arup devised a new system, based on a 'box-frame' principle, which, as John Allan summarised it, brought 'an intelligent and logical evolution in response to demands of use and economics'.[16] Later on Arup constantly preached the togetherness of architects and engineers.[17] Another leading London engineer, Felix Samuely, assisted the LCC with their most daring project of the late 1950s, the Brandon Estate towers, with their unprecedented height of 18 storeys. They were soon outdone, however, by the Hide Place project in Westminster, with its 21 storeys, whose structural design was directed by Charles Weiss, 'an engineer with inexhaustible energy and initiative'.[18]

What seemed to be needed, in the view of the younger Modernists, was co-operation on an even wider scale. In reality the engineer's task became more and more identical with that of the builder's' task. A model for such a close relationship already existed, namely, the Hertfordshire County Schools experiment of around 1950.[19] Clients, architects, engineers, contractors and building component manufacturers had worked there in the closest possible co-operation. One member of that team was A.W. Cleeve Barr, who took the spirit of the 'Herts Schools' into the LCC Architects' Department, His LCC pilot project for the new approach was Picton Street, in south London, whose slab blocks were devised from 1954 onwards, with Arup acting as the engineer. Following a precedent first established in wartime contracting, one major step to take was to give up the traditional sequence of first producing the complete design for the building and then inviting open 'tenders' from building contractors. It was replaced by a 'negotiated contract' with a 'nominated builder', the chosen firm here being John Laing & Son Limited, who had already

established itself as a favoured contractor for 'progressive Modernist projects' and was commanding considerable experience with low-cost housing. The hope was that by getting together early, the design could benefit from the views and experience of the contractor in arriving at an optimal structure and the most speedy and efficient performance. Apart from the LCC's research team, the national Building Research Station was also involved. However, as often happens with such kinds of experiments, the Picton Street blocks took an exceptionally long time, around four years, to complete – by which time it was, of course, difficult to arrive at any realistic assessment of the architects' claims regarding their collaborative practices. One thing was certain: costs were 'high'.[20]

Another LCC undertaking which had been completed just before Picton Street was the Trinity Road development (Fitzhugh Estate) in Wandsworth, with its five 11-storey blocks. Here another major firm, Wates, had won the contract through the conventional tender process, but they were then invited by the architects and the engineers, Arup again, to engage in complex discussions,[21] so as to to work out further the details of the building process. One of the results was to achieve completion seven months before schedule. This was also due in considerable measure to the most dramatic mechanical advance, the tower crane, which could easily reach above the 100 foot height of the blocks. Britain was, in this respect, catching up with France and Scandinavia. Not only did the crane often make scaffolding unnecessary, but it also brought discipline to the job, through its efficient handling of all prefabricated elements, cutting down on messy trades milling around the site.[22] By the mid-fifties the way appeared clear for major advances in construction – which at the same time meant a new area of contractor power.

'Package deals'

'Was there any industry where designers and producers were kept separate, other than building?' – or so asked the *Architects' Journal* in 1956.[23] In Cleeve Barr's view, it was eminently feasible for the architect to eventually become a staff-member of a contractor's organisation. By contrast, 'the Renaissance individualist is today a public menace'.[24] Barr foresaw that in the end, the 'manufacturers will probably force the pace'.[25] Indeed, if one was to ask for an authoritative statement about buildings that were designed by Cleeve Barr alone, such information would be difficult to obtain. With the 'package' blocks to come, names of the designers were only very rarely mentioned, nor, for that matter, were those of the engineers.[26]

Already, by the late 1950s, contractors were beginning to promote the construction of high blocks entirely designed by themselves, building on the obvious precedent of the plethora of low-rise prefabricated proprietary designs of two-storey houses that briefly flowered in the three or four years after the war. Importantly, many of these unconventionally-built houses could be procured on a more or less 'package-deal' basis, serviced by a small number of large firms, such as Laing and Wimpey. In 1954 Wates had advertised their 'Wates system' when presenting models for three-storey flats, and in 1957 they claimed to have 'developed a system of building multi-storey flats'.[27] Laing, while completing the Picton Street blocks, proposed a system called 'High-Structure', which could be 'offered to local authorities ... in the form of a fully designed and specified series of multi-storey blocks'.[28] Wimpey used the term 'off the peg' in relation to its 'no-fines' building method for 6–8-storey mini-tower-blocks in Birmingham.[29] However, none of all this led to any large-scale practical outcome as yet.

All the greater, therefore, appeared the impact of 'industrialised' building production from 1962–64 onwards. Historian Brian Finnimore called it a veritable 'revolution', with building joining other calls for a comprehensively modernised and better-off Britain.[30] The subject here is the organisational framework, whereas the actual modes of construction will be dealt with in Chapter Ten, in the context of the broader constructional issues of high-rise building. There was a more material impulse, a severe general building-industry shortage, but there was also a more politically-idealistic concept, namely that, in order to speed up modernisation, the Welfare State should be in a position to avail itself fully of the resources that competitive capitalist industries had to offer.

Naturally, in capitalist Britain there was no question of introducing the rigid concentration and standardisation characteristic of the state house-building combines of the USSR. Indeed, in Britain the building industry was far less concentrated than many other industries. Even when counting in new dwellings of all sizes, not just high blocks, the five largest firms, Wates, Laing, Wimpey, Bison and Tersons supplied only one quarter of the total. The remainder was distributed among a great number of national, regional or local firms. Overall the proportion of wholly prefabricated, or 'factory produced' high blocks amounted to hardly more than one third.[31]

As so often with catchwords, there can be a glaring mismatch between rhetorical intent and tangible meaning. 'Industrialised building' actually meant very little that was new, as virtually all building components in Britain had already been mass-produced for some time. At the same time what needs stressing is that putting these parts together on site could require a new kind of individualised precision workmanship. Moreover, the term 'industrialised' was not, in practice, restricted to pure factory-based work, but was also commonly applied to any rationalised and mechanised site practice, such as the use of more sophisticated formwork for casting in-situ. Much the same vague meaning was carried by the term 'rationalised construction'. Likewise, as already mentioned, the 'prefabrication' of dwellings was nothing new at all: after all, the 'prefabs', the small temporary bungalows of the mid 1940s, were completely factory built and famously fitted with all mod. cons. However, 'prefabrication' did acquire a new emphasis in relation to those parts of a building that used concrete, and to the casting which was done away from the site, either in a special workshop close to the site, or in a factory at any distance.

The important catch-all term was 'system', or 'system building'. This could serve as the most elevated expression, conjuring up complex intellectual concerns which referred to production and design alike and which nurtured an ideal of completeness. It was a concept which postulated a sharp reduction of the number of components which could then fit together optimally, for instance a piece of a wall would come ready fitted with all duct work. The most 'complete' mode of prefabrication, the factory production of whole rooms, was known from the Soviet Union but was not used in Britain. In the 1960s, the term 'system' was often also directly attached to the name of a firm, such as the 'Wates System', or to a brand name, such as the 'Bison System'. Its meaning could subsequently be broadened even further, to be used as a catchphrase, denoting all large-panel modes of construction, especially in a negative context, after such a construction method failed in the Ronan Point disaster of 1968. Lastly, the term 'package deal' did not necessarily imply factory or even industrialised production per se but referred to the way in which building firms could do the whole job, from the preparation of the site to supplying the design and right through to the handing over of the keys of the finished building, comprising the tasks of the architect, the engineer and the contractor, something that proved eminently useful for short-staffed smaller authorities. All the municipality had to do was to provide the site and the finance.[32]

Taken as a whole, the projects that came under the labels 'systems' and 'package deal' greatly varied in their realisation. On the one side were cases in which building firms offered complete construction methods, or 'systems', for the building of housing schemes in collaboration with the municipal architects, who were still in charge of the overall design; on the other side were 'packages' in which firms sold the municipalities blocks that were complete in every respect.

A 12-storey block of **Wall Frame flats** could be built here in **4 months...**

CONCRETE LIMITED the largest structural precast concrete specialists in the world
LONDON Whitehall 5504 · BIRMINGHAM Midland 0321 · LEEDS Leeds 73211 · GLASGOW City 3392

BISON

Whatever the weather... there are nine Bison factories in continuous production

BISON
CONCRETE LIMITED the largest structural precast concrete specialists in the world

Bison advertisements of 1965 and 1966 (cf. p. 96).

The actual rise of 'systems' in Britain in 1962/3 came quite suddenly, and was widely supported by all the agencies involved in housing, including all Housing Ministers, for instance by Keith Joseph, who spoke out, with characteristic verve, at the beginning of the Cement and Concrete Association's 1962 conference 'Housing from the Factory', hailing 'system-building' as 'a movement ...which has the greatest significance for the happiness for the people of this country'.[33] In 1965 it was Labour's turn, with Richard Crossman's endorsement, 'giving the industrialised building programme the best conditions to get on its feet'.[34]

In the 1930s and 40s British housing providers had studied planning in other European countries carefully; now the interest turned towards foreign building methods. Councillors and local authority officials undertook extensive study trips to the Continent. The actual beginning of the British season of 'systems' was marked by a number of high-profile developments, extensively reported on in the professional press. During 1963 the LCC chose the Danish system Larsen Nielsen, Liverpool the French system Camus and Manchester adopted Sectra, equally French. The licensed Larsen Nielsen contractor for the LCC's Morris Walk Estate in Woolwich was one of the largest British builders, Taylor Woodrow. Their factory for the production of the large wall components was unusually far away, at Lenwade, outside Norwich. Actual building took a fairly long time, from 1964 to 1966. Recently the *Survey of London* has praised Morris Walk as a 'heroic experiment', stressing that it 'holds a distinctive position in the history of mass housing'.[35] Much attention in the architectural press was attached to the way in which the LCC architects had maximised their design input at the Morris Walk project. Ultimately, however, the LCC's ingrained design individualism and industrialised production could not make for good bedfellows. By far the best known Taylor Woodrow/Larsen Nielsen was, once again, West Ham /

New Ham's nine towers in Canning Town, which included the fateful Ronan Point.[36]

The years 1962/63 also marked the launching of the only large panel production method in Britain which really deserved the epithet of the ubiquitous industrialised mass producer, offering as it did a radically rationalised kit of parts. This was Concrete Ltd, acting mostly as a structural subcontractor to local builders, producing its own brand, the 'Bison System', or 'Bison Wall Frame'. The firm eventually accounted for a total of 306 high blocks containing 31,668 dwellings, built between 1963 and 1979, and it duly called itself the 'biggest structural concrete specialist in the world'. Production was located in London (Hounslow), Lichfield, Leeds and Falkirk and blocks can be found in sedate Eastbourne as well in Scotland and Northern Ireland; but in inner London Bison's clients were only the Boroughs, not the LCC or the GLC. The firm's first three twelve-storey towers were opened in 1963 in medium-sized Kidderminster, 'on time' and 'under budget'. At the ceremony Sir Keith Joseph, the Minister of Housing, promised that 'within ten years a modern .... or a decently modernised home ... would be in the reach of every citizen'.[37]

Next to Bison comes Wimpey; both Bison and Wimpey can be understood as 'package dealers' in the fullest sense of the term, in that they did not just sell building methods, but buildings as such. George Wimpey was Britain's largest building firm altogether, and it also built by far the greatest number of multi-storey blocks in the country, totalling almost 900. Moreover, Wimpey could look back on several decades of experience of a vast number of homes, overwhelmingly two-storeyed houses. The firm acted as a contractor for many blocks designed by local designers, but it based its claims as an efficient provider principally on its own building method, 'no-fines'. Wimpey's dwellings, however, marked an exception in that they were

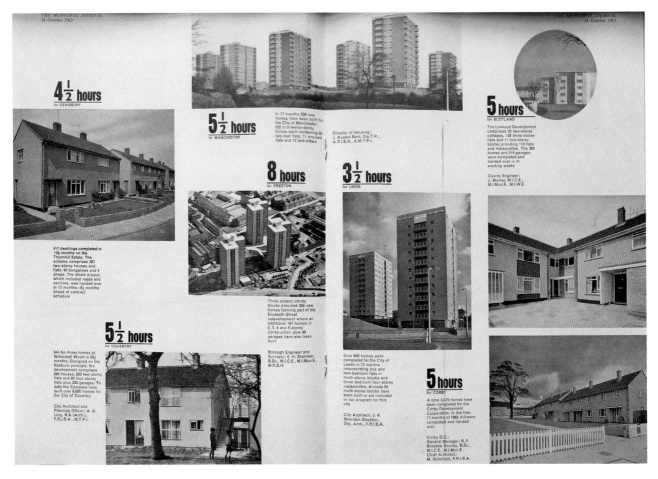

Wimpey advertisement feature in the *Municipal Journal* in 1963. It starts off on the previous page:
'The Mechanisation of Building; ... contracts carried out with an almost stopwatch efficiency. A new home every ... '

not 'from the factory': 'no-fines' denoted nothing more than a special way of producing in situ concrete efficiently by using only a coarse aggregate. Wimpey's most popular package-deal was the '1001/6', a twin-tower, usually of 15 or 16 floors, and which was spreading throughout the country, very often in medium-sized towns, such as Norwich or Ramsgate. In Greater London, as with the case of Bison, it was only the Boroughs that employed the firm.[38]

Another long-standing firm in English housing was Wates; its story was different again. Wates was active principally in London where it built around 15% of all high blocks, among them many of the LCC's most prestigious estates. The firm carefully cultivated a double face, on the one hand as a constructor in charge of almost everything, and on the other hand as 'the one system of industrialised building which allows the architect freedom of design'. Wates firmly believed in prefabrication on site, in its 'mobile manufacturing unit'.[39] In this area a general consensus was never reached: was it better to avail oneself of fully protected precision conditions, but incur expensive transport costs and the risk of damage, or was it better to produce the parts in less than optimal conditions but right next to the building?

A range of large firms continued to build package deals in various permutations of in-situ construction and prefabricated elements. The next best known firm was Reema, which laid great claim on having used a large proportion of prefabricated panels early on in blocks in Leeds and then in a LCC maisonette block in Battersea (see cf. p. 88). Truscon, or, rather, the 'Trussed Concrete Steel Company Limited', was a firm that frequently worked for medium and smaller towns. A further number of foreign systems found limited, but all the more determined application in the later 1960s, controlled, as they were, by design-conscious authorities, such as the Balency System at the LCC's satellite town of Thamesmead, and the 12M Jespersen system employed by Southwark Council for the giant Aylesbury Estate. By 1964/5, no less than 280 'systems' were said to be on offer in Britain, but only about a dozen of them could be used for multi-storey construction – although this number was set to grow somewhat during the following few years.

The mid-sixties also saw a new cleavage as regards the attitudes towards 'systems'. It was largely brought about by the architectural profession, by all those who resented what they felt as the power of the commercial firms. A rhetorically-charged opposition was posed between two types of system: the contractor-led 'closed system', in other words, the 'package' that was supposedly impossible to modify

A Wates advertisement in 1963 (cf. p. 73).

16 years of
housing acceleration by

REEMA

REEMA CONSTRUCTION LTD.,
Milford Manor, Salisbury. *Tel. 6233.*

REEMA (CHESTERFIELD) LTD.,
Storforth Lane, Chesterfield. *Tel. 4195.*

REEMA (SCOTLAND) LTD.,
106 Crown Street, Aberdeen. *Tel. 22328.*

Reema supply housing of all kinds from
their factories near Southampton, Bristol,
Chesterfield and Glasgow.

You are cordially invited to
visit our Stand No. 21 at the
NATIONAL HOUSING and
TOWN PLANNING
EXHIBITION, Scarborough.

Reema's principal stress, like Bison's, was on factory
prefabrication (cf. p. 93).

or customise architecturally, and the architect-led 'open system', seen as a 'kit of parts' which could be assembled in any way the architect wished. All this resulted in a number of very diverse modes of building devised principally by the municipal architects, such as the high towers built in the Lift-Slab method in Coventry or the extraordinarily daring SF1 method devised by the LCC for towers clad in plastic panels, or the rigid system of the direct labour-built towers in the London Borough of Enfield. In this book these efforts will be presented in a later chapter, within their local contexts. A further solution, based on the model of CLASP, the school building system, was for several local authorities to get together to form 'consortia', such as when the major Yorkshire and Midland authorities, Leeds, Sheffield, Hull and Nottingham jointly founded the YDG, or Yorkshire Development Group system. One of the primary aims of the resulting intricate deck-access complexes was to look different from the boxy kinds of commercial package deal blocks. By 1967 the group's leading architect, Martin Richardson, was publicly voicing his strong dislike of system-built high flats, a type which Richardson knew well, having worked on the just mentioned LCC/Taylor Woodrow Morris Walk Estate only a few years previously.[40]

Ever since the 'sixties, the combination of 'systems' and 'package deals' has been associated with multi-storey council tower blocks. John Laing & Sons could stress in 1964 that 'multi-storey flats ... are particularly suitable for industrialised building'.[41] It must be remembered, though, that since the 1940s industrialised building had also applied to normal-sized suburban houses and continued to be so in greater numbers during the 1960s. However, a large block does comprise many dwellings of exactly the same shape, and repetitiveness was what an 'industrialised' building firm was primarily seeking. Ostensibly systems were intended to facilitate the efficient production of good modern dwellings of all kinds. It was numbers that dominated the discourses, at least initially. The threshold of 'profitability' for any industrialised undertaking was said to lie at 500 dwellings. This would apply to, say, five blocks of twenty storeys each. However, many systems developments were much smaller than that. Furthermore, local authorities invariably demanded at least some small changes, so as 'to make each building a little different and claim credit for it'.[42] Conclusions about costs in comparison with conventional construction were kept tactfully vague: '...a little dearer, e.g. 3%'.[43] But successes were frequently claimed as regards construction times, especially when these could be calculated in months, rather than years. The ever-optimistic Cleeve Barr calculated an overall 25 to 40% saving in building time.[44]

All in all, the building world as regards large blocks of flats in the 1960s had gone through an enormous development and had reached a diversity of approaches never known before. There were still the traditional shapes and constructions in brick, and equally the bespoke designs by private and municipal architects using new, individualised solutions, with a strong input from a consulting engineer and often from the builders as well; but there were now also the 'industrialised' modes of construction in which the work of the designer and the engineer were part of a single 'package'. A selection of commercial firms in the world of British municipal high flat building follows.

A selection of firms and organisations in the world
of British municipal high flat building

Contractors / **S**ystems
*SYSTEM NAME | FIRM'S NAME | Type of building method | country of origin | name of contractor, if different from
system | date and place of first use in UK high flats | total number of high blocks in system built in UK |maximum
height of blocks built.*
SYSTEMS: RISC = rationalised in-situ concrete | LLBP = large load-bearing panel (concrete)

S Balency LLBP and RISC / France / Holland / Hannen Cubitts / 1966, GLC Thamesmead, London /
29 blocks / 13 storeys

S Bison Wall Frame System / Bison High Wall Frame Concrete Ltd
LLBP / UK / Concrete Ltd (plus various local main contractors) / 1961, Pollokshaws CDA,
Glasgow / 306 blocks (including 89 in Birmingham) / 23 storeys

C Bryant: LLBP and RISC / C. Bryant & Son / West Midlands / 173 blocks / 24 storeys

S Camus LLBP / France / various; in Liverpool: Unit Construction Company Ltd. /1963,
Liverpool sites / 70 blocks / 23 storeys

C / S Concrete Ltd., Concrete Northern, see under Bison

C Crudens (mainly Scotland) RISC and LLBP / 182 blocks

C DL, DLO municipal 'Direct Labour' organisations

S Jackblock RISC / UK / 1964 / Barras Heath Coventry / 1 block / 17 storeys

C / S John Laing Ltd. see Sectra, see 12 M Jespersen; also: 'Storiform'; 'Easiform' (houses) / total C and
S 245 blocks

S Larsen & Nielsen LLBP / Denmark / Taylor Woodrow-Anglian / 1963, LCC Morris Walk,
Woolwich / 64 blocks / 23 storeys

S / C Liftslab: British Lift Slab Ltd. RISC / UK (USA) / 1962, Middleborough Rd Coventry / 6 blocks / 17 storeys

S / C Reema Construction Ltd. / Reema (Scotland) Ltd. 'Reema System' / LLBP / UK / Reema / 1956,
various Leeds sites / 67 blocks / 26 storeys

S Sectra RISC / France / Laing / 1963, Heywood, Lancashire / 37 blocks / 15 storeys

S SF[1] **(Indulex)** LLBP (plastic) / UK / F.G.Minter / 1965 Walterton Road, Paddington / 4 blocks / 24 storeys

C Shepherd Building Group Ltd (North East) RISC / 94 blocks / 17 storeys

S Skarne LLBP and RISC / Sweden / Crudens /1966, Sighthill, Edinburgh / 94 blocks / 24 storeys

S SSHA No-Fines No-fines RISC / UK / Scottish Special Housing Association DL / 1955, Toryglen,
Glasgow / 15 blocks / 10 storeys

C Taylor Woodrow Anglian Ltd. See Larsen & Nielsen

C / S Tersons Ltd. RISC and LLBP / 'Tersons' heavy concrete system' / total S and C 180 blocks / 24 storeys

S Tracoba LLBP / France / Gilbert-Ash / 1964, Charlemont Farm, West Bromwich / 41 blocks / 24 storeys

C / S Truscon Trussed Concrete Steel Company Ltd. 1950s: 'Plate System'. 1960s; 'The Truscon Complete Building
Service' / total blocks 116

C / S Wates Ltd. 'Wates Build', 'Wates System': RISC and LLBP / total blocks C and S 503

C / S Wimpey 'Wimpey **No-Fines**' (for houses)**,** 'Wimpey [No-Fines] System Building': RISC / UK / Wimpey / 1953,
Tile Hill, Coventry / 884 blocks / 25 storeys

S YDG (Yorkshire Development Group) Mk.I LLBP / UK / YDG, many Shepherd plus various local main
contractors / 1966, Leek Street, Leeds / 134 blocks / 7 storeys

PROGRESS IN INDUSTRIALISED BUILDING

Norfolk builds flats for London

INDUSTRIALISED housing, on the biggest scale yet in Great Britain, is beginning at a factory at Lenwade, near Norwich.

From this six-acre factory, set in the Norfolk countryside, are to come the massive room-size components for 562 flats at Morris Walk, Woolwich, one of the L.C.C.'s biggest housing schemes, costing more than £2 million, and the first in London to use fully-industrialised construction.

From the factory, built specially for Taylor Woodrow-Anglian Ltd., at a cost of over £250,000, will come at first two flats a day, then four, scaled to keep pace with the rate of erection at Woolwich. The ultimate capacity of the factory will be six flats per day.

The system, used exclusively by Taylor Woodrow-Anglian in Britain under licence from Larsen and Nielsen of Copenhagen, is based on a technique which has been used and improved over a period of 15 years on the Continent. It is extensively used in eight countries in Europe—Austria, Denmark, Germany, Holland, Iceland, Norway, Sweden and Switzerland—and has lately been introduced in South America and the U.S.A. It is the subject of review at technical conferences held two or three times a year by all the countries using it. Great Britain has thus been able to reap the benefit of much international experience and to adapt the system to British needs.

Among advantages of the Larsen and Nielsen system is that it has been developed in Denmark under conditions similar to those in the United Kingdom with strong competition from traditional construction and has become established as a standard method of building. The all-important jointing method, tested and proved over a number of years, is generally accepted as the best among several other systems.

THE FACTORY

The factory, first of its size and kind in Britain, has been specially designed and constructed for the sole purpose of manufacturing industrialised building components. It is divided into four shops to make varying types of units requiring different manufacturing techniques.

Each shop is provided with two fast-operating 10-ton overhead cranes, giving complete coverage of the factory and extending outside over the whole of the 200,000 sq. ft. stockyard.

The stockyard has special racks for storing complete units and each area is provided with a rail siding and facilities for loading on to road transport. This dual loading ability increases the area of economical delivery.

The raw materials for the concrete are delivered to a central batching plant where the cement is stored in four 30-ton overhead silos and the aggregate in underground hoppers. The aggregates are weighed and fed by conveyor to the mixer which has an output of two cubic yards of concrete every 30 seconds.

The mixed concrete is carried to the factory in specially made trucks and discharged direct into the moulds, with the exception of the floor casting shop where a conveyor is to be used.

The factory was designed, manufactured and erected in under six months by Anglian Building Products, whose factory, 500 yards away, is working at full capacity for road, hospital, school and university programmes. Units can be seen awaiting despatch to the Chiswick-Langley Motorway, Birmingham-Preston Motorway; Northern Link Road, Worcestershire; Slough-Maidenhead Motorway; Blackfriars Bridge reconstruction; various bridges for British Railways; and St. Thomas' and Guy's Hospitals. This company has made bridge beams of lengths of up to 128 ft. long (in one piece) and is planning longer ones for the future. St. Catherine's College, Oxford, much in the news, has Anglian structural columns and 75 ft. pre-stressed concrete beams with a marble-like finish.

THE MOULDS

Ninety steel moulds are being used for forming the concrete units for the Woolwich contract. They weigh anything up to five tons and are precision-made with machined edges and contact surfaces, the maximum tolerance (deviation from specified measurement) on all the dimensions and in the plane of the unit being only two millimetres.

This degree of accuracy in manufacture is necessary to ensure that the various components readily "slot in" to one another on the site.

All the special Larsen and Nielsen joint details are provided for in these moulds.

To start production for Woolwich as early as possible the moulds in use now were obtained from the Continent (Denmark and Germany). They cost from £1,000 to £1,700 each. Much foresight has to be used in their design for they have to allow for the casting without further alteration, of every feature in a wall or floor, including door and window openings, conduits, pipe sleeves and fittings for the water, gas and electrical services, and even appropriately placed points for radio, television and telephone.

COMPONENTS

These are room-size—that is they are storey-high and can be as long as 24 ft., weighing from one to nearly five tons each. The only limitation on the size of a unit is that imposed by transport and ease of handling at factory and site.

Six main types of components are made: face walls up to 8 in. thick, with an internal layer of polystyrene

14

An account of an 'industrialised building' process, at the Morris Walk Estate, London, from the *Journal of the National Housing and Town Planning Council*, 1964 (cf. p. 91).

for thermal insulation; cross walls (which are the main load bearers) up to 6 in. thick; partitions 2½ in. thick; floor slabs of hollow construction 7⅛ in. thick with an economic span of 18 ft. and a width of 8 ft. 6 in.; stair-flights and landing slabs.

The components leave the factory complete with wall and floor insulation installed, with conduits ready for electrical wiring or water services, door and window frames cast in and painted, and windows glazed. When the panels are fitted together on the site the only jobs remaining are the hanging of doors, electrical wiring, wall papering and final painting.

The outside surfaces of the concrete walls may be patterned, moulded, painted or aggregate exposed in an infinite variety of designs. The finishes for Morris Walk, chosen by the L.C.C. Housing Committee (from a number which may be seen on the lawn in front of the offices of Anglian Building Products at Lenwade) consist of 1 in. to 1½ in. Norfolk flints.

FACTORY LABOUR

Most of the men are local and some come from Norwich. They have nearly all been trained by Anglian Building Products at Lenwade on the production of large concrete components and the first of a number of teams has just returned from training in Denmark.

Numbers employed in the factory in turning out the components for the Woolwich scheme will be about 120.

RAIL TRANSPORT PREFERRED

The factory is 120 miles from London.

For such large components and regularity of delivery so that the components arrive in their correct sequence for "phasing in" to the building programme, rail transport has been chosen for Woolwich and probably will be for many other sites.

A train consisting of 15 wagons, specially adapted at the Ashford Works of British Railways and carrying components for four flats, will leave Lenwade every other night for Charlton sidings where road trailer units, also specially designed, will be used to the site about half-a-mile away.

Two of these trains will be in constant shuttle service between Lenwade and Charlton, completing each journey overnight—the first "Night Specials" for the building industry.

ERECTION METHOD

Erection and jointing of the components of a block of flats is normally carried out by a superstructure gang of approximately 15 men working with one crane. The probability is that at Morris Walk two such teams will be at work and the key men in each are being given training in Denmark by Larsen and Nielsen.

On site, mobile cranes are the only items of plant required. No scaffolding is needed, as each floor will be erected and jointed complete before a start is made on the next floor. Rigidity of the structure is obtained by in situ concrete joints between the main elements such as floor panels and main cross walls.

As soon as flats are completed on one floor, the erection team will start on those above while at the vacant flats below other teams will move in to complete the finishing jobs such as hanging doors, connection of wiring, wall papering and final painting.

At Morris Walk, Woolwich, a start will be made first on the tall blocks, to contain 40 flats each. Structural completion of each of these will take about a month, and a further 10 weeks or so will be required for the lift installations at each block. The three-storey blocks, without lift installations, will be erected within a few working days each.

Industrialised building methods such as this show a saving in the site labour employed of 25 to 30 per cent.

THE L.C.C. MORRIS WALK FLATS, WOOLWICH

This will be the first large-scale industrialised block of council flats in Britain and the first built by Taylor Woodrow-Anglian.

At Morris Walk on the 16½ acre site 562 homes are being provided in seven 10-storey blocks and 47 three-storey blocks. The first residents will move in next year and the whole scheme will be completed in 1965 accommodating about 1,800 people.

The rooms to be provided vary from one (for bedsitters) to five, but more than 60 per cent of the flats will be of the three- or four-roomed types. More than 100 will be old people's dwellings, generally on the lower floors of the three-storey blocks.

The slopes of the site, which adjoins Maryon Park, have been utilised to plan underground garaging for about 140 cars. Garages or parking spaces for a further 180 cars approximately are to be provided, together with tenants' stores, a children's play area, and an old folk's clubroom. The scheme also includes road widening. A community centre, a public house, and shopping premises are among other facilities planned or proposed.

Blocks will be warmed by a gas space heating system (with a separate unit in each dwelling) and electric-heaters will provide the hot water.

The tall blocks will be constructed in two wings, connected to a central lift, staircase and service tower by a short access bridge. Each wing will have two dwellings on each floor—one day's factory production.

15

PART TWO – TOWER BLOCK DESIGN

6 The 1930s: a new kind of economic dwelling for the *Existenzminimum?*

In the long history of British public and charitable housing, the 1930s marked an increased concern for new kinds of plans and new methods of construction. By 1934 a new rallying cry had emerged: 'Reduce the cost of housing through the fuller use of modern structural methods and materials' – so we read in a long report, entitled *Slum Clearance and Rehousing,* issued in that year by a newly-created Council for Research on Housing Construction. The CRHC was a very large body indeed, comprising over seventy members, chaired by the Earl of Dudley, later noted as presiding over the Government's housing design committee, when he cautiously advocated the building of flats in his 'Dudley Report' of 1944. Apart from a number of the most eminent architects, such as Francis Lorne of Sir John Burnet, Tait & Lorne, who had designed Sydney Harbour Bridge and the British Museum extension, or G. Topham Forrest, architect of the LCC, the bulk of the Council's membership was recruited from the construction and building supply industries. The lavish volume of 1934 was also to serve the industry's, that is principally the steel industry's, self- promotion.

Equally significant were the CRHC Report's new proposals for planning. The avowed starting point was what was happening on the Continent, principally in Vienna and Berlin, as well as Rotterdam. In architectural research circles, in Berlin in particular, a new conception of mass housing had been developed under the heading 'the dwelling of the *Existenzminimum*'.[1] The basic assumption is best expressed as that of 'standard needs'. These, it is assumed, are the same for all human beings, and they can all be reliably defined. Following this logic, a dwelling that serves these needs is guaranteed to be a satisfactory dwelling, and therefore all dwellings not only can be, but also should be, planned in the same form, down to the last detail. At that point the notion of the minimal enters the equation, in that this standardized approach is assumed to lead to financial savings, which, in turn, help to guarantee that there can be enough satisfactory dwellings for all.

All this kind of reasoning formed part of the strictly rationalist trend in International Modernist architecture. To define the actual standards and needs on which it was based did not appear difficult at the time: they were largely those of physical health and prowess. The building forms thought to be most conducive to these aims were those that guaranteed a maximum of 'light, air, sun [which] make life possible' – words accompanying the opening of a Swiss documentary film on design in 1930, as cited by Paul Overy.[2] Neither did there seem to be any problem in defining the look of the actual dwellings that would serve and express these needs. They simply needed to be light, light in their construction and light in every aspect of their appearance. Lastly, it greatly helped to keep all this in mind when contrasting the modern look with the image of the 'slum': a world of dirt, darkness, disorder and, most disturbingly, irregularity and unpredictability.

The *Existenzminimum* dwelling concept seemed to lead inexorably to a certain shape of building, a shape that was held by its advocates to be undeniably rational, namely a new type of free-standing block of flats which formed a basic rectangle of a certain length, and nothing more, which in Germany had begun to be called 'Zeilenbau', literally building along a line. Above all, this kind of planning would be best suited to admitting the newly-desired qualities of light and air. It could then be arranged in rows in any numbers. The Report, too, presented a number of its own models for long 5-storey blocks.

Most significant is also the Report's model design for 10-storey blocks, though here the *Zeilenbau* shape is given up in favour of a cross shape, doubtless to in order to maximize the use of the lifts. The crucial step towards height could here be taken because of a new use of the steel frame. A year later the concrete building industry launched a counter-effort with a 'Competition for Working Men's Flats' which likewise produced outline plans for ten-storeyed blocks.[3] However, neither it nor the CRHC Report succeeded in catching wider attention, though some of the names involved in the concrete competition, such as Lubetkin/Tecton and Edward Armstrong, were to rise to prominence in post-war London housing architecture.

However, while serving on the CRHC, Burnet, Tait & Lorne were already busy constructing one small estate in reinforced concrete, a social housing development named Evelyn Court in Hackney, comprising ten five-storey blocks of flats. These, in

Left: London, Evelyn Court, Amhurst Road,
Hackney, E8. 1933–34, by Sir John Burnet,
Tait & Lorne for the 4% Industrial Dwellings
Company (cf. p. 51).
Below: Block plan for Evelyn Court.

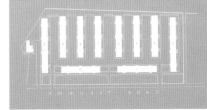

their block plan, superficially resemble the German *Zeilenbau* models; but they also differ significantly in that each block gives out onto a street on both sides, and not, as the newest Berlin blocks, to greenery. The most significant factor here is density. It amounts to above 300 persons per acre. In the 1934 Report it is held that new 4 to 5-storey blocks can accommodate 60 dwellings, or 250 to 300 persons, per acre 'without serious congestion'.[4] In the case of the proposed 10-storey flats the density would amount to 120 flats on a 1 acre plot, comprising perhaps 400 or 500 persons.[5] As the Report itself states, these are figures that apply commonly to urban slum areas.

In Chapter 9 the discussion will return to density figures. The essence of it will be that the official upper density figure for British post-war municipal developments was 200 persons per acre, with most new urban and inner suburban housing in Britain having to lower densities still, at 130, 100 p.p.a. or even less. Without actually overtly referring to the notion of an

Existenzminimum, the Report's proposals of 1934 clearly represented an extreme position. Neither did Britain ever resort to the very high degree of standardization of dwelling form that the Report suggested.

All these factors lead one to ask how much Britain was, even at this early stage, destined to diverge from the wider international context of mass social housing, which would witness in some places the most rigid cost systematization and plan standardization, as for instance in 1940s-60s American and in 1950s-80s Soviet public housing, and in the unimaginably high densities in some other places, including those blocks comprising between 2,500 and 7,000 p.p.a., built, actually, under British colonial auspices, in 1950s-90s Hong Kong.[6] Of course, there was no question of a disregard of 'economy' in post-war British housing; to save costs was certainly a constant preoccupation, but the ways of doing it kept changing all the time. A completely standardized '*Existenzminimum*' was never a serious proposition in Britain.[7]

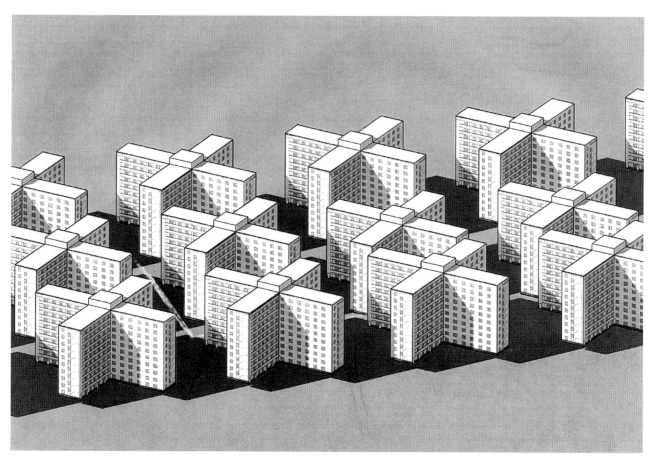

Housing proposed by the Council for Research on Housing Construction, London 1934.
Computer simulation of those 1934 proposals by Nicholas Warr 2016.

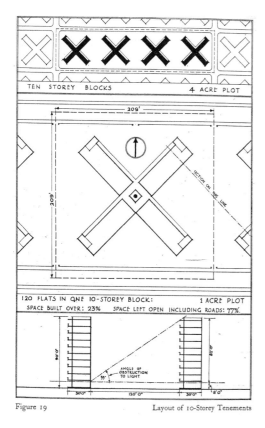

Berlin housing proposal 1928, by Marcel Breuer.

TEN STOREY BLOCKS   4 ACRE PLOT

209'

209'

SECTION ON THIS LINE

120 FLATS IN ONE 10-STOREY BLOCK: 1 ACRE PLOT
SPACE BUILT OVER: 23%   SPACE LEFT OPEN INCLUDING ROADS: 77%

80'-0"

80'-0"

ANGLE OF
OBSTRUCTION
TO LIGHT

33°

30'-0"   120'-0"   30'-0"   8'-0"

Figure 19   Layout of 10-Storey Tenements

7 High-rise stories: from six to thirty-two

Pioneers of the 1940s and 1950s

For an overview of the drive towards height in council blocks the Council for Research on Housing Construction's *Report* of 1934, with its tentative ten-storey blocks, marks a good beginning. During the following years a greater number of factors began to come together. New private, mostly stylistically indifferent blocks of flats were being built in London with eight, ten or even more storeys; there was a small number of internationally-known housing blocks of up to fifteen floors in Germany, Holland and France and an equally small number of distinguished English examples in the new International Modern style, both philanthropic and public, which appeared in London and which went up to seven or even nine storeys; Leeds City Council's massive Quarry Hill complex of 1934–38 reached eight floors.[1] It was then the *County of London Plan* of 1943 which codified high blocks of flats, of 7 to 10 floors.[2] Height was presented as the logical outcome of the decision to combine a high density with extensive open green areas. It meant a sanctioning of these formulae in the context of town planning. Town planning was at that time a quasi-public institutional force; one of its major policies, country-wide, was the preservation of open agricultural land, which led to a new contempt for suburban low-density housing. In that way, high blocks were becoming part of state and municipal policy, and they were henceforth financially supported by the central state for well over two decades. A crucial early step to make possible a greater height on a larger scale was the promise, in the Housing Act of 1946, to help with the financing of lifts.[3]

The accepted official definition in Britain for post 1945 'multi-storey' or 'high rise' blocks is six storeys plus; the very occasional definition of 'five plus' need not concern us here as it appears to be based just on the fact that the newest five-storey blocks were being fitted with lifts, too. After 1950 the building of five-storey blocks in England decreased considerably, precisely because of the less economic use of the lifts. Thus the lift was not only something that resulted from the desire for building upwards; one may also see it as a cause of greater height.[4] In the very densest inner suburbs of London, such as Shoreditch, the hitherto common London type of five-storey block groupings was being superseded by single slab blocks of six to eight floors, while still adhering to the customary solid and stolid brickwork. But 'Modern' architecture, as understood by a still very small elite of adherents to the Continental International Modern style, was something quite different. A new beginning was made in 1946 with Holborn's ten-storey steel-framed Dombey Street slab block and, in the same year, Westminster Council's large Modernist Pimlico development, called Churchill Gardens, mostly of nine storeys, was won in competition by the young team of Powell & Moya. By 1950 Frederick Gibberd was completing the much publicised block, 'The Lawn', at Mark Hall in Harlow New Town, reaching ten storeys although, because of its width, one hesitates somewhat to call it a tower.

A breakthrough to the high tower in 1950 came in the context of the most radical development inside the London County Council, when the reorganised Architect's Department 'recaptured' the design of housing from the Valuer and Housing Manager. Here, the chief task of the group of council architects was now seen as not just the provision of dwellings but the design of new types of dwellings. A major innovation of the early 1950s was the long block divided into maisonettes, piling five of them on top of each other, resulting in a total of eleven storeys. But the most radical shift had come in late 1950. Chief Housing Architect H. J. Whitfield Lewis presented his model of the Princes Way development (Ackroydon Estate) in Wandsworth, including eleven-storey 'point' blocks in reinforced concrete frame construction. For the next ten years, or, arguably, for the next twenty years, the slim point block – a new term in itself – was the principal aspiration of British public housing design. The way in which the Akroydon blocks' eventual construction drastically changed the early plans indicates the difficulty and novelty of the task at that time. Daring, too, must have been their cost, with only three flats per floor and two lifts. A special interest in the LCC's eleven and twelve-storey slab blocks and point blocks was maintained during the whole of the 1950s, culminating in the later, even more celebrated Roehampton estates.

The basic formula regarding all high blocks was: a higher density needs higher blocks. But there was also now a more complex formula, the 'mixed development' argument: higher density can combine high and low formations, there are always at least some dwellers who prefer a house to a flat, and it is precisely through using high blocks that land could be freed for small houses with gardens, and even a few bungalows for the aged. In any case, it could be stated plainly that 'the tall block had arisen from the work of Whitfield Lewis's Housing Division in 1950',[5] that is, from the architect's lobby and its elected supporters, the councillors, within the 'progressive' LCC.

Meanwhile some of the Metropolitan second-tier boroughs were trying hard to keep up; in Paddington MBC the Borough Architect, Major Rolf Jensen, propagated fifteen-storey point blocks in 1954; Finsbury MBC completed twelve-storey blocks at the Stafford Cripps Estate in 1954, designed by the older avant-garde architect Joseph Emberton, and not far from it the City of London, a Metropolitan Borough Council of a very special kind, completed its Golden Lane Estate, with its sixteen-storey Great Arthur House, in 1957; its height having been raised by four floors from the competition plans of 1951/2. Here, too, a private firm had been chosen, Chamberlin Powell & Bon, later of Barbican fame. Remarkable both for its height and its highly individualistic design was the private architect Denys Lasdun's seventeen-storey 'Cluster Block' at Claredale Street (Keeling House), for Bethnal Green Council, planned from 1955.

Reflecting the primacy of the LCC in these debates, Whitfield Lewis duly acted as the first major speaker at a large conference at the RIBA, entitled 'Symposium on High Flats', the most thorough architectural exploration of all the issues of multi-storey flats so far. Here Duncan Sandys, the Housing Minister, put it in a nut-shell: high blocks 'save land' and provide 'aesthetic opportunities'.[6] Dame Evelyn Sharp, one of the top administrators at the Ministry, pleaded for high blocks within mixed developments. But Sandys and Sharp also warned about cost and the architect-planner J.H. Forshaw remarked that the 'present cost of flats is quite fantastic'.[7] The engineer Peter Dunican then ventured a guess: '15 to 20 storeys would be the optimum for the next decade or two'.[8] As if they had been waiting for the LCC to push the boundary forward, from 1955 many of the Metropolitan Boroughs took up the eleven-storey concept and during the next fifteen or so years the LCC and its successor, the Greater London Council (GLC), together with the boroughs, built over 200 blocks of that height.

As regards public and professional attention, London's fame, and especially that of the LCC Architect's Department, almost totally overshadowed the contributions made by other large cities. True, many of them took five years, or even a decade to join in, but some, notably Birmingham, Coventry, Sheffield and Bristol, contributed new models of housing almost as original as the capital, especially if one does not apply too rigid a definition of 'Modern'. In fact, as regards height some cities' aspirations were bolder than those of London. During the war, Birmingham's City Engineer Herbert Manzoni outdid the *County London Plan* with his vision of a ceremonial road, flanked by enormous seventeen-storey towers. Their realisation could hardly be expected, but in 1950 Birmingham started building a number of large, twelve-storey blocks at Duddeston and Nechells, even though with their wholly exceptional shape one hesitates to call them towers; the somewhat less complex twelve-storey towers of the Aston Reservoir (Holte) Estate followed from 1952. Around 1958 Birmingham started planning sixteen-storey short slab blocks. Coventry began its three eleven-storey point blocks at Tile Hill in 1953. The concept of Sheffield's best known contribution, the Park Hill complex of linked slab blocks, was being worked out from 1955, the highest reaching thirteen storeys, with the later Park Hill Part II, or Hyde Park complex rising higher still, and in 1958 the city started its massive programme of thirteen-storey point blocks. Bristol initiated a very considerable campaign in 1953/4 with

its linked slabs, up to thirteen-storeys in height; the T-shaped Barton House of fifteen storeys, planned and built from 1954–8, brought the city neck and neck with London. By contrast, Leeds's and Liverpool's blocks of the mid 1950s only reached ten storeys. By the later 1950s some middling towns had begun joining in this 'race', such as Bedford, with twelve-storey and Birkenhead with fourteen-storey blocks. All these pioneering undertakings had one thing in common: they took two, three or even four years to come on stream, and their cost appeared to be nobody's business. Arguably, one can speak convincingly of a 'tower' only when a building has reached around thirteen storeys and does not contain more than four small flats on each floor. Such a thinking may have governed the planners in Sheffield from the mid-1950s onwards, leading them to avoid the ten or eleven-storey formula altogether. The same applied to Manchester in the 1960s.

Clearly, by the mid-1950s the big intent was to create a far greater number of towers, and that one should go higher than eleven storeys. London surmounted a crucial hurdle: the fire safety precautions. There had for a long time been a general London rule: so that a fire could be fought from outside, no building should exceed 100 feet, that is, thirty and a half metres, or ten or eleven storeys. But by the mid-fifties these rules were modified, or, rather, made 'less onerous'.[9] It was now emphasised that the firefighters had to be able to get up inside the block, via a ventilated staircase or a 'fireman's lift'.[10] Most importantly, the height limit thereby disappeared. Blocks of 'any height' were now permitted.[11] At the same time, a complex of considerations emerged. Incombustible materials were needed throughout: certainly concrete scored highly in that respect. Blocks of flats were understood in terms of individual 'cells': fires were assumed to occur in a very localised manner, and not all occupants would have to leave when a fire broke out within a 'cell'.[12] At the same time escape routes did require careful consideration. The straightforward and frequently practised solution was to have two staircases. But under certain conditions, mainly taking into account the possibilities of ventilation, one set of stairs was deemed sufficient. If there was only one staircase for a long maisonette block, an additional small escape balcony attached to the bedroom floors could be required (see ill page 71). Concluding, Cleeve Barr writes 'the details of any individual case is considered on its own merits.[13] Finally, what was stipulated for London appeared to apply to the provinces as well.

At the RIBA Conference in 1955, Whitfield Lewis pronounced that he harboured '... no prejudices about going higher', higher than eleven storeys, that is. In 1956 he became a little more precise: going above eleven or twelve, he argued, did not mean changes in 'physical effect', as the 'effect of insecurity' did not increase beyond this height.[14] In any case, almost all towers, that is, most towers of the point block type, now had internal staircases, in contrast to the slab blocks with their external access balconies, a factor which made point blocks appear somewhat superior dwellings. Another reason for building at a greater height had entered the discussion by 1955: the task of rehousing inhabitants of high-density slum areas. Planned from 1955 onwards, St. Anne's Neighbourhood in the London

East End was to include one fifteen-storey block, similar in shape to the Roehampton point blocks.

From the mid-fifties London towers began edging up further. At the Brandon Estate, the LCC's boldest group to date, begun in 1955/6, they reached eighteen storeys. The announcement of a 'Nineteen-storey maisonette block at Tidey Street', in Stepney, came in 1956. Just as much as with height, the designers were now also grappling with the new plan types. A key challenge was to devise a maisonette block which could go beyond eleven storeys. Here, the principal trend was now towards complex combinations of flats and maisonettes in short slab or wide point blocks. 1958 saw the first LCC plans for the Warwick Crescent redevelopment, which was to breach the twenty-storey mark, as well as the first plans for Draper House, in the Elephant and Castle CDA, which was to contain eleven tiers of maisonettes within a total of twenty-five floors, though its completion took until 1965. Finally, 1960–61 saw the emergence of the last major set-piece of the LCC's experiments in high-rise planning, the 'scissors' or 'split level' tower-slabs at Deptford and elsewhere – another new planning idea, which was also taken up to twenty-five storeys. And yet, in 1960, the LCC had been beaten by a Borough, St Pancras MBC, with the completion of their nineteen-storey tower at the Regent's Park Estate, one floor higher than Brandon.

All in all, however, by the end of 1959 one was still far away from anything remotely approaching a landscape of towers. There was a sprinkling of eleven and twelve-storey point blocks, none of them placed in the more accessible and prominent parts of London; only Golden Lane's Great Arthur House did rise impressively above the medley of the City of London. Bristol and Birmingham were in second and third position. But many major cities, including Nottingham, Leicester and Manchester, had not shown any interest in high blocks at all. The building of towers had so far been driven by a number of highly specific impulses, town planning, sociological and aesthetic, and each tower had arisen from a unique co-operation between enthusiastic clients, designers and builders.

1960s Ubiquity

In 1961 A. W. Cleeve Barr voiced his conviction that multi-storey flats would be 'the dominant form of urban dwelling in this century'.[15] The towers of the 1960s, indeed, appear in a very different light. First of all, the whole of the 'provincial' world was now coming into its own, and London no longer dominated, as it had done so far. The new ubiquity of towers means that their story cannot be any longer just one of a sequence of a few major undertakings. Hence one should begin with sheer numbers: How did the years 1958 to 1972 see completion of no less than 343,000 council flats in high blocks, counting all blocks of six floors and above, compared with the years 1945 to 1957, when only 49,000 such dwellings were built? How did high flats as a proportion of all council housing increase so dramatically, from 3% in 1953 to 20% in 1960 and to a peak of 26% in 1966?[16]

The plain answer was that a high building could deliver, at a stroke, a hundred or more new dwellings on a small site, a total which would go a noticeable way to reduce a town's housing waiting list, and thus add to its 'housing yield'. There was, among central government politicians and civil servants at the time, a strong dissatisfaction with the country's performance in public housing production: from a peak of over 200,000 new council dwellings in 1953 the figure had come down to well under 100,000 by 1961.[17] At the same time the housing shortage appeared more acute than ever. There was an increase in the demand for smaller dwellings, to accommodate the growing number of smaller households. General living standards were rising and with them the demand for more modern facilities all round. An added impetus to hurry up and to organise an effective performance came through the way in which land prices and general building costs were sharply rising – the latter being paralleled by crippling materials and labour shortages. By late 1961 the *Architects' Journal* wrote of a 'tragic situation'.[18] Build homes 'in quicker and more economic ways of building ...' demanded the International Union of Architects' Congress in London in 1961,[19] and shortly later the *Architects' Journal* adumbrated this issue even more starkly: '...for the immediate relief ... building more cheaply ...'[20] – which might indeed sound like the procedures which Khrushchev had been pursuing a few years earlier in the USSR. But for British public housing this could hardly have meant reducing standards, merely the hope of reducing building costs somehow. In any case, successive Housing Ministers, whether Conservative or (after 1964) Labour, demanded a vast increase in output, double or treble the current numbers. Their rhetoric could still be as strong as in the early post-war years: new housing was to be 'of the greatest significance for the happiness of the people ...'.[21] The year 1967 finally brought a new peak of public housing production, with over 159,000 completions. Yet exhortations continued, with some still demanding, in 1965, 500,000 new dwellings by 1970.[22]

The single most important driving factor was slum clearance, and its unique force in Britain. As was explained in Chapter 4, millions of older dwellings were considered unfit. Their replacement started from the mid-1950s, initially on a piecemeal basis and then, throughout the 1960s, on ever wider and all-embracing lines, with architects working in close conjunction with planners in CDAs (Comprehensive Development Areas), creating new districts which often comprehensively changed the street patterns of the old areas. Height was now a decisive factor in the new buildings that replaced the slums. 'Building upwards is now the most urgent need', so read a headline in the *Municipal Journal* in 1959.[23] No major slum clearance project could be imagined without at least one tower – for aesthetic reasons as well as for its obvious practical advantages, in facilitating decanting and phased clearance. Once again, Whitfield Lewis's voice in 1956: 'One tall block on an immediately available site gives enormous housing profit, and facilitates the more rapid clearance of the remainder of the site'.[24] In Salford's Ellor Street, one of the most impressive redevelopments, the towers loom large, helping, as they did, to re-accommodate all the original inhabitants within their original area.

For those who could not be rehoused on, or close to the same site, their officially mandated fate was 'overspill' – that is, the 'decanting' to sites sometimes well beyond the boundaries of the authority undertaking the clearance. In 1962 a figure of two million people was given for whom overspill accommodation needed to be found during the subsequent 20 years.[25] The early post-war solution most favoured by the regional planners was that of concerted removal into completely 'New Towns', or to existing, often far-flung 'expansion towns'. But by 1960 doubts about this programme were growing, especially because of the vast expenses incurred. A better solution, at least for the biggest towns, appeared to be the creation of quasi-self-contained new 'satellite' communities of council housing, either at the edge of the city, or just beyond, such as Birmingham's two massive developments, Castle Vale and Chelmsley Wood, containing over 20,000 dwellings, almost all of them council owned. At the same time the older kinds of planning admonitions, regarding health and community spirit, or the protection of open land and green belts, continued.[26] What was to be avoided at all costs was the 'uncontrolled sprawl of the inter-war period'[27] of low-rise dwellings in a 'no-man's land between town and country', often dubbed 'subtopia'.[28]

Once again, the best solution that offered itself was to build high. One of the most astonishing facts regarding redevelopment and resettlement was the way in which high blocks increasingly also served suburban or out-of-town areas. Here the model of Roehampton, in turn based on late 1930s International Modern ideals of towers in a park, must have still played a role. Towers could furthermore be placed prominently on 'gap sites' adjacent to open areas or even carved opportunistically out of parks or golf courses, as for instance in a succession of early 1960s sites in outer north-west Glasgow in and around the low-density interwar council garden-suburb of Knightswood. There did not always have to be the full complement of a mixed development, as, after all, there were more than enough cottage-type houses or two-storey flats in those outer suburbs. A sub-category of the outer suburban high rises was the individual tower, or couple of towers, of a very great height and individualistic design, as at Nottingham's Clifton and Leeds's Cottingley. One may see these towers as part of a broader logic of 'mixed development': if one strives for houses in or near the centre, a quid pro quo would then involve tower-building on the outskirts.

None of all this could have happened without the new developments on the supply side. These were principally due to the greater expertise and to a more streamlined organisation of the building industry, and partly also in response to the overload conditions afflicting 'traditional' building in the early 1960s. In 1962 the Minister still felt he had to admonish the builders, 'don't be afraid of new methods'.[29] Only one or two years later a considerable number of national firms, about a dozen, were offering new advanced building 'systems' which allowed the highest blocks to be built seemingly without any fuss, without stress for the municipality and, as some firms prided themselves, completed not within years, but within months. Many of the highest blocks were now identified directly with the name of the building firm or a 'system', such as 'Bison', 'Wimpey' and others. For a few years, around 1961–64, continuous advancement through technological research appeared entirely plausible. While the promise of a general reduction of costs remained elusive, there did appear to be a new calculability as regards timing, not only for blocks of eight or eleven storeys, but for those of seventeen or twenty-two storeys, too.

And thus, within half a dozen years or so, urban Britain started to become a land of towers, or, to be more precise, of point blocks. This type was generally preferred over the long slab blocks that prevailed in some continental countries, although the latter did occur in some very prominent locations in Britain, too, such as at Sighthill in Glasgow or Ardler in Dundee. Naturally, the slab block normally offered the more economic solution, simply because lifts could serve a larger number of flats. But the designers of point blocks tried their hardest to increase the number of flats per floor, from four to six or even eight, while also making every effort to avoid the look of a massive slab. These oscillations between slab and point blocks greatly contributed to the variety of architectural solutions overall.

Throughout the 1960s the average height of newly-built blocks was on the increase. One may guess a rough countrywide average height of new council towers of 15 or 16 floors by 1962–65.[30] Of great significance was the twenty-storey mark. This was hardly ever explicitly stated by the professionals, yet the evidence is clear: hardly more than two dozen nineteen-storey blocks were built, and there were a few more of eighteen storeys, yet the total of blocks of twenty to twenty-eight storeys came to a massive 478 in the whole of Great Britain, including 230 in London, 102 in the rest of England, a single block in Wales, and 145 in Scotland. Of the latter no less than 127 were located in the City of Glasgow – over a quarter of the total in the whole of Britain, which the last chapter will return to. But the odd high tower could now be found in virtually every part of the country, and not only in the larger cities. From 1965 the new London 'upper-tier' authority, the GLC, built some 300 blocks of eleven storeys and below, as well as 32 at twenty storeys, but hardly anything in between. Liverpool and Birmingham both showed a sizeable number of twenty-storey blocks, but no nineteen and very few eighteen-storey ones. In the latter city the chief engineer, Herbert Manzoni, reportedly argued for twenty storeys so as to most effectively rehouse central area slum dwellers.[31] One motive must of course have been the practical one of 'site yield', but the symbolic importance of the twenty-storey mark was also clear, as was made explicit by Liverpool councillors in 1957: 'The housing committee take the view that there was no reason why the twenty-storey mark should not be passed and we regard this as important a step in the construction of domestic dwellings as was the breaking of the sound barrier in the world of aeronautics'; in London, the Liverpool councillors noted, the LCC were considering blocks of nineteen storeys.[32] In 1960 Liverpool announced a twenty-two-storey block and a few months later Leeds launched a project for a twenty-three-storey tower, though it took Leeds until 1970 actually to begin construction of its two twenty-five-storey towers at Cottingley. By that time a total of 27 towers of twenty-five to twenty-eight storeys had been built by a number of British municipalities, but only eight of them in England, the rest of them in Glasgow.

Finally, with thirty floors the story comes to a close. Glasgow was completing its eight thirty-one-storey towers from 1967 onwards. In the same year the tiny authority of Whickham Urban District Council, adjacent to Gateshead, began building the thirty-storey Derwent Tower, in a wholly exceptional shape, as one would expect from the maverick London architect Owen Luder. London's only comparable block, Ernö Goldfinger's thirty-one-storey Trellick Tower for the GLC, equally exceptional in its architecture, was likewise started in 1967, as were Birmingham's Sentinels, initially envisaged at thirty storeys. A total of only twelve blocks of thirty storeys and over were built across the whole country. The much higher blocks of the City of London's Barbican development with over forty storeys, one has to be reminded, were not 'council housing' in the strict sense, but market-rental prestige apartments for elite tenants. At an early stage the Birmingham Sentinels' designers decided to add another two storeys – possibly once it was realised that other similar towers were going up elsewhere. At thirty-two floors the Sentinels were, and still are, the highest 'Council Towers' of social housing in Britain; right in the centre of the city; next to the famous, the notorious Inner Ring Road, which was completed around the same time, they trumpet, and document for posterity, the presence of British council housing like nowhere else. The great irony was, of course, that by the very late 1960s, towers had gone out of fashion altogether and the provincial blocks just mentioned received virtually no public or professional recognition at all.

8 Debating the aesthetics of tall buildings

'London's Houses', title vignette by Kupfer-Sachs, 1939: a rare
pre-International Modern concept of height.

Before delving into the complexity of the many new technical
details which every tower block presents, it might be fortifying
to hear something unequivocally positive, some simple words
of visual praise. Plenty of these could be heard at the RIBA
Symposium on High Flats in 1955. Basic eulogies came right
at the beginning: high blocks are 'a thing of beauty', claimed
the first speaker, Dame Evelyn Sharp, Deputy Secretary of
the Ministry of Housing and Local Government.[1] Indeed, this
kind of lofty language can be traced some years further back;
speaking to the strongly left-wing Association of Building
Technicians in 1945, Aneurin Bevan held that when 'experimenting with high buildings in the countryside ... no one is
complaining that [a] scene is spoilt by a lovely church spire
... [thus] high buildings can be an adornment if they themselves are aesthetically correct'.[2] More fervently aestheticiz-
ing was a comment in *Wimpey News* in the early 1960s on an
eleven-storey block in Mersey Street, Wallasey, rhapsodising
that '... the clean lines of this block break impressively into
the sky'.[3]

However, praising the mere look of a building in the 20th century
could never be a straightforward matter. Politicians could use
common epithets freely because they did not trouble themselves with architectural theory. Professionals could never
be so certain. For most Modernists, all judgments of aesthetic
value provided a problem; hence the striking complexity of
the pronouncements that one meets. One of the practitioners
who also wrote theoretically was Frederick Gibberd, whose
own scheme of council towers at Harlow New Town we will
meet later; here he, too, compared tower blocks with medie-
val spires. Although Gibberd had counted amongst the most
ardent Modernists in the 1930s, by the 1950s he had adopted

a curious in-between position, arguing that 'modern architecture is no different from Greek, Roman and Renaissance in its
fundamental principles ... a building needs to be a complete
harmonious whole'.[4] At times, he chose an overtly hedonistic
tone: 'the truth is, and like most truths it is quite simple, it is
this: The building of tall flat blocks gives more pleasure to more
people. That means just what it says'.[5]

But for most other mainstream Modernists, such as the critic
J.M. Richards, words like 'beauty' and 'harmony', let alone
'pleasure', used in any straightforward way, practically did not
exist. Neither can one find them in Nikolaus Pevsner's important contribution on Roehampton; here was an art historian
who proudly supported the cause of the present, but it had to
be done through a strictly historical account of the past developments of the point block. What was most significant for him
was the new LCC concept of towers in a park, which he linked
back to the 18th century English concept of the picturesque.[6]
Earlier, in his book *The Englishness of English Art*, published
in 1956, Pevsner's last two illustrations show the LCC's new
housing in Wandsworth, at Roehampton and Ackroydon, which
for him served as examples of 'picturesque principles applied
to urban [sic] conditions'.[7]

Many Modernists saw it as their task to downplay aesthetics
and to valorise only the buildings' fulfilment of all practical
aims. For example, the fulsome architectural praise of the
famed Hertfordshire schools, up to that time Britain's most
respected Modernist architectural undertaking, avoided
any specific aesthetic evaluation. Among the often small
circles of practitioners and their attendant architectural
commentators, especially in the LCC Department in the

LANDSCAPE AND BUILDING

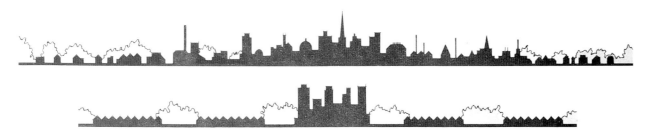

Frederick Gibberd's diagrammatic vision of the vertical accents in town centres, old and new, Harlow, c.1960 (cf. p. 156).

1950s, architectural issues were instead discussed through the medium of more oblique catchwords, such as 'Hard' vs. 'Soft' or 'New Empiricism', or 'New Humanism'. Here, 'hard' meant the exclusion of aesthetic considerations altogether, while 'soft' meant a stress on the visual, largely in the tradition of picturesque aesthetics. Probably the most ambiguous catchword of all was the slightly later 'Brutalism' (or 'New Brutalism'). Here the questioning of the legitimacy of any kind of separate visual realm was dramatized though a polarised formulation: 'ethic or aesthetic?'

The relevance of these debates for the design of council towers of the 1950s and 60s is hard to assess. The decision to go for Modernist towers as such was not directly related to any of those party lines. 'Mixed development', with its insistence on diversity, fitted more into the 'soft' camp. If the term 'Brutalist' is more narrowly associated with the Smithsons and with the Park Hill housing scheme in Sheffield and its horizontal character, then it can be at least partly held responsible for the eventual demise of the council tower in the later 1960s. All categories kept mutating: by the early sixties, the LCC's principal housing architect, Kenneth Campbell, had shifted from the 'softs' to the 'hards', to judge from his defence of standardisation and his approval of the rough surfaces of Larsen Nielsen panels at the Morris Walk development. The direct association, axiomatic for many present-day (2016) commentators, of 'Brutalism' with council tower blocks and reinforced concrete construction must, however, be treated with caution, not least because few council towers, in their original condition, actually displayed surfaces of raw concrete ('beton brut') to any extent. The new planning trends of the mid 1960s, including high-density medium-rise and the growing preference

for brick in England, were already leaving all these debates behind.[8] Many of those practitioners who were not inclined to take part in such complex debates nevertheless periodically stated, as did, for instance, Cleeve Barr, that terms like 'architectural design' or 'aesthetic solutions' were at least worth a mention.[9] One may also cite Sheppard Fidler in Birmingham who demanded that '"design" was not to be relegated'.[10] With the tower block, it seemed that it was impossible to leave out purely aesthetic-formal considerations; moreover, it appeared to be a type of building for which clear delineations could be drawn between practical planning and constructional issues on the one hand, and purely aesthetic ones on the other. However it must be noted that the definition of 'design' remained unclear at most times, as Chapter 10 on construction will demonstrate. Taken together, all of this could of course be understood simply as an attempt to ennoble the council block: economically built, serving an unarguably mundane purpose, a council house could nevertheless be classified as art. Typical was a circumspect formulation by Duncan Sandys, the Housing Minister in 1955, who was well versed in contemporary architectural discussions: high flats provide savings of land as well as 'aesthetic opportunities'.[11] However, there were also those who saw a problem precisely at this point: cheap buildings could not be aesthetically satisfying: '... between aesthetics and economics ... a battle had to be fought', argued Robert Matthew.[12] Yet at least many of the LCC's designs – in which Matthew himself had an important early involvement – attracted all-round praise: LCC estates were 'properly balanced visually and sociologically', proclaimed a laudatory book, *Achievement,* published at the time of the 1965 reorganisation to celebrate the council's legacy.[13] With as glib a pen as Robert Furneaux Jordan's, one could even conclude, categorically, that 'a correct architectural

RA Exhibition. 1960.
Drawn by Basil Spence.
BASILDON TOWN CENTRE. ANTHONY DAVIES, CHIEF ARCHITECT; BASIL SPENCE, ARA, CONSULTANT

RA Exhibition, 1960.   Model by McCutchon Studio.
PROPOSED CIVIC CENTRE, HAYES, MIDDLESEX
CLIFFORD E. CULPIN, ARCHITECT

RA Exhibition, 1960   Model by W. Starzewski.
NEW OFFICE PREMISES, VICTORIA, SW1
GORDON TAIT, ARCHITECT

RA Exhibition, 1960.   Drawn by J. D. M. Harvey.
CONVALESCENT HOME AND FLATS, BOURNEMOUTH
ARTHUR BAILEY, OBE, ARCHITECT

RA Exhibition, 1960.   Drawn by T. L. Fraser.
PROPOSED 22-STOREY FLATS, LIVERPOOL
RONALD BRADBURY, ARCHITECT

A section of the 1960 London Royal Academy Exhibition devoted to designs for high buildings included a number of council blocks.

solution would have proved a correct social one.'[14] It was the LCC Architects' Department which around 1956 provided the principal starting point for about five years of discussions on the aesthetics of high buildings of all kinds.[15]

Altogether there was a climate of intense anticipation of visual urban change. Once again it should be remembered that most areas of London were singularly lacking in high buildings that reached above the norm of five or six floors, other than churches. What was needed, so J.M. Richards argued in 1958, was '...nothing less than a revolution in the visual character of London which has always been a horizontal city'.[16]

Considerable attention was created by a number of visionary schemes proposing groups of massive skyscrapers, including 'High Paddington' in 1952 and 'The Glass Age Development in Soho' of 1954.[17] With their giganticism and complexity, these could hardly serve as direct models at that time, although the very first proposals for the Barbican Scheme which appeared in 1954 and 1955 were hardly less daring.[18] By 1959, when several skyscrapers were at least under way in London, the architect–planner William Holford wrote: 'the tall building is in fashion'; 'it is also architectural news wherever it appears in project or reality. This could hardly be otherwise, since it draws attention to itself.' [19]

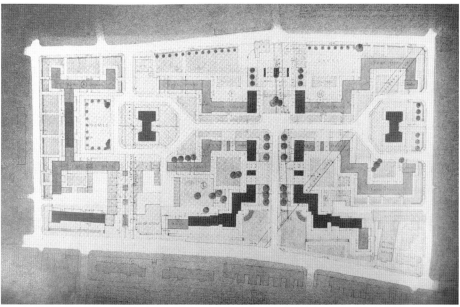

London, Lansdowne Green Estate, Wandsworth Road, SW18, 1954–59 by Arthur Kenyon for Lambeth MBC. The roofs are largely new. Exceptional is the use of an older, highly symmetrical 'Beaux Arts' form of layout. The towers' dominating effect Is helped by their isolated positioning.

When considering the single high building, it was important that it could be called properly a tower. This meant that the principal model for housing that had come with Continental Modernism, the slab block, was no longer really welcome. An over-large slab block could have the effect of a 'cliff of a building blotting out the sky'.[20] A 'proper' tower had to be a 'high spine' tower,[21] standing by itself. It is only the point block for which there were no rules regarding maximum height. A few commentators, like Eric Hollamby, pleaded for 'the soaring quality, the aloofness of genuine towers'.[22] For Holford, on the other hand, 'absolute height does not seem to be a criterion in itself.' What mattered was slenderness. Height, for Holford, 'has to be read in conjunction with thickness and depth'. Whitfield Lewis tried to be more precise: point blocks, if they were to retain the 'tower characteristic', should not be more than 60 feet wide if their height went up to 100 feet.[23] These were, indeed, the dimensions of the point blocks at Roehampton's Alton West estate. For Robert Matthew, however, this was not slender enough; his demand was for a height five times the width, arguing that only then can 'elegance be achieved'.[24] This degree of slenderness was not often reached, certainly in council housing, where economy demanded the maximal number of flats per lift stop. Further deliberations regarding height and slenderness will follow in the section on the 'point block' in the next chapter.

3. Imprisonment

This is the danger. Spaced out buildings of medium height (150'-200') would appear from this angle to form a solid wall and sharply define the edge of the park, ending all illusion as to its size

flow between the groups of towers and the edge of the park remains undefined.

4. Solution

Contrasting groups of high blocks, from Kenneth Browne, 'High London', in the *Architectural Review,* 1960.

Beyond the image of the single accent at 'strategic points', the 'interesting and beautiful landmark',[25] there was the issue of the ensemble of towers. International Modernism had brought the regular formation of blocks in rows, especially of slab blocks. But by the mid to later 1950s serried ranks of blocks of the same height, placed at the same distance from each other, were beginning to be criticised. The celebrated Roehampton / Alton West Estate, completed in 1958/9, still remained faithful to this formula, but here a diversity of views was provided by the old trees and the undulating grounds. But by now groups of blocks of different heights begun to be preferred. According to Robert Matthew there could be a number of ways of placing groups of blocks: they could be 'scattered more or less evenly throughout the city ... or located singly at visually strategic

points, or grouped in clusters', the latter being a relatively new term, introduced in the 1950s.[26]

The siting of towers within existing built environments became a much-discussed issue in itself. This included admonitions as to where not to place towers, where they might work as a disturbance. Interestingly, the Queen and the Duke of Edinburgh were reported not to be opposed to seeing high blocks from the Royal palaces.[27] In general, though, Dame Evelyn Sharp stressed 'contrast'. Gibberd expressed his preferences in his characteristically bold language: a tall block 'gives "punch" to the design', yet it should not be too large because the overall unity of all the dwellings of a mixed development needed to be preserved.[28] The conviction shared by most council house designers and many town planners was that public housing towers could fit in almost everywhere, into any kind of surroundings, into the very centre of towns; naturally, in the inner suburbs, but also at the edge of towns, or even in the countryside. Sheppard Fidler formulated this belief confidently: towers simply prevented 'dullness' in central areas; but 'really tall blocks' could also be effective when sited 'adjoining a river, a reservoir, ... an existing park or open space, a major arterial road'.[29] In the 1960s two special scenarios emerged: firstly, very tall blocks amidst a sea of low-rise housing, and, secondly, very tall blocks helping to mark the centre of a town, usually tied in with a commercial hub. There had to be a 'positive visual or civic significance in relation to the town as a whole'.[30] Chapter 11 will return to the latter issue.

The visual concepts directing tower design and placing can of course be followed by considering the pictorial presentation of the actual blocks in the professional press. One notes that the relationship between the new blocks and photography was far from straightforward. Art-conscious Modernist photography often indulged in rendering complex and dynamic spatial configurations and textural effects. A front-on, all-in view of a council tower, or a group of towers, was not a favourite subject, quite in contrast to the way in which a new high office block was illustrated, always seen proudly through the wide angle lens, as a singular, complete structure. Council towers were shown preferably in the context of their estates, with an emphasis on the surrounding natural or urban environment, at least in the *Architectural Review* and the *Architects' Journal*.

During the 1950s a new term was being added to the criteria of the 'civic' and the 'urban', namely 'townscape'. This entailed an appreciation of a mixed urban scene, grounded essentially in the aesthetic of the picturesque. Like the new urban sociology, which was now less concerned with shaping a new urban society, but, instead, with an understanding of the already existing social groups in towns, the townscape movement was happiest with varied older urban scenes which might well include a number of aesthetically banal, even ugly structures. It was a perspective that was now strongly opposed to the image of the isolated, assertive, single building. New tower blocks, too, should be seen as firmly integrated into the urban scene. At first the movement manifested itself in sketchily drawn illustrations, by a number of artists such as Gordon Cullen, mostly published in the *Architectural Review*. But soon photography joined in and produced similar kinds of casual scenes. Sometimes new council towers were included in the views, and this meant that these towers were seen in a totally new way. Basically, they now looked old, or, at any rate, they appeared to have lost their sparkling newness.[31] Inevitably this kind of view then became adopted by all those who were now critical of the towers' existence. It meant that by the later 1960s the period of visual dislike of tower blocks and, with it, many other kinds of Modernist housing, had firmly begun.

An unidentified street in South London, c. 1972 (cf. p. 258).

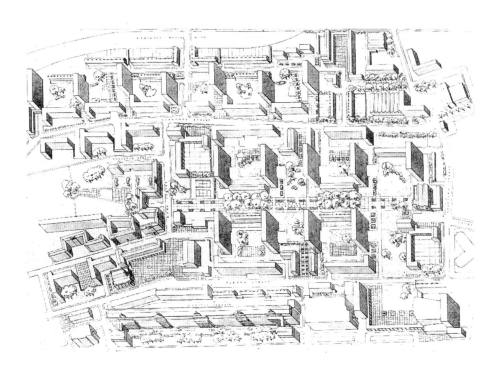

LONDON WAYS OF GROUPING
TOWERS IN THE 1940s AND 1950s

Top: Regent's Park Redevelopment
Project, 1948, Frederick Gibberd
(cf. p. 67).
Bottom: The Brandon towers
in c. 1990 (cf. p. viii).

AND IN THE 1960S

Top: Swedenborg Gardens, late 1960s (cf. frontispiece).
Bottom: Tustin Estate, Old Kent Road, Camberwell, SE15,
  LCC Architects, 1964.

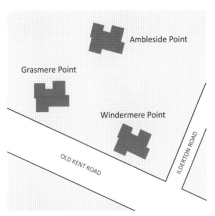

9 New types of flats and maisonettes in London

The case for the flat

During the past few decades new high blocks of flats, all of them built privately, have become ubiquitous in or near the centres of all large British cities. There appears little argument about their appropriateness or usefulness. Yet going back fifty or sixty years, living in a tower block was something very new indeed. While large medium-rise blocks of flats had been built in London for many decades previously and had been growing considerably in numbers and in size during the interwar period, flats in towers were a veritable invention of the post-1945 years. What makes the story exceptional in Britain is that the new kind of high living was essentially the creation of the latest modern Welfare State public architecture.

In his introduction to the first serious history of flats in Britain, Anthony Sutcliffe called them 'arguably a deviant, inferior type'.[1] But as Sutcliffe's book reveals, a fairer assessment would be to speak not of an inferior, but of a rarefied type of home. The Scottish story is, of course, very different, the flat having been the common dwelling in all towns of any size for several centuries. The British name for this abode is, in fact, derived from the earlier Scottish 'flet', denoting a floor in a domestic building. Clarity is not helped by the fact that in Scotland 'house' can also mean a flat. In London 'flat' then came into common use during the nineteenth century.

In the story of European 20th century housing as a whole, English and Continental modes of dwelling are complicatedly intertwined. Early in the century, the Continentals, especially German planners, flocked to England to admire the way every family appeared to live in a self-contained suburban house, in utter contrast to the massed, densely packed, contractor-built 'rent barracks' of the German cities. An immensely powerful 'housing reform' movement after 1918 then led the Continentals to completely abandon the 'barracks' type and replace it with the simple rectangular block of flats embedded in garden suburb kind of greenery. From the 1930s all this, in turn, impressed the British housing reformers, many of whom henceforth preached a reining-in of suburbia and its individual dwellings, and thereby extolled what they saw as the virtues of flat life.

More basically, what is highlighted by a comparison between all common kinds of flats on the Continent and English blocks of flats is that the hesitant ways of flat building in England meant the opposite of routine design. English flats were invariably architect-designed buildings, and that applied to blocks specially built for the lower classes just as much as for high-class abodes. It also meant that flats in England were always 'modern', in the sense that they were fitted out with the latest sanitary technology. Such a new flat, compact and practical, could in many respects compare favourably with the rambling older, multi-storey terraced house or even the older type of villa. From the early 1900s, and especially from the 1920s onwards, privately-built blocks of flats grew rapidly in number in certain favoured parts of London, such as Maida Vale, where many of them served as metropolitan pieds-a-terre. Their architectural treatment varied considerably, but from the 1930s many joined in with the latest Art Deco or Moderne fashions. The areas around these free-standing blocks were often carefully landscaped, at least at the front. A generic classification was attached to the blocks, that of 'mansion flats'; in addition, each block was given a prominently displayed generic tag, such as 'court', coupled with a unique name. Each block gave the impression of a marked individuality. There was, as one might assume, a strong contrast between these elite private flats and the groups of blocks built for the lower classes – mostly situated, of course, in different parts of the city, and commissioned not by private speculators but by charities, from the middle of the 19th century, and by local authorities, in great numbers, from 1918 onwards. But, once again, these blocks, too, were always one-off undertakings. The estates mostly consisted of quite a number of blocks, arranged in a carefully spaced-out way, though until about 1930 there would normally not be any greenery. Naturally, it was for all to see that these blocks, whose flats were often called 'tenements', were inhabited by the lower classes, but in their case, too, there was a world separating such a purpose-built estate and the old, run-down and multi-occupied, speculatively-built row of houses. Building a group of blocks of flats never meant placing them just anywhere, in any numbers, in the way row houses, or smaller semi-detached houses were usually placed, but it always meant a very specific, individual, carefully

LONDON
Chaucer House, Churchill Gardens, Pimlico, SW1. (1946) 1950–51, Powell and Moya for Westminster Borough Council.

The rejection of common suburban
development: From F.R.S. Yorke and Frederick
Gibberd, *Modern Flats* of 1937; the provocative
caption runs: 'we are giving this [top left] up
for this [top right], rather than for this' [left],
i.e: the 'Project by W.A. Eden'.

planned undertaking. Hence each 'estate' had its own name
attached to it and was individualised, in that way, too, like the
'mansion' blocks. The specific British custom of naming a
group of houses or flats, with all its subtle class connotations
and inversions, will be taken up again in Chapter 11.

A major impetus to build more flats came in the 1930s, when
Modernism, that is, the International Modern style, entered
Britain from the Continent, creating an architecture which
dazzled with its pure forms of shining whiteness. Now, for a
few years, the block of flats was the highly individual manifestation of an avant-garde spirit in domestic design, devised
by a coterie of young architects and their patrons. By the
later 1930s, books by these avant-gardists, accompanied by
striking photographs, extolled the 'civilising' effects of comprehensive technical advancement, especially with regard
to physical health, acting as a guarantee of a future 'health-
ier, more virile race'.[2] The young F.R.S. Yorke and Frederick
Gibberd's lush volume *The Modern Flat* of 1937 further elabo-
rated a general sociological and environmentalist discourse

'Flats in a Country Park', illustration from Thomas Sharp,
Town Planning, 1940.

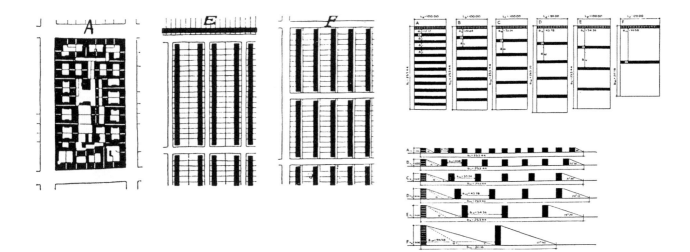

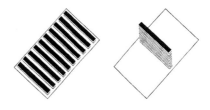

The advantages of *Zeilenbau*-formation and high slab blocks, extolled by Continental designers from the late 1920s onwards. By repeating the same kind of dwelling (cf. p. 34), by eliminating the public street as far as possible and by increasing height, more public green spaces and more light can be provided, and that in equal measure for a relatively large number of people on a relatively small piece of land.
Top right: Diagrams published by Walter Gropius in 1935 in London.

of flat design. Their architects were now fiercely opposed to semi-detached suburbia, deploring both its cottage styles of design as well as the way its estates 'swallowed' up the hallowed English landscape. The idea that Modern design fits in with a park or an open landscape was powerfully reinforced in 1940 by Thomas Sharp in a visionary drawing of a single eight-storey slab 'in a country park'. Sharp's argument at this point was that such a block could take the place of a demolished country seat; and rather than developing the ground with suburban-typed houses, building a single block of flats would enable the dwellers, as well as visitors, to properly 'share the beauty' of the park.[3] By the late 1930s a number of strictly International-Style Modernist blocks had been completed, or were being built, by young architects, such as Max Fry, Berthold Lubetkin and Fredrick Gibberd. These pioneers were to carry over their daring Modernism into the public housing of the late forties and early fifties. They were supported by the professional press but also by government officials, such as Evelyn Sharp. One might thus conclude, along with a number of recent histories of 1930s architecture, that however much the first post-war years liked to see themselves as starting from scratch, the scene had in many ways been set in the years just before the war.[4] Most certainly the case for the flat had been convincingly made.[5]

Zeilenbau / slab block

When discussing the 1930s earlier, we emphasised both the new fervour for planning reform and the close interest in what was going on in some Continental countries. By the early years of that decade the Germans had built a very considerable number of new kinds of flats, made up of freestanding four or five-storey blocks which formed a basic rectangle of a certain length, and nothing more. These blocks would be laid out in parallel rows, as many as were required. Most radically, blocks were now placed at right angles to the public street and could thus be surrounded by greenery on all sides, apart from small access ways. Moreover, there is no longer what one may call a front and a back to the house. One may see all this as a garden city of flats, while another origin can be seen in the later 19th century health-conscious, air-craving layout of the pavilion hospital. The new German term for this urban formation was *Zeilenbau*, '*Zeile*' being the word for a line of writing on a page. The already mentioned blocks of Evelyn Court in Hackney of 1934 superficially resemble the *Zeilenbau* formation, but they lack the essential ingredient of the elimination of the normal street space and its replacement by greenery. On the other hand, a principal aim of the earlier London 'reforming' estates, as for instance the massive early 20th century Bourne Estate in Clerkenwell Road,[6]

LONDON
Top: Blemundsbury, Dombey Street, Great Ormond
    Street, WC1, 1946–48, Robert Henning & Anthony
    Chitty, for Holborn MBC.
Left: Minerva Estate, Bethnal Green Road, E2,
    by the LCC Valuer's Department, 1948–51.
Right: Woodberry Down Estate, Stoke Newington,
    N4, 1946–49; LCC Architects.

was the elimination of the old heavily enclosed small private back courts, a reform which clearly ran parallel with, or even preceded the Continental efforts. It was only during World War II when the *Zeilenbau* concept really took hold and found its application in the vast plans of the *County of London Plan* of 1943. Yet, in practice Britain, and certainly England, very rarely actually followed the *Zeilenbau* concept on a very large scale. But the slab block type and the *Zeilenbau* formation seemed to play a decisive role in going higher. During the 1930s Walter Gropius published, in London, his arithmetically and geometrically sharpened demonstrations of the fundamental advantages of taller blocks, up to ten storeys. One could thereby increase the number of people housed on a given plot, while guaranteeing the maximum amount of sunshine and greenery, at a density equivalent to that of any big town. It all formed part of the conviction that one could conceive of a mass-produced dwelling that could also be the optimal dwelling, in the way it shares out its health benefits to all in equal measure.[7] The greatly idealized views in the 1943 *County of London Plan* abounded with seven to ten-storey slabs of a very considerable length. The first long, 'pure' slab blocks of six to ten storeys were actually built from 1946 onwards. By the mid-1950s their height consolidated itself at eleven storeys, as exemplified in the highly-publicised LCC maisonette block. Britain still differed in this respect from some Continental countries, especially France, where blocks of flats in slab form soon came both longer and higher.

Great Arthur House.

1952 competition entry.

WEST ELEVATION

1954 project.

GOLDEN LANE ESTATE CORPORATION OF LONDON
Golden Lane EC1. Built 1955–57, by architects Chamberlin, Powell and Bon, engineers Arup and contractors Wimpey. There are 146 maisonettes in the six-storey blocks and 120 flats in the tower. At the time of completion, the 16-storey Great Arthur House was the highest council tower in the land. With its internal corridor access it might also be classified also as a point block, and with eight flats per floor a most economic one. The prehistory is complex: the winning design (by Geoffrey Powell) in the competition of 1952 envisaged 11 storeys, the greatly modified design of 1953 went up to 14. As with the first LCC point block in Ackroydon the modernity of Great Arthur House lies principally with its glazed elevations. The density of the estate, at 200 persons per acre, is high, yet there are large areas of semi-public lawns and shrubs (cf. p. 114).

County of London Plan 1943 Mixed Development with high slab blocks.
Birdseye view of a district by William Walcot, following the plan below.

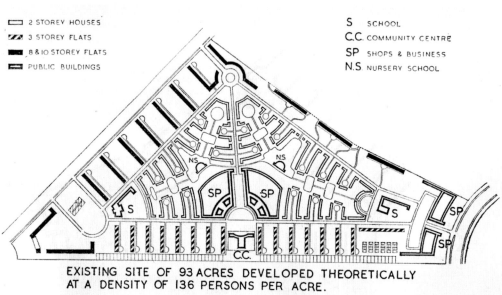

2 STOREY HOUSES
3 STOREY FLATS
8 & 10 STOREY FLATS
PUBLIC BUILDINGS

S   SCHOOL
C.C. COMMUNITY CENTRE
SP   SHOPS & BUSINESS
N.S. NURSERY SCHOOL

EXISTING SITE OF 93 ACRES DEVELOPED THEORETICALLY
AT A DENSITY OF 136 PERSONS PER ACRE.

POPULATION APPROX. 9143   CHILDREN APPROX. 1143 [3-15]
DENSITY (a) - 136 - 67·2 ACRES
DENSITY (b) - 98 - 93·0 ACRES
DENSITY (c) - 71 - 129·87 ACRES
IN HOUSES AND FLATS OF NOT MORE THAN 3 STOREYS - 3461 - 38%
IN HIGH FLATS - 8 AND 10 STOREY ·························· - 5682 - 62%
OPEN SPACE REQUIRED - AT 4 ACRES PER 1000 - 36·57 ACRES.

Density (a) - area of housing site including service roads only
Density (b) - area of (a) plus main roads, schools, shops and community buildings.
Density (c) - area of (b) plus open space at 4 acres per 1000 persons

100 0   200   1000
                                        FT
1 : 2500

HIGHEST AND LOWEST DENSITIES
Left: London, Dolphin Square, Pimlico, SW1, 1935–37.
Right: Birmingham, part of Weoley Castle Estate, 1930s.

High density, mixed development

A relatively new term in the planning and designing process of a larger housing estate was 'density'. When there were only a few types of housing to choose from, and each estate normally contained only one type of dwelling, naming the type sufficed for a description. But the new, more complex kinds of town planning from the late 19th century onwards brought also a new kind of arithmetical thinking which described the formations of housing in abstract figures. Mention '12 houses per acre' and the professionals knew that this marked the way the cherished garden cities were laid out. For anybody planning a scheme of slum-clearance it also appeared vital to know the density of the existing buildings, as well as that of their replacements. Most importantly, the density figure conjured up also the look of the immediate surroundings of the dwellings, the amount of open land or greenery. An elaborate scheme of figures came into use. 'Houses per acre' was soon replaced by the measurement of 'persons per acre', or 'p.p.a'. With this change flats could be brought into the calculations.[8] Just to be awkward, two other terms were also increasingly used from the 1960s, namely 'bed-spaces per acre' and 'habitable rooms per acre'. However, given a tolerable margin of imprecision, they could both equate with 'p.p.a'. For the equivalent figures per hectare, the number of persons should be multiplied by two and a half.

What the new preoccupation with density measurement in the post-war years entailed was also a desire to *increase,* wherever possible, the density in all urban environments. 'Close and compact development ... is often more satisfactory than loose and open development ... without sacrifice of desirable standards [it can lead] to some actual improvement in the overall design', argued Ministry planners in 1952 in a Government handbook, *The Density of Residential Areas*. A continuing important national political corollary was, once again, the desire to protect agricultural land: 'save every acre that can be saved' wrote Harold Macmillan, the Housing Minister.[9] Thus the ambition was to provide a high quality of accommodation at the highest possible density. A scale of figures was devised for the 'net' density of new housing areas – in other words, for groups of dwellings and local roads only, excluding other functions such as schools or shopping centres. Garden city houses came in at 40 p.p.a.; anything up to 80 or 90 p.p.a. could still permit a garden city kind of layout, but now using two-storey or three-storey houses, built in rows. Around 130 or 140 p.p.a. was the density level normally used for building in the inner suburbs, now necessitating a preponderance of flats. 160 p.p.a. would reduce the number of houses to a minimum, while 200 p.p.a. layouts would not only be entirely flatted but most likely be dominated by high flats at that. Certainly, the challenge of operating with these measurements and correlating them with the special conditions of each site, while at the same time providing a 'variety of accommodation', all this presupposed a 'designing skill of a high order'.[10]

The LCC, in its capacity as 'planning authority' for the County of London, considered 200 p.p.a. to be the highest desirable density in council housing, and the Council attempted to impose a three-level maximum density scheme not only for its own new housing projects but on those of the boroughs as well, the maximum being 200 for the inner zone, 70 for the outer suburbs, and the idiosyncratically precise figure of 136 p.p.a. for the inner suburbs.[11] Some architect-planners, such as Major Rolf Jensen, Borough Architect of Paddington, did attempt, unsuccessfully, to challenge the LCC regime by proposals for higher-density developments at the very centre of cities. Urban housing of a greater density had been permitted in London before World War II, notably with private blocks of flats. This had been achieved largely by the blocks' uniform height of ten storeys or more. But the way they followed the street perimeter was the very kind of layout to which the new *Zeilenbau* mode was now strongly opposed to.

The driving issue in the new ways of thinking about housing layout was to look beyond the individual block of dwellings. The authors of the *County of London Plan* J.H. Forshaw, the LCC's architect, and Patrick Abercrombie, Professor of Town Planning at University College London, who had also been trained as an architect, as well as some other younger architects who called themselves 'architect-planners', such as Frederick Gibberd, saw it as their principal task to tie in the individual development with their concepts for the town as a whole. All this, in turn, meant a new kind of thinking for each individual estate. So far, the natural order of things meant a polarisation between highly concentrated dense blocks of flats in the centre and loosely spread 'cottages', mushrooming on the outskirts. There was, of course, a widespread awareness of a dilemma: which type of home is the better one? The new planning thinking had no time for simplistic statements, such as that of the 1934 *Slum Clearance and Rehousing Report*, to the effect that houses were a matter for the private sector and that councils should therefore concentrate on flats,[12] nor for musings, like those of a planner in 1941 on 'Houses or Flats? ... a time-honoured controversy ... flats are things one likes or does not like'.[13] The planning of housing had to be put on a more sophisticated footing than that. Forshaw and Abercrombie had made a start with their detailed analysis of the needs of all dwellers. Most definitely council housing had to offer a much greater variety of dwelling types.

In response to these quandaries, a new concept emerged fairly rapidly during the 1940s, that of 'mixed development'. Once formulated, its main point appeared simple and eminently logical: every major new development, catering for a 'normal' sector of the population, would comprise a diversity of people and thus would require a mix of dwelling types. The beginnings of this argument may be seen in a speech on slum clearance by Elizabeth Denby in 1936, advocating high blocks, but also pleading for denser versions of cottages nearer the centre of towns; if somebody preferred a house, they should not be banished to the edge of town.[14] In her history of Mixed Development, Ruth Owens traces early formulations of the idea, apart from the *London Plan*, in the recommendations supplied by the RIBA to the authors of the Government's 1944 'Dudley Report'.[15] Mixed development's first built manifestations emerged in the late forties in London, as in the Lansbury Estate in the Stepney-Poplar redevelopment zone of the East End, in an area which, had the normal LCC procedure prevailed, would have been

filled uniformly with five-storey blocks. Lansbury, however, did not yet include high blocks. The first 'complete' mixed development, that is, the first that sported a tower, was the Mark Hall district in Harlow New Town in 1950.

'Mixed development' had thus become a distinct sociological and architectural theme. It was seen as a template which could be used to realise an ideal that town planners had long been calling for, the harmonious 'neighbourhood', or, as the sociologists put it, 'a true community'. Stressing the mix of dwellings also meant a stress on the diversity of people and on the full span of ages; a case in point was the dwellings for the old: a row of bungalows was the preferred habitat for this group, though in practice their accommodation in towers was much more frequent. Visually, mixed developments became exercises in 'grouping', in the formal, compositional sense of the term as discussed in the last chapter. Crucial was the apparent happy fusion of both aspects: 'Flats, maisonettes and houses have been fully integrated both visually and to give a better sociological balance in the use of the varied types of dwelling'[16] – so ran a comment on the completion of the LCC's first such complex, the Ackroydon Estate on Putney Heath in 1954. What matters here is that from the early to mid fifties onwards virtually all developments that deserved the epithet 'mixed' were to include towers; Ackroydon claims a first in this respect, too. Throughout the 1950s the LCC proceeded with its numerous mixed development estates and with many of them to great acclaim, notably those in Roehampton. It was for their towers that they were principally admired. As Ruth Owens concluded, 'mixed development was a way to make high flats more acceptable'.[17] And yet, by the same token, its rationale served the argument for the low rise types of housing equally well. Planners simply could not disregard the house altogether. Ultimately the fascination with the new concept might appear as a fresh response to deep-seated cultural conundrums. If one takes, for example, any ordinary, older Paris suburb, one notes the complete, quasi natural mix of blocks of flats of all kinds with individual houses of all shapes and sizes – in stark contrast of the custom in Britain, especially in England, with its rigid division of housing types, complete with an entrenched nomenclature, and its domination of large areas by one dwelling type only.

In the late fifties, the Ministry's housing design guide booklet, *Flats and Houses 1958,* marked the high point of the belief in mixed development. For a given piece of land of about 12 acres, the book presented eight detailed studies, with several solutions for each density range, 100, 140 and 160 p.p.a. The basic principle, that of variability, is demonstrated by the fact that the lowest and the highest density proposals both contain houses with gardens and high flats: in the case of the 160 model the flats reach sixteen storeys. The variety of types in each plan, houses, low flats, maisonettes, high flats, and in addition smaller differences, such as the number of bedrooms, is almost impossible to count. Amongst the drawings, one layout permutation is singled out as unfavourable, that which consisted solely of five-storey blocks: because 'the effect is monotonous'.[18]

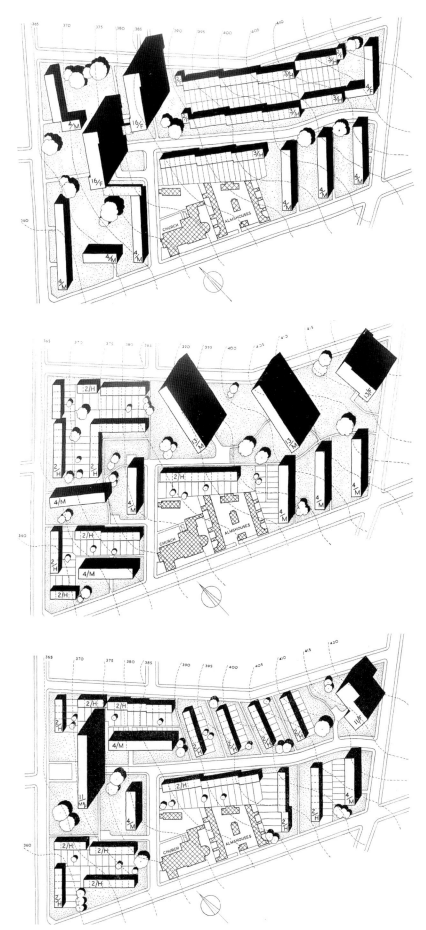

Three ways of planning a mixed development on the same site. *From Flats and Houses 1958;* the densities, persons per acre, are (from top down) 160. 140, 100.

MIXED DEVELOPMENT
Inner suburban, London, Loughborough Road Estate, Brixton, SW9. LCC architects, 1952–57.
NewTown, Harlow NewTown, Mark Hall, Frederick Gibberd, Architect and Planner, 1949–51.

MIXED DEVELOPMENT
Halesowen, Worcs. Highfields Development, Andrews Road, 1961.

Lastly, it was patently obvious that mixed development solutions tended to be relatively expensive. But by now a clear contrast makes itself felt when comparing the attitudes of the 1950s with the discourse of the 1930s, where the principal stress was on methods to provide dwellings for the working class cheaply, 'to bring as much of the housing field as possible within the measurable economic terms is vitally necessary'.[19] Of course the *Flats and Houses 1958* booklet admonishes councillors and architects to build economically. The report's author, Ministry architect Alec Bellamy, had himself felt torn, when undertaking a study of new housing in New York, between admiring its systematic organisation and being appalled by its utilitarian appearance.[20] The fact was that *Flats and Houses 1958*, with its subtitle of 'Design and Economy', came from what one may call the architectural 'interest-grouping' within the Ministry. As the Housing Minister, Henry Brooke, put it in his foreword, mixed development aimed 'to achieve the complete combination of attractive buildings, a happy variety of form and skyline' and he concluded that 'reasonable cost and high architectural quality can both be secured, there is no doubt, if only one takes enough trouble to study how'. In the end, the new Welfare State would take care of all the costs.[21]

And yet, again, like most utopian concepts, mixed development rapidly began to run itself into the ground through its own aporias. The problem was that there always needed to be a close need-fit relationship, and the right kinds of people were to inhabit the right kind, and the right size, of dwelling. If the tenants' life-situation changed, logic required that they should immediately change their dwelling, for example moving from a house into a flat, or vice versa; all this requiring a very

considerable degree of flexibility overall – and liable to create a nightmare for the housing manager. A very different problem for the towers was the vertigo factor, which was said to increase with the way tower block dwellers looked down onto the roofs of houses. Yet another major new and complex problem arose with overshadowing. When high blocks followed the street layout, or a widely-spaced regular *Zeilenbau* formation, there was no need to be concerned. But where there was a densely built group of houses mixed with high blocks, the latter's shadows might well cause problems. Help was provided in *Flats and Houses 1958* through a complex new variant of the time-honoured daylight and sunlight indicators: they now became diagrams and calculations of a very considerable complexity.[22] By the mid-sixties a new trend occurred, aiming, simply, to reduce densities altogether, with 200 now appearing too high.

As a result of all this, even by the early 1960s the whole concept of mixed development was beginning to lose its rhetorical power. On the other hand, it remained perfectly plausible to demand that every large new housing estate should be planned with at least some diversity of dwellings. At the height of the demand for high blocks in 1962, the Minister of Housing, Keith Joseph, reaffirmed the importance of mixed development.[23] A late version was practiced in some large cities, such as Hull, Leeds and Nottingham, namely to offset the mass of small houses in distant suburbs with a contrasting landmark of one or two very high point blocks. A further variant for the mixing of various flats and maisonettes, that of 'conglomerates', will be considered at the end of this chapter. Yet another solution was to devise densely packed complexes of low-rise dwellings, for instance on the courtyard principle.[24]

Punkthus: the high point block

All Modernist types of planning and building seemed to share one characteristic: they wore out quickly in architectural-reputational terms. With regard to the slab block, already by the early 1950s a scepticism had set in, although to call it a 'revulsion', as one architect put it in 1952, was probably an exaggeration.[25] One could certainly speak of dreariness in the case of many of the blocks built by the Metropolitan Boroughs directly after 1945, those which showed little more than sheer, clean brick walls interrupted only by smallish metal windows (cf. p. 112).

In Britain, advocacy of tower-like structures for flats can hardly be found in the housing discourses before the late 1940s. A short, narrow, squarish block of six to nine storeys, with a lift, while remaining below the London 100 feet limit, would not have made economic sense for public housing. All this was probably also related to the general perception that high buildings, in tower form, were not for English cities, in contrast to much of interwar continental Europe, when, for instance, the largest German cities had built at least one *'Hochhaus'*, an office structure of ten to fifteen storeys, and occasionally a new housing estate could feature accents with six or eight-storey corner blocks.

And so it happened that the tower block, like the slab block and like the *Zeilenbau*, became yet another Continental import. Among the examples known from the mid-thirties onwards were the group of slim fifteen-storey blocks at La Muette at Drancy of 1931 and the somewhat lesser known and rather squat and solid-looking twelve-storey public housing block, the 'Wolkenkrabber' on Amsterdam's Victorieplein, of 1930.[26] But the chief influence came from Sweden. The country's welfare state system as a whole had found much admiration in early post-war Britain. In 1946 the *Architects' Journal* was fascinated by a number of eight to ten-storey towers of small flats near Stockholm, especially the, admittedly still rather stumpy, and privately-built, Danviksklippan of 1943–45.[27] The Scandinavians called them *punkthus*, and the *AJ*, at first, translated this literally as '"point houses"'.[28] The novelty of it all can still be felt in 1950 and 1951. By 1950 an internal LCC document reports on 'the new type high block of flats ("point block")'[29] and even in 1951 the Council still used inverted commas for '"point" block' when referring to the plans for the first Ackroydon towers.[30] Cautious deliberations carried on for a few years; for instance, the young Hugh Casson mused about Stockholm in the *Observer* newspaper in 1952, as follows: 'a 20-storey point block ... sculpture in space, visually more exciting than the long continuous slab. But so far incomparably more expensive to build.'[31]

The point block is a type with a number of clear characteristics which can all potentially be called advantages. It is, in fact, in many ways *the* high type of dwelling par excellence. There appears absolute flexibility in deciding on its overall height, while a long slab block above a certain height could easily appears incongruous. Secondly, there is great flexibility in the way it can respond to uneven land, while a long slab block needs a generally flat site. The *punkthus* can also fit in more

'It is generally thought that to have fresh air blowing through a flat is an advantage'

Margaret Willis, the LCC's Sociologist, on 'Living in High Blocks of Flats', 1954.

easily with a mixed development; in groups with many low rise blocks, one high tower can greatly increase the overall density, in fact, the point block became one of the defining elements of mixed development. As regards landscape situations of any kind, the high block is more likely to fit in well with pre-existing high trees. It likewise fits easily into any small site in a town, one speaks of a 'gap-site' filler. As regards overshadowing, any number of point blocks can be grouped freely, as their smaller shadows move on quickly. One critical issue was aspect. Naturally, every block has a side that faces north, and thus an exact north-south alignment was to be avoided; alternatively, the flats could be planned so as to look out on two sides, or there could simply be windows around the corners of the block (cf. p. 164). Lastly the views from a point block are usually the most varied. Accordingly, the early blocks, especially, tend to have large windows. As regards access to the flats, the point block introduced something quite new to English public housing: an enclosed entrance lobby, entirely located internally, in front of the lift doors. As will be discussed in Chapter 11, access was a crucial issue: the dominant method of access to working-class flats up to that time had been by means of open galleries, which was now widely held to be unsatisfactory. Finally, in contrast to slab blocks, point blocks offer a much wider range of possibilities in their plans. Their exact methods of construction, as will be seen in the next chapter, varied accordingly, in contrast to the slab block type with its highly standardised method of construction, as do the forms of the elevation. The issue of costs always loomed large: the more flats served on each floor by the lift, or lifts, the better. With eight flats and more per floor, however, the point block gradually turns into a slab block.

Lastly, it was felt that the views of the users should also be cited. In 1954 the LCC's in-house sociologist, Margaret Willis, presented a summary of some voices with regard to the new heights: it took some time to get used to it, she reported, but certainly the blocks offered privacy, fresh air and, of course, the best views.[32] More significant than these findings themselves was the very fact that the inhabitant's view were being publicly recorded. But what was sensational was the national and international accolades for Roehampton, beginning in those years. Roehampton's praise upon its completion during 1959 has already been cited (cf. p. 40). A clear model of Alton West was first shown in early 1954. There is a possibility that it provided the inspiration for the layout of the celebrated 1957 Internationale Bauausstellung in Berlin ('Interbau' / Hansaviertel) which showed a very similar way of presenting a group of slab blocks, contrasting with a group of point blocks, though there were in Berlin no further housing types that would give the whole the character of a mixed development, at least not in the new London sense of the term. The height of the point blocks, with around 16 stories exceeded the London models. Their plans and elevations differed wildly, being designed by an accolade of celebrities.[33]

Drancy, near Paris, Cité de la Muette, 1932–34.
Stockholm, Danviksklippan, 1943–45.

London, Roehampton model of Alton West, 1953/4.
Berlin Interbau, 1957.

POSITIONING THE POINT BLOCK

Top: Norwich Darrell Place, Dereham Road, 1958. City Architect David
  Percival. In the sea of two and one-storey houses in outer suburban
  Norwich a compacted block of four storeys of flats may not be called
  a tower, but, in effect, it acts like a point block.
Middle: Reigate, Surrey, 16-storey point block proposed for the town
  centre; architects Bridgewater and Shepherd. 'We are convinced
  that one tall block rising above the trees would be an interesting
  and beautiful landmark in itself', 1957. It was not built.
Bottom: 'Gap-site' development: Leeds, 1961.

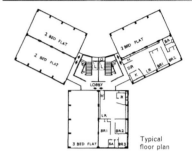

Harlow New Town, The Lawn, 1949–51.　　London, Claremont Estate, West Ham, 1955–57.　　London, Perkins Heights, Paddington, 1954.

EARLY POINT BLOCKS

London, Fitzhugh Estate, Wandsworth, 1953–56.　　Bath, Berkeley House, 1955–58.　　Coventry, Tile Hill, 1954–56.

LONDON, ACKROYDON ESTATE

Top: Princes Way, Wimbledon Park Side, SW, 1950–54.

Right: LCC Chief Housing Architect H. John Whitfield Lewis, Architect in Charge H.G. Gillett. The first LCC Modernist Mixed Development incorporating towers: 11-storey point blocks; also comprising 4-storey maisonettes, 4 and 5-storey blocks of flats and 3 and 4-bedroomed houses. The overall density of 100 p.p.a is high for this outer-suburban situation, and yet, today at least, the general impression is one of diversity, leafiness, even affluence.

Bottom left: Plan, 1950–51.

Bottom right: Presentation of model: (right to left) Whitfield Lewis, Reginald Stamp (Housing Committee Chairman) and Cyril Walker (Director of Housing and Valuer), 1950.

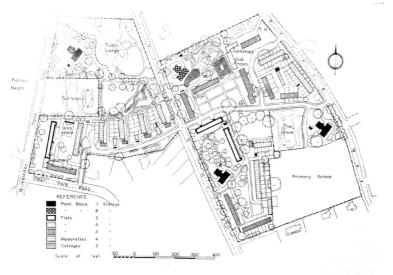

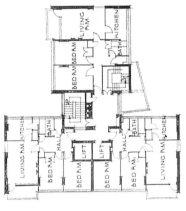

ACKROYDON ESTATE
Top: Oatlands Court, Wimbledon Park Side.
Left: Mynterne Court, Victoria Drive, Swanton Gardens.
Plan upper: 1950, plan lower: 1954.
Bottom right: Interior 1954.

Top: The model of 1951.
Above: Air View 1959.

Cadman Point, Dilton Gardens.

LONDON ROEHAMPTON ALTON EAST
Roehampton Lane, Alton Road, SW15 (formerly Portsmouth Road), (1951) 1953–56; LCC
Architects in Charge: M.C.L.Powell, A.W Cleeve Barr, Oliver J. Cox, Rosemary Stjernstedt,
engineer W.V.Zinn, contractor Kirk & Kirk. Mixed development, with only 10% houses.

LONDON ROEHAMPTON ALTON WEST
Roehampton Lane, Danebury Avenue, SW15, 1954–58 . LCC Architects,
in charge M.C.L. Powell, Colin Lucas, engineers Arup, contractor Wates.
The classic LCC mixed development: 53% dwellings in high blocks, 30%
in four-storey maisonettes and 17% in two and three-storey terraces and
single-storey old persons' dwellings. Overall density 100 p.p.a. Famed also
for its landscaping effects on the edge of Richmond Park (cf. pp. 61, 70).

The high maisonette block and its variations

By 1952 LCC architects were devising another new type of block of an unprecedented size, as high as the eleven-storey point block, but also of a very considerable length, which could measure more than 250 feet, or 76 metres, and contain 100 dwellings or more: the maisonette slab block.[34] The word 'maisonette' had marked compromise solutions between traditional English house plans and types of flats for quite some time. The late 19th and early 20th London maisonette, the Tyneside flat, not to mention Scottish equivalents, looked almost like ordinary suburban row houses, but each 'house' was divided into independent dwelling units, one on each floor. The new London 'superimposed maisonette' block after World War II appears exactly as the reverse: it looks like a block of flats, but it is divided into dwelling units which comprise two storeys each. What English planners wanted to create was a greater measure of privacy, a 'house' quality[35] and therefore the maisonette was held to suit families with young children better than the flat, although, in the case of the two-bedroomed version, it had to be a small family.

A beginning had been made during the late 1940s with four-storey blocks containing two maisonette units. The advantage of this frequently built version was that it did not need a lift, which was becoming de rigueur with four-storey blocks of flats. A large number of six-storey blocks were also built during the next two decades. When they were planning their new higher version, the LCC architects, on the initiative of Deputy Architect Leslie Martin, took the highly unusual and expensive step of constructing a full-scale model, fully fitted out like a real-life dwelling.[36]

High slab maisonettes use the cross-wall constructional principle, which means that the principal supports also form the separation between the dwellings. Rooms tended to be long and deep, and sometimes their width, the space between the party walls, only measured 11 feet, 3 inches, or 3.4 metres, as in the Picton Street blocks (cf. p. 23).[37] The dwellings normally face out to both front and back, like the normal row house, while flats in high blocks might face only in one direction. Many maisonettes also have small balconies on the upper floor. Altogether the LCC maisonette became a quite heavily standardised dwelling type. Most fortunate of all were the dwellers in the bottom maisonette, as they could have a small private garden, even though that is something possible with any block of flats. And yet the new eleven-storey version of the maisonette block mostly gave up the ground floor to collective uses, such as sheds, car spaces, or entrance lobbies, or simply kept the space open, boldly demonstrating the lightness of the building's construction.

Of great significance is the access to the individual 'house'. Here the maisonette block continues the tradition of English philanthropic or public housing blocks for the 'working-classes', with its open access balconies. But because this balcony now occurs only on every second floor, rather than on every single floor as with the old-fashioned flats, it usually has a much more open feeling. The opportunities this gave for constructional variety will be explored in Chapter 10. Crucial is the fact that lifts could serve a great number of dwellings, strung along the length of the block. It was the principal reason for their costs being lower than those of the point blocks.

From the mid-fifties onwards the LCC built large numbers of the eleven-storey maisonette blocks. Exactly at the time when the type was being devised, Le Corbusier's Unité d'habitation was nearing completion in Marseille. It created enormous attention among British avant-garde designers. However, with its giant size it could hardly serve as a direct model, certainly not in any cost-saving way. But a number of elements were of particular interest: the daringly open ground floor (cf. p. 103), the quasi-curtain wall treatment of the main elevations (cf. p. 89) and the internal access corridor (cf. p. 76).[38]

LONDON
Picton Street, Maisonette Block, showing the side with the private balconies. LCC Architects, 1954–57 (cf. pp. 23, 83).

LONDON

Top left: Kingsgate Estate, Tottenham Road, Hackney, N1; four-storey maisonette
   block, 1959; Frederick Gibberd for Hackney MB.
Top right: Interior of maisonette, Roehampton, Alton West.
Bottom: The LCC's experimental two-bedroom maisonette unit, 1952.

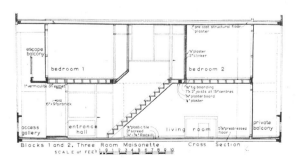

LONDON

Left: Bentham Road, Hackney, Cassland Road, E9,
   Maisonettes, 1954–59; LCC Architects P.J. Carter, A.H.
   Colquhoun, Colin St. John Wilson and others. One of the
   largest and most tightly calculated of the 11-storey maisonette slab blocks, each unit is only 12' 3" (3,7 m) wide.
Below: Plans of the lower and the upper floors of the
   maisonettes.

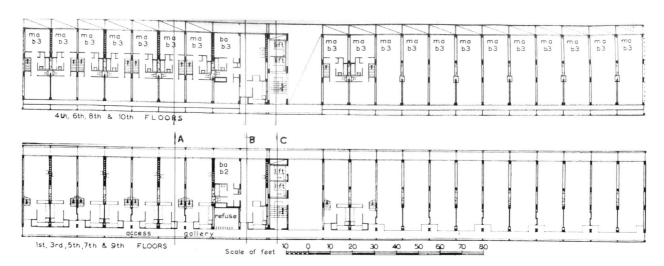

4th, 6th, 8th & 10th FLOORS

|A |B |C

1st, 3rd, 5th, 7th & 9th FLOORS

Scale of feet   10 0   10   20   30   40   50   60   70   80

Right: Charcot House, Roehampton Lane,
Alton West, SW15, 1954–58 (cf. p. 67).

LONDON
Top: Taylor Court, Hillgrove Estate, Dorman
Way, Finchley Road, Hampstead, NW8
(1952) 1955, by Louis de Soissons (?) for the
LCC. On the right are the private balconies.
Bottom: Yates House, Bethnal Green, Gosset
Street, E2; LCC maisonette block, 1957;
the passages on the upper floor serve as
escape ways (cf. p. 188).

With eleven storeys, the long maisonette slab seemed to find its natural limit in London. To be exposed to all weathers on a tenth-floor open access-way, and that on the northern side, could be tough. Yet the LCC designers wanted to go higher, with this type, too. Thus a new solution had to be devised for the entrance problem. It was found by locating the entrance corridor inside the block. Now the block contains on each floor a short row of four maisonettes on one side, and another row of four maisonettes on the other side; both are accessible from the same corridor in the middle. Clearly, a major benefit of the slab block is thereby lost: the dwelling no longer faces both directions. Thus the whole of the interior of the dwelling is lit only from one side. But the way to the lifts is now a short one, to the end of the corridor. At that point the block also accommodates two flats on each floor. Thus the block as a whole contains 80% maisonettes and 20% flats. The great advantage, having eliminated the open access way, is that one may now go further upwards. Instead of five tiers of maisonettes one may now have seven, as in the LCC's 16-storey blocks at Rotherhithe New Road in Bermondsey in 1958[39] or eight, as in the developments in Stepney, planned from 1957. In the twenty-one-storey blocks at the Warwick Estate, Paddington, this adds up to 72 maisonettes and 36 flats, making them large blocks by any British standards.[40] The culmination was the tallest block at the Elephant and Castle CDA, first planned from the same year, 1958, but not completed until 1965, with 25 floors, piling up eleven layers of maisonettes and totalling 133 dwellings.

The exterior of all these blocks must be judged as eminently 'legible': there are the prominent tiers of maisonettes on the long sides, while one of the short sides is punctuated by a small window on every other floor, indicating the high corridor between the maisonettes; the other short side, with its many windows and balconies, indicates the flats. Point block or slab block? It naturally depends on the block's length in each case. Many more variations on this theme will be encountered in Chapter 12 of this book. Something that specially lent itself to a great number of variants was the type's vertical access. In many maisonette blocks it became a distinct element, a quasi-separate slender tower structure attached at one of the ends.

The next, and last, major type of high block devised by the LCC's architects is of a different kind again. It actually appears simpler, that is, much more unified on the outside, while being very much more complicated inside. At the same time it represents a follow-up to some of the themes just discussed, not least in that its basic accommodation unit is still the 'maisonette'.[41] This 'scissors', or 'split level', or 'cross-over' plan type was not actually invented by the LCC's architects. Early proposals for '"cross-over" maisonettes' came from the Ministry's architectural team in 1951,[42] and there was a somewhat less complicated model, the nine-storey Lister House at the Fulbourne Estate in Stepney of the mid-1950s.[43] Another similar example is Sceaux Gardens in Camberwell, completed in 1959.[44] The first LCC-designed project was announced in 1956, the nineteen-storey Tidey Street development in Poplar.

LONDON
Crone Court , Carlton Vale, NW6, Willesden MBC, 1963. A block containing maisonettes as well as flats on the lower floors.

LONDON, LCC FLATS AND MAISSONETTES INTERLINKED
Top: Warwick Estate, Paddington (Warwick Crescent Site), W2;
 (1958) 1960–64.
Left: Stifford Estate, 'High Stepney', Clive Street, Jamaica Street, E1;
Below: Maisonettes and flats, from 1957 (cf. p. 8).

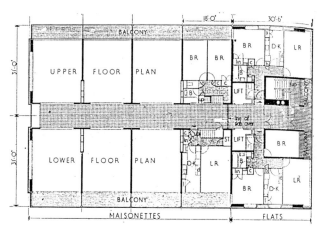

LONDON LCC
Left page: Princethorpe House, Woodchester Square, Paddington, W2, 1961.
Above: Draper Street Block (Draper House / Estate), Elephant and Castle,
    Southwark, SE1. (1958) 1962–65.
Right: Proposals for the Elephant & Castle area, c. 1960.

LONDON
Left: Tidey Street project,
Lincoln Estate, Poplar, E3,
1956. LCC Architects.
Bottom left: Le Corbusier, schematic section through Unité
d'habitation, Marseille 1947–52.
Bottom right: LCC Scissors /
cross-over / split-level type,
schematic section.

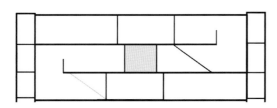

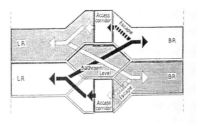

An explanation of the LCC's scissor blocks of the early 1960s can only be attempted with the help of diagrammatic illustrations. The three rooms of each dwelling unit are on two floors. But these two floors are not all on top of each other, as with the maisonettes; instead, the dwelling is spread in a complex way across the width of the block. When one goes up from the living room to the bedrooms, one also goes across the centre of the block. That centre of the block, and this is the principal innovation, also contains the access corridor. The dwellings are, so to speak, intertwined around that central access way, which, as with the straightforward maisonette, occurs only on every other floor. There is further complexity in this central area, as it contains, apart from the public corridor and the internal steps, also the bathrooms and toilets, and, finally, there is another flight of steps serving as the fire-escape route. The exterior of the block, by contrast, is now extremely uniform: just the same row of windows all the way up, and that on both sides. There are normally no private balconies. If there had still been faint remnants of a sense of a front/back contrast in the eleven-storey maisonette slab block, here they have disappeared completely. Scissor blocks are mostly extremely slim slab blocks. Finally, there is no place inside the block for the main staircase(s) or lifts; they have to be added in a separate small unit.

There is a hint here of Le Corbusier's 'rue intérieure' of the Marseille Unité, but the spaces there are far more lavish, as Le

Corbusier adhered to his old model of the double height living room. The London scissors plan really does utilise the available space to the very maximum. The smallish corridor avoids one disadvantage of the maisonette–cum-flat block just described: the wasted space of the two-storey height of its access corridor. At the same time all this meant that a crucial feature, if not the basic feature of the maisonette was effectively lost, namely the likeness to a house and the inkling of a feeling of individuality. Indeed, the elevations of the high scissor blocks show a degree of small-scale uniformity and repetition never seen in Britain before.

A confident statement by the LCC in 1962 regarding the scissors type summarised the whole sequence of LCC planning endeavours described in this Chapter, which had spanned a dozen years. The scissors plan, it pronounced, was the successful conclusion of 'a long search for methods of planning dwellings that [combine] the essential objectives of maximum flexibility in site layout, maximum economy of site use at high densities, a maximum of flexibility in accommodation build-up and economy in constructional cost.'[45] At this point, it would perhaps have been more apposite to summarise the situation as one featuring a maximal number of solutions, rather than just one optimal solution, as by that time the number of major and minor variations of types of council dwellings in London had become uncountable.[46]

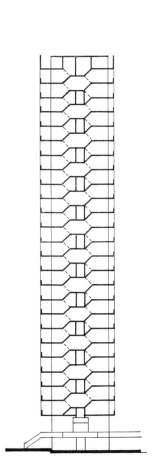

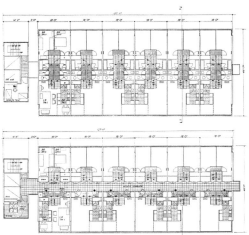

LONDON
LCC Scissors type. Pepys Estate, Daubeney
and Eddystone Towers, Deptford, SE8, 1962–63.

LONDON
Maydew House, Abbeyfield Estate,
Bermondsey, SE16, LCC scissors
design, 1964.

At the end of this process, one can turn back, once again, from the single block to the wider context of the whole estate. The 1960s became increasingly dominated by large conglomerate designs, though this was not a term used at the time. The term 'megastructure', so popular during the 70s, could also potentially be used for this approach, but it was normally applied to mixed-use complexes. As regards the 1950s' pet notion of mixed development, this now seemed to mark something self-evident, namely that every estate of any size should contain dwellings of various sizes, from the one-roomed studio flat to the one-bed-roomed flat up to flats or houses with three or four bedrooms. At the same time, two major preferences of the 1950s were, by the early sixties, beginning to fade, preferences which gave 'mixed development' such a clear visual specificity: firstly, the demonstration of diversity through the use of strongly varied dwelling types; and, secondly, the positioning of the blocks in open spaces. To start with, many estates of the 1960s were of an unprecedented size. 500 dwellings and more were no rarity. Many of the developments also seemed to demand the highest allowable degree of density, namely 200 persons per acre. That meant that two-storey houses had to be excluded, which left only two types of dwellings, lower-to-medium height kinds of flatted blocks, and high point or slab blocks. The former would accommodate the maisonettes and the larger dwellings, while the towers would contain the smaller ones. The City of London Corporation's Golden Lane development, with its six-storey maisonette blocks in combination with a seventeen-storey point/slab block of one and two bedroom flats, can be seen as a major model. Later noteworthy examples in London include Broadwater Farm in Haringey, from 1966, with over a thousand dwellings in towers and lower deck blocks, while a provincial development was Wolverhampton's Heath Town, built from 1967, very large by any British standards, housed 4,537 persons in its

1,265 dwellings. Its programme was formulated not in terms of types of dwelling, but simply by stating percentages of house-hold units: 30% of dwellings would be for two persons, 50% serve four persons, 17% 5 persons and 3% for 7 persons.[47] The architectural result can be a most complex amalgam, a con-glomerate, of horizontal and vertical blocks (cf. p. 195).

But the trend towards both higher density and greater height in the 1960s was not just the result of practical-economic con-siderations, but also entailed a growing demand for a general sense of the 'urban'. It did not mean that greenery had to be excluded altogether, but everything now appeared more tightly confined. The basic spatial value is now that of feeling rela-tively 'enclosed'; this is matched by a demand for horizon-tal connectivity within the whole of the estate. At the West Chelsea (World's End) development, built from 1969, one of the few London Borough projects to successfully breach the LCC/GLC 200 p.p.a. ceiling, the plan was to make it 'possible to push a pram from any flat to any flat'.[48] The result of all this, in many cases, was massive rectangular grids of long medium-rise slabs, of six to eight storeys, with or without interlinking high blocks. A veritable denial of height can then be felt with the pronounced horizontalities of Alexandra Road in Camden, or at Central Hill in Lambeth, presenting immensely sophisticated versions of the row house, or even, as with Lillington Street in Westminster, where one meets an amalgam of all dwelling types so that one speaks neither of slabs, nor of point blocks, nor of row houses or even maisonette units. All these com-plexes, nota bene, come under 'mixed development', providing, as they do, the most complex combinations of diverse sizes of dwellings.[49] From the plain *Zeilenbau* rectangles, imported from the Continent in the 1940s, British public housing design had come a very long way.

LONDON
Broadwater Farm Estate, Haringey LBC , N17, 1967–73.

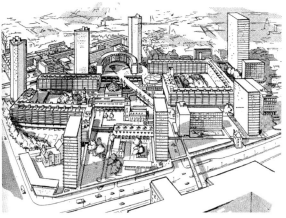

Barbican Centre, Chamberlin Powell and Bon for the Corporation of London, 1955–82, view at the planning stage, end of the 1950s.

10 Construction / design: a continuous experiment

Frame or box?

The decision, the determination, to build high opened up totally new fields of construction and design. This was inevitable, as for structures above five storeys, and certainly above seven or eight storeys, the traditional methods of building would simply not do any more. British urban commercial architecture had already, for some time, been using more experimental methods, but there was little to be learnt from them; the building of high rise council flats developed within its own sphere. The principal reason for this was that economic considerations weighed much more heavily. 'Structural economics', an expression used by Peter Dunican, a member of Ove Arup's team of engineers – was the paramount consideration at all times. It was prefaced by all post-war commentators that all kinds of flats, even medium-rise walk-up blocks in traditional construction, always cost more to build than houses; in 1955 flats in twelve-storey blocks were said to cost 80% more. But cost was not the only uncertainty. Everything concerning higher blocks, argued Cleeve Barr in 1957, still appeared 'a complete new experience,' not only construction-wise, but also as regards lift speed, water provision, to which one might add foundations and wind pressure.[1] A sense of uncertainty was palpable throughout.

All this provoked an intensely experimental spirit among many architects. The new Modernist radicalism demanded openness, all-comprehensiveness, a holistic approach in the demonstration of modernity; it was not sufficient to just lay on 'mod. cons.' like hot and cold, or to use metal and concrete construction internally and then hide it away behind brick walls, as it had been the case with some of the large mansion flats built since the thirties. Modernist council-house architecture demanded that everything had to be radically exposed. 'Design', if one defines it summarily as the 'architectural' look of the outside of the block, was now seen as almost completely identical with a block's method of building. On occasion the absolute primacy of construction was openly declared: 'Birmingham puts structure before plan'. Accompanied by effective illustrations, Birmingham City Architect Sheppard Fidler commented on his Millpool Hill project of 1956 as follows: 'The normal procedure for flats which subordinated structure to planning was wasteful ... [now the architect] was anxious to test the effect of

reversing the process and design dwellings to fit an economic structural frame'[2] (cf. p. 184). In any case, there should be 'continuous experiment in plan, plan form and structure'.[3]

There was the very occasional attempt to use brick walling for blocks above the normal limit, but that required special techniques. By the 1940s, the well-established method for building high was, of course, that of steel framing. With such a thin, but very homogeneous and fairly dense framework, one did not have to worry much about going up ten, twenty, or thirty storeys. All the metal components came ready shaped and standardised from the factory. The walls and floors could then be fitted around them as individually required. A spectacular 1930s example of a steel frame in public housing was Quarry Hill in Leeds; in 1946 came the steel frame for one of the first, and, in fact, with ten storeys, the highest block so far: Holborn MBC's Dombey Street block (cf. p. 52) An equally ambitious example of building in steel, albeit completely hidden by homogeneous brick walling, is Birmingham's Duddeston RDA Unit 1 group of 1950 (cf. p. 184). Nearer the end of the story came Glasgow's soaring Red Road development of 1962–69. However, steel was generally in short supply and remained expensive throughout the period. (cf. p. 238)

By contrast, concrete and even steel-reinforced concrete ('r. c.') were relatively cheap and easily procurable, and their basic materials, at any rate, amounted to half, or even less, of the cost of steel. Constructions could proceed flexibly, though that was likely to add expense.[4] Sheppard Fidler enthused that 'there are endless possibilities for experiment in the field of reinforced concrete construction'[5] but he might equally have stressed the endless problems that the material brought in its train. The most urgent of these was the horizontal bridging of space, as concrete lacked tensile strength. However, with the right kinds of metal reinforcements, ceilings that could span the relatively narrow spaces in public housing were possible; in the thirties, some floors in blocks of flats were already using concrete. A quite different challenge was posed by the use of concrete floors within a system of r. c. column supports. By the fifties, the favoured solution was to use a continuous, homogeneously flat and relatively thin ceiling, sandwiched between the columns, the so-called 'flat plate' or 'plate floor'.[6]

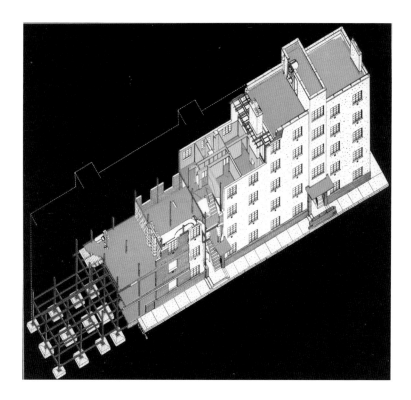

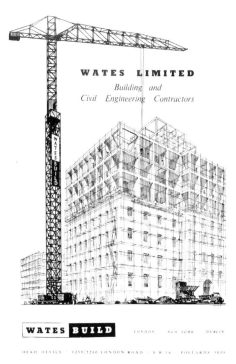

Left: The steel industry's proposal for housing, 1934 (cf. p. 84).
Right: A builder suggesting a seemingly straightforward
frame-cum-infilling method of construction, as well
as stressing the novelty of the tower crane, 1954.

Reflecting all these constraints, the 'normal' kind of concrete construction, the seemingly most efficient method, was a homogenous, regular kind of skeletal r.c. framework. This broadly behaved like a steel frame, but in tall buildings it needed to be calibrated more carefully. The guiding spirit overall was 'rationalisation': the task of making all processes of production and building more efficient. A major innovation for all high structures was the use of tower cranes, cranes that were higher than the building to be constructed, and which were first brought in from France in the early 1950s.[7] In contrast to prefabricated steel framing, concrete structures were normally produced on site, through a process of pouring into moulds – for which the special term is 'in situ'. To create the formwork for a frame in situ was a complex task, certainly in the case of high blocks. There was now a slowly developing alternative, namely, to make the parts of the framework off-site and assemble them on-site. Prefabrication became a general battle cry, especially in the sixties, although the question of where it was best for the prefabrication to take place, whether in a made-up workshop close to the site, or in a more distant factory building, remained an open one.

Once the basic, load-bearing framework of a high block of flats had been constructed, a wide range of further issues arose. How was one to fit the walls into the framework? How could these walls be made soundproof and show other insulating qualities? Inside the block, arrays of regularly spaced, but ubiquitous columns might not easily conform to the mostly complicated dwelling plans, especially those of the smaller flats, and one might find a column blocking one's way, as in the case of some of the living rooms in the twenty-one-storey LCC point block type, that was used in 1962 in the Canada Estate. (cf. p. 136)[8].

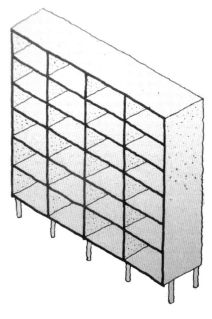

The basics of box frame construction, 1945.

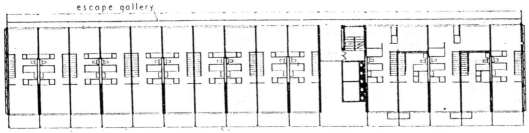

escape gallery

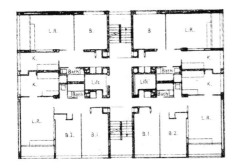

Top: cross-wall construction for an 11-storey maisonette block, London, Picton Sreet, 1954–56 (cf. p. 23, 68).

VARIATIONS IN THE CONSTRUCTION OF POINT BLOCKS (CF. PP. 63, 65)
Left: Point blocks at Roehampton, Alton West (cf. p. 63, 67).
Right: Brandon Towers (cf. p. viii).

These considerations, in turn, bring us to a different kind of constructional thinking, one that starts not with the frame, but with the actual walls. There could, of course, be any kind of combination of framework and walls. But a newly emerging trend was to conceive of a multi-storey block, and more especially a council block with small flats, purely as an assembly of walls, in the form of panels. Here, each panel would be large enough to form a whole wall of a room; floors and ceilings were likewise conceived as panels. Thus a normal room is made up of six panels: four walls, floor, and ceiling. The wall panels would usually have a thickness of 6 to 7 inches, or 15 to 17 centimetres. The major new idea of those panels was that they fused the functions of wall-membrane with those of the frame. It was one of those constructional concepts that took some time to emerge, but once it had, it seemed eminently plausible. The floor panels and wall panels together could then be looked at as a kind of framework, or as a 'house of cards', but one with all the cards firmly and stiffly fixed in place, and this framework could all build up to a considerable height, certainly to twenty floors or more. The immensely tricky problem was, however, that of joining the panels to each other, and the methods of doing this varied accordingly. In the case of England, John Allan has described in detail the way in which the idea crystallised and was developed in a succession of blocks designed by Lubetkin, greatly helped by his engineer, Ove Arup.[9] The term that British designers finally settled on for this new mode was 'box frame', or, more rarely, 'egg crate'. This should, however, not be confused with 'box' construction, that is, the pre-production of entire rooms, which was not practised in Britain.

There was one further new kind of structure, closely related to the box frame, namely the 'cross-wall' method. Here, the key constructional element is a regularly-spaced series of un-pierced walls which reach through the depth of the block as well as right to the top of the block. The dwellings are sandwiched in between. If the block was only of four storeys, the cross-walls could be of brick,[10] for higher walls concrete or r. c.

had to be used. As already mentioned, cross wall construction had become the logical procedure for the high and long London maisonette blocks. Naturally, the higher the cross walls, the more they had to be strengthened by horizontal components, the floors, so that, in effect, the cross-wall system became a box frame system. Such long high blocks had to be further strengthened by an in situ-cast core block, containing lifts and staircases, or by specially strengthened end walls. Another way of adding strength was, very simply, to join on another slab block at right angles, an approach that was, for instance, popular with new council blocks in Bristol in the 1950s. (cf. p. 173). And yet, like all 'systems' that were based on geometrically simple procedures, the cross wall mode, like the box frame mode, had its limitations; it made most sense for blocks which were long but not deep.

For square blocks, that is, for point blocks, a pure box frame is hardly conceivable. Naturally, the more the point block shades into a slab block, the more the constructional principle also becomes that of a slab block, either in its cross-wall or its box-frame mode. Square point blocks can either be of pure skeletal construction, or they may use studs of cross walls mixed with columns, which can be laterally elongated. As with the slab block, or indeed with any block of flats, the principal, thicker structural components serve at the same time as effective separations between the flats. The story of the first proper point blocks, at the LCC's Princes Way development, or Ackroydon Estate, planned and built from 1950 to 1954, very precisely illustrates this spirit of experimentation (cf. p. 65). Originally there were to have been a series of strip columns, but in the built version there are solid stud cross walls in the centre and at the ends, augmented by lesser elements of support. More than with the slab block, with the point block it is the core of the block that matters, the lift shafts and solid stairwells. In effect, in complete contrast to the repetitive slab block pattern, the plans of point blocks never seem to repeat themselves in Britain.

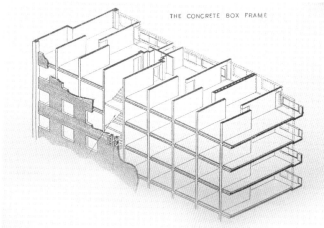

THE CONCRETE BOX FRAME

Left: Berthold Lubetkin / Ove Arup: Demonstration drawing to show the
complete independence, designwise, of the external walls from the
construction behind, or of any kind of construction on the ground.
Right: Spa Green Estate, Finsbury, EC1, 1957.

So far the issues were those of the interior of the block. It was part of the holistic ideology of Modernism to demand that the exterior forms of a building should correspond exactly to its interior divisions, or at least present some kind of reflection of the method of internal construction. But the shaping of the elevations of council tower blocks turns out to be a most complex issue. The salient fact about the different modes of construction – whether framework, box frame or cross-wall is that they do not present an idea as to how the outside of a block should be formed – other than leaving it as a series of gaping holes.

Modern architects' attitudes to that challenge were conditioned by a fundamentally new understanding of a building as a whole, which was diametrically opposed to the old kinds of thinking under which the determination of the shape, for instance, a wall of bricks, comes first, which is then assumed to fulfil, at least summarily, the required functions. The new mode of thinking, which became more widespread during the 1950s, starts with the consideration of the various purposes that a wall has to fulfil, rather than with the description of predetermined forms. One begins with listing the tasks of the exterior covering of a block, which are, in random order, to let in light, to keep warmth in and the cold and wet out; it should also be durable, and the purely aesthetic aspect is a concern, too, as well as, naturally, cost.[11]

When it came to erecting a high block there were a number of ways of creating its outside 'skin'. Up to a height of five to

THE MUNICIPAL JOURNAL
26 April 1963

SfB Kk4
UDC

STRAMIT
INTERNAL
INFILL-PANELS

Whether applied to brickwork beneath windows of conventional design or incorporated into modern curtain-wall structures, STRAMIT internal infill-panels offer many advantages. Not least of these is the inherently good insulation value of the STRAMIT slabs, eliminating the need for a separate insulating material and thereby reducing costs. STRAMIT also offers an exceptionally good surface for decorating purposes or can be supplied with special facing materials, such as coloured plastic sheeting or veneered plywood, if desired.

Recommended Application to
CURTAIN-WALL UNITS

WINDOW GLAZING

TIMBER FRAME

EXTERNAL CLADDING

2″ STRAMIT INFILL-PANEL

SIDE ELEVATION

CAVITY

TIMBER FRAME

VENTILATION TO CAVITY

D.P.C

BRICKWORK

This drawing shows the recommended method of construction where it is desired to incorporate STRAMIT internal infill-panels into curtain-wall units.

PROPERTIES

THERMAL CONDUCTANCE: At 2″ standard thickness 0·30; better than an 11″ cavity brick wall.

SOUND INSULATION: The mean sound reduction factor is 30 dB.

FIRE RESISTANCE: STRAMIT has excellent fire-resistant qualities. Copies of official Fire Test Reports available on request.

STOCK SIZES
2 in. thick × 4 ft. wide × 6, 8, 9, 10 and 12 ft. long.
Special sizes made to order

STRAMIT BOARDS LTD. COWLEY PEACHEY, UXBRIDGE, MIDDLESEX : : Telephone: West Drayton (WE3) 3751 (10 lines
One of the TOMO Group of Companies

New industries serving the cladding of blocks, 1963.

seven floors one could simply use a traditional loadbearing wall. Interior and exterior construction constitute one homogeneous mass. Above that height this method will not do any more. The most likely construction inside is now a framework, which results in the structure with holes described above. At this point the covering of the outside starts to pose choices. What can now be highly deceptive is the way many high blocks are given a solid-looking, smooth external surface that appears to rest on the ground – whereas in fact this 'wall' is actually just a thin layer tied on to the internal construction (cf. p. 132). There is of course a very different way of treating the elevation, namely to expose the frame on the outside and to insert into it pieces of wall or whatever else is needed, windows or balconies: this was the time-honoured mode for French architects,

who, after all, were the inventors of r. c. framework construction. The third method is 'cladding' – the use of exterior elements, invariably prefabricated, which are now understood as separate entities that need to be fastened on to the inner construction, as well as having to be tied in with windows and balconies in complex ways. Terms related to cladding in general, though not much used in the housing context, were 'screen wall' and 'curtain wall'.[12]

If we return to the Modernist conundrum that demands clarity in showing how a building is constructed, we can see, once again, that the different techniques cited above resulted in quite different kinds of elevational designs. A homogenous wall covering, whether it is built up from the ground or is attached to the frame,

Left: Colour, another subsidiary
  industry, 1956.
Right: Frame construction, clad
  with concrete slabs, Hide Tower,
  Westminster, 1960 (cf. p. 127).

shows nothing of the frame at all. This is how Lubetkin understood the elevations in his Finsbury blocks. The second, one
might, again, call it the 'French' infill method shows the frame
most clearly. In Britain many designers, especially around
1960, were particularly interested in the third method, cladding, which ultimately allows the inner structure of the block
to 'shine through', but it did this in very diverse ways. These
new panels for cladding which were made from a plethora of
materials, selected according to their insulating qualities, their
weight and, of course, their cost. A great number of terms had
emerged for cladding: 'heavy cladding', 'light cladding', 'solid
panels', 'activity panels', 'sandwich panels', 'waffle panels',
and more. The materials used for cladding included concrete,
in various mixtures, plastic, plywood, coloured glass, fibreglass

and, frequently, asbestos, 'with its high insulation powers' (cf.
p. 237).[13] Every aspect of cladding was critical, not to say prob-
lem-laden, most especially the jointing, the ways of attaching
parts firmly, yet unobtrusively.

Once again, the exterior treatment of a block can thus be
assessed largely as a technical, a practical-constructional
issue. But there are other ways of evaluating the exterior, in
particular by considering the materials used purely according
to their appearance, and certain ways in which the architects
exercised their visual preferences. Construction was held to
be determining 'design', but at the same time 'design' also
carried a meaning as something that pinpoints visual – aesthetic preferences in their own right.

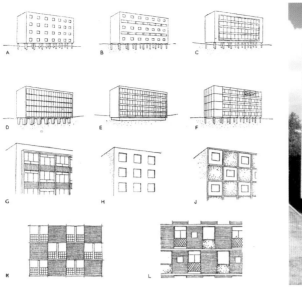

Left: Frederick Gibberd's 'Expression in Modern Architecture' emphasizes the very diverse kinds of relationships between internal construction and external treatment, 1952.
Right: Tecton, later Drake & [Denys] Lasdun, London, Paddington, Hallfield Estate, from 1949.

Regarding the surface of the primary building material, concrete, there were unexpectedly complex issues at play. For a start, 'raw' concrete, concrete of the kind found in the basic cast in-situ construction at the core of a block, with its relatively smooth, yet hard surface, was not something that would normally be exposed to any extent on the outside of domestic buildings. Its 'ordinary Portland' grey colour would not be considered attractive. It would be limited to the edges of the frame, or the floors, or to details at the base or the top, where it could be given an extra colouring and described as 'fair-faced'. 'Béton brut', that is, concrete left strongly marked by rough-surfaced shuttering – as found, for instance on Lasdun's National Theatre[14] – was not seen as desirable in British housing, either. On the whole though, a certain variety of ways of treating the surfaces of concrete did occur, such as bush-hammering, as at Ernö Goldfinger's GLC projects at Edenham Street (Trellick Tower, from 1967), where the contractor, F.G. Minter, was given the most detailed instructions by the architect. There was tooled concrete, the creation of strong relief patterns, and there was a wide variety of materials that could be mixed into the aggregate as a 'facing mix'. Finally, one could add colour to the concrete mix of large components, although how often this happened is hard to say today.[15] Prefabricated component production must have facilitated the application of all these treatments – a significant factor especially with many of the 'package' blocks in the 'sixties.

In England, in particular, there was also a continued widespread external use of brick as a cladding material, even though Cleeve Barr maintained that its insulation qualities were deficient.[16] This did not, once again, mean the same as creating a brick wall from the floor up: rather, the bricks were fixed together into panels usually of a thickness of 4½ inches, which were lifted and placed into position by a crane, just like any other cladding, or infill element. Sometimes the brickwork covers the walls completely, sometimes only in certain zones. A quite popular mode, in London at least, was to let the edges of floor slabs show on the outside, appearing as lightly

coloured thin strips, sandwiched between the broad bands of brick walling (cf. p. 149). This lent the whole block a horizontal look, somehow contradicting the essence of a tower – its verticality. More rarely, the outside walls were covered with coarse mosaic work.[17] The most frequent method of all was still also the most traditional one, especially in Scotland – rendering or roughcast. This, again, made possible a choice of colour, though the traditionalist ochres or beiges seem to have prevailed. Lastly, and relatively rarely, the very opposite to large and comparatively uninterrupted surfaces was the foregrounding of the metal frames of the balconies and windows, often linked with the display of large areas of glass, a look of overall lightness that was central to the most common perception of a 'Modern' high block (cf. p. 84).

There was thus a sliding scale in the shaping of elevations, ranging from those forms which arose entirely out of the choice of materials and of their constructional possibilities, to forms that were derived from purely formal considerations, not to say from a desire for decoration. Under the heading 'expression in architecture', Frederick Gibberd produced a range of schematic compositional exercises emphasising the multiplicity of formal possibilities for the design of elevations.[18] A particularly uncompromising example of freely designed patterns, completely disregarding the internal framework, was Lubetkin's Rosebery Avenue (Spa Green) project of 1946 in Finsbury, whose eight-storey slab blocks feature layers of variously coloured bricks. Lubetkin explained that these were grounded in 'abstract principles, with formal expression ... principles of composition ... [aimed at] the emotional impact of the visual'.[19] A little later, Lubetkin's firm Tecton, with the young Denys Lasdun as project architect, further developed this approach with a much greater formalist intensity in the Bishops Bridge Road (Hallfield) Estate in Paddington, from 1949. This prompted the critics Rayner Banham and Robert Furneaux Jordan to politely chide the architects for producing 'decoration'[20] and thereby contradicting the ethos of Modernism – and Lasdun duly gave up this approach.

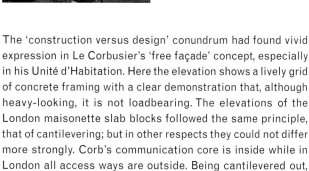

LCC MAISONETTE SLAB BLOCKS
Top left: Fixing the prefabricated screen elements to the Aegis Grove
   block, Reema Construction.
Top right: Symington House, Deverell Street, Southwark, SE1, 1957.
Lower left: Maisonettes, Aegis Grove, Battersea, SW8, 1960–61.
Opposite page from left to right: Raynham House, Globe Road,
   Massingham Street, E1 1958; Withy House, Globe Road, E1, 1959;
   Torridon House, Kilburn Park Road, NW6, 1966.

The 'construction versus design' conundrum had found vivid expression in Le Corbusier's 'free façade' concept, especially in his Unité d'Habitation. Here the elevation shows a lively grid of concrete framing with a clear demonstration that, although heavy-looking, it is not loadbearing. The elevations of the London maisonette slab blocks followed the same principle, that of cantilevering; but in other respects they could not differ more strongly. Corb's communication core is inside while in London all access ways are outside. Being cantilevered out, the stress in London is on the lightness of these walkways,

and thus the additional support they are given by the attached, quasi hanging framework is also very light (and cheap), sometimes almost filigree-like. All this provided opportunities for considerable variation. In general terms, the varied elevational patterns of the London maisonette blocks was appreciated by J.M. Richards, who wrote that 'the two-storey units of which maisonettes are composed have effectively reduced the monotony. Since alternate floors are different, and broken down, they scale into something more human'.[21]

The 1960s: individualisation or standardisation?

During the 1960s the diversity of British council tower design was reaching a climax. An utterly different situation had prevailed less than ten years before, when few architects had any idea what it involved to build higher than twelve storeys, not least because of a fear of the associated 'fantastic costs'. Now everything appeared to be available: the number of planning types was very considerable and the choice of materials and the constructional possibilities, including cladding, was wide. The resulting diversity of blocks defies systematisation. Part Three, and Chapter 12 in particualr, will present a small selection.

But the 1960s also brought a cleavage, namely with the rise of the big building firms. In Chapter Five, we traced the new ways in which architects attempted to co-operate with the construction industry, which could then end up with the industry seemingly taking over, resulting in the 'package deal' phenomenon: the whole 'product' was supplied by the industry, ready-designed and engineered. The designers of those kinds of blocks, normally salaried architects and engineers on the contractors' payroll, were hardly ever publicly named.[22] It was to be expected that architects, some clients and certainly the architectural critics would soon begin to voice their dislike, and even contempt for this situation. However, at the beginning of the 'systems boom' in Britain, in 1961–3, there was ample support from practically all sides. Pre-casting concrete brings variety, argued the engineer Felix Samuely in 1950.[23] By the late 1950s, Cleeve Barr was propagating ever more strongly his materialist understanding of architecture, stressing now that the use of prefabricated parts was something that helped to avoid the designer being 'employed as a stylist'.[24] One could now plausibly portray 'system-building' as the final, decisive realisation of the longstanding Modernist ideal of architecture as 'pure construction', or, even, in this case, 'pure manufacture'. In the case of the point blocks at Roehampton and also with the Hide Place tower in Westminster in 1960, much stress was put on the way the exteriors were clad in prefabricated panels. At the commissioning stage of their first experimental project as UK licensees of the Danish Larsen Nielsen system, the LCC's Morris Walk development in 1962/63, the contractors Taylor Woodrow proposed to the LCC's architects that they should design the project first, and the firm would then produce the buildings accordingly. But architects proposed instead a more complex and interactive approach: 'We want to know how the system is produced, what are your technical limits, and we will then design the blocks accordingly, as well as from the client's point of view'.[25] Kenneth Campbell, the LCC's Chief Housing Architect, stressed the architects' enthusiasm for the new systems movement, repeating for emphasis the key ideal: 'precision, precision, precision'. Reproaches, such as that of 'monotony', he considered 'practically meaningless'; the architect should divest himself of any kind of 'sentimentality'.[26] The ever optimistic, yet always circumspect Cleeve Barr maintained in 1962, in this case regarding designer-co-ordinated prefabrication(see below), that 'the main results in using repetition and standardisation ... must surely be that relatively more money and a higher degree of skill can be put into design and working efficiency'.[27] As so often, the precise meaning of 'design' remained elusive.

All these pronouncements stemmed from a generalised architectural discourse of economy and efficiency, and thus its relationship to the practical realities of building organisation could sometimes be quite remote. Our main concern here, however, is the ways in which the actual 'systems' of the 1960s fitted in with the constructional models that had been developed for high blocks during the 1940s and 50s. Taking a basic morphological view, most 'systems' used the box frame formula described above; each room being composed of a number of panels. The first firm in Britain that made a strong claim of using a 'large panel system' was Reema, with its many eight and ten-storey blocks in Leeds from 1958 and its eleven-storey maisonette block for the LCC at Aegis Grove, Battersea, from 1960. (cf. pp. 88, 213) In their blocks in Leeds, though, the joints between the panels are quite hard to see; with the Larsen-Nielsen blocks they are much stronger, visually driving home the facts of prefabrication.

Much the same applied to the Camus system, the object of much early attention from visiting British council delegations in Paris and finally introduced in Liverpool on a large scale from 1963/64 (cf. p. 281). Camus was more up-front in stressing their factory-like production methods, already underway in many countries by 1957, but appeared less interested in creating a specific external 'look' for their buildings. The third major early import was the French Sectra system, used by the contractor Laing, beginning with Manchester in 1963. Its construction, in this case site-fabricated, came closer to the basic box frame method; usually the blocks were only one, very long panel deep – the panel being cast in situ – and the system was thus best suited to slab blocks.

Above: London, Morris Walk Estate, Maryon
  Road, Woolwich SE7, 1963–66. Detail of one of
  the ten-storey blocks. Builders: Taylor Woodrow
  Anglian / Larsen-Nielsen System with LCC
  Architects (cf. pp. 30–32).
Left: Model of 1962.
Opposite page: Morris Walk Estate, sketch, 1964.

In all this, the ideal of speed and 'simplicity' was prominent, yet there was one issue that proved persistently complex and tricky, namely the joining together of the panels. Precast floors and walls were usually linked together by metal parts protruding from each component. Each firm devised its own methods of doing this. Discussions about these joints, which, after all, nobody could see from the outside, remained entirely within the circle of specialists – until the 16th of May 1968, the day when part of Ronan Point, part of a a twenty-three-storey Larsen-Nielsen block in the London Borough of Newham, collapsed following a gas explosion. The final verdict of the lengthy investigation into the causes concluded, cautiously but firmly, that there was an 'absence of reliable scientific evidence on the effect and stiffness of such structure'.[28]

By far the largest suppliers of 'manufactured' blocks were Wimpey and Bison, producing more blocks than all the other major nationally active builders put together. Like all firms they could act as contractors for designs that were supplied to them by architects, but their principal activity was to produce 'packages', that is, blocks designed and engineered by themselves. In that respect they were the most successful firms, in the sense that their 'products' appeared strongly branded, on most occasions, as a specific kind of construction and a specific look. That said, their methods of construction constituted polar opposites, respectively involving in-situ frames and precast large panels.

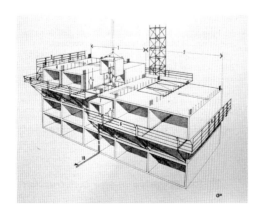

Model of a 'Sectra System' block. Demonstration of a Sectra construc tion process: walls and ceilings are cast in-situ under special conditions.

Ronan Point collapse in 1968.
London, Newham, Canning Town, Clever Road RDA, E16, 1966. Ronan Point in front.

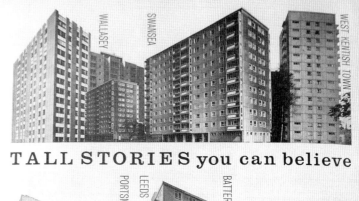

TALL STORIES you can believe

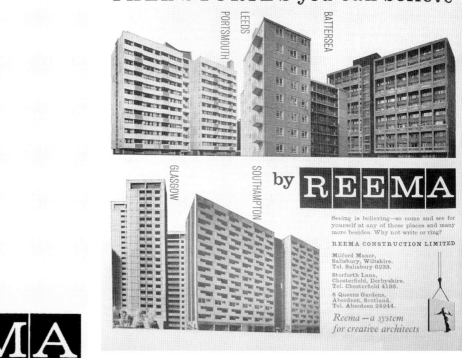

by REEMA

Seeing is believing—so come and see for
yourself at any of these places and many
more besides. Why not write or ring?

REEMA CONSTRUCTION LIMITED

Milford Manor,
Salisbury, Wiltshire.
Tel. Salisbury 6233.

Storforth Lane,
Chesterfield, Derbyshire.
Tel. Chesterfield 4195.

8 Queens Gardens,
Aberdeen, Scotland.
Tel. Aberdeen 24244.

*Reema — a system
for creative architects*

REEMA
USE
CONCRETE
to build faster
and cut costs

616 houses built in 686 working days at Portsmouth.
19 blocks of high flats now going up in Leeds. More to
come in Swansea, Wallasey, London and Southsea.
Church halls, youth centres, swimming pools,
churches, synagogues and chapels for communities
throughout the country.

Almost everywhere you go REEMA is being endorsed
by wise men, who see the sense of a system that uses
concrete to its utmost. With strength in clean, simple
lines. With quick erection to weatherproof stage
resulting from pre-casting large elements in controlled
factory conditions. With slashing economy in man
hours and material. Without scaffolding: No fuss.
No clutter. Anywhere.

And REEMA is flexible. Fitting the most advanced
ideas with simple grace. Lending itself to initiative
and opening new opportunities. Even in finish, there
is hardly a limit. Almost any material can be used on
a REEMA panel. Some have just been made, faced with
amber glass, some with vitreous china. They are
brilliant, permanent, self-cleansing.

REEMA is worth knowing, if you want to build fast
and save money on fine building that is both revolu-
tionary yet in sympathy with our tradition. Send the
coupon, and have REEMA tell you more.

Above: Reema Advertisement 1965: from top left: three private blocks in
   Wallasey: Swansea: Sketty Park; London St. Pancras MBC: West Kentish Town;
   Portsmouth: Wingfield St; Leeds: Ebor Gardens Stage 1; Battersea: LCC Aegis
   Grove Area & Site (cf. p. 88); Glasgow: Maryhill CDA Area B, Southampton:
   Bevois Street Redevelopment.
Left: Reema Advertisement 1960 (cf. p. 28).

TYPE 1001/6
WITH FEATURE PANELS IN BRICKWORK
TO FULL HEIGHT OF BLOCK

This design
comprising four 2
Bedroom and two
1 Bedroom Flats per landing
is an economical block
of pleasing appearance and
meets the popular demand
throughout the country.

TYPE 1001/6   TYPICAL FLOOR PLAN

WIMPEY
Wimpey advertisement, c.1963.
Ramsgate Staner Court, Manston Road, 1963.

Norwich, Winchester Tower, Vauxhall Street, 1964.

Wimpey's 'No-Fines Concrete': The raw exterior of the wall and some of the surface coverings offered by the firm. Left to right, 'Ham River Gravel', 'Portland Stone', 'Dalbeattie Granite'.

Wimpey's was the in-situ method, based on a kind of poured aggregate which had been tried earlier in thousands of houses, under the rather opaque term 'no-fines'. This referred to the lack of sand and the preponderance of coarse material, which meant less moisture in the mix, which, in turn, allowed for larger and cheaper units of shuttering, simplifying and speeding up the building process as a whole. Wimpey blocks can often be recognised externally in the way that two floors were poured together. For blocks above five floors Wimpey enhanced its method by creating a new kind of framework, calling the whole procedure 'Wimpey industrialised systems building'. The resulting complex process is described thus: 'Within these shutters [for the walls] are fixed special core shutters where the vertical columns are required, and in these cores the reinforcing steel is placed. The process is then to pour the No-fines concrete panels between the column positions, remove the column cores, then pour the dense concrete [i.e. denser than the no-fines concrete] into the recesses that have been so formed. This is followed by placing the reinforced steel required for the horizontal beams on top of the No-fines panel walls, again followed by pouring the dense concrete for these beams. Thus the No-Fines supports the reinforced concrete frame until it hardens, after which the framing supports the No-Fines'.[29] In other words, first comes the infill and then comes the frame that holds up the infill! Externally, though, the frames merged with the walls and were not visible as such; all was contained within a unified surface and all windows gave the impression of holes cut into the wall. With the coarse appearance of no-fines concrete, Wimpey's walls could never be left bare but had to be rendered, providing a certain breadth of choice with regard to texture and colour.

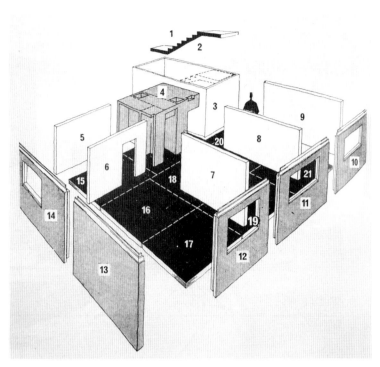

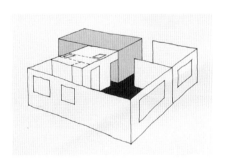

BISON
Above: 'Bison Wall Frame', the most publicised image of any 'system'
in Britain, the twenty-one components two-bedroomed flat, from 1962.
Below: The scheme reduced to a one-bedroom unit, 1964.

Above: London Haliday House, Mildmay Park,
Islington, N1, 1969.
Below: Nottingham Willoughby Street Area, 1965 (cf. p. 193).

Bison – the firm's actual name was Concrete Ltd. – first claimed originality for their method of pre-casting parts of a concrete framework in Barking in the late 1950s,[30] but the actual 'system' was developed only from 1961–62 onwards, when it came into its own under the brand name 'Bison'. The technical label was 'wall frame'. This provides the clue: it amounts to a continuation of the Lubetkin / Arup large panel 'box frame'. But Arup's 'frame' did not constitute a complete flat, whereas this was exactly what Bison now endeavoured to supply. Implicit in systems thinking was the aim of creating a maximal completeness with a minimum of parts. Bison's pride was its two-bedroomed flat, which managed to do it all with an astonishing total of only 21 parts, comprising not only all the walls and floors, but also a staircase unit, the bathroom and the toilet, each of the latter being prefabricated as complete units. As with most of the other systems, the wall panels contained the ducts for wiring and services, and the internal walls were ready for any surface treatment desired. The number of possible variations also appeared astonishing, whether regarding the size of the flats, the number of flats per floor and room sizes. The number of floors in a block could range from four to over twenty.

Bison Wall-Frame also incorporated one minor revolution – albeit one that was shared with Larsen Nielsen, Camus and other French systems: the external wall panel. As we saw above, what was novel about the external covering of a frame construction in post-war Modern blocks was that it could be treated either as infill or as cladding, both involving components *sui generis*, attached in complex ways to the frame. With Bison the external panel is treated in the same way as all the internal panels – even though it differs somewhat in its materials – and this external panel is tied in firmly into the rest of the 'house of cards'. The exterior of a Bison block shows relatively wide jointing gaps between the panels, which give the clearest indication of the mode of construction.

Late Bison: London Dickens House and Blake Court, Kilburn Park Road, South Kilburn RDA, W9, for Brent LBC, 1970: a variation of the Bison system, here relying also on the cross-wall method.

Left: Bison publicity: 'A block ... with more elaborate elevational treatment', from c. 1962.
Right: Bison at Kidderminster, Stourbridge Road, Coniston House, Derwent House, 1962–63.

THE FIRST FULLY INDUSTRIALISED HIGH FLATS TO BE COMPLETED IN BRITAIN

BISON WALL FRAME at Kidderminster

When, in 1963, it came to the opening of the very first Bison wall frame block, Coniston House in Kidderminster, there was, as could be expected, maximal praise: all agreed on the importance of it as being the first all-British system block; the Minister underlined the new comforts, 'bath, basin, lavatory ...'; the firm stressed the savings in man-hours. Only the Midland correspondent of *The Times* issued a challenge: 'Not good looking ... the main objection ... may be on aesthetic grounds. From the outside the flats do not appear to be either elegant or distinguished'.[31] As regards 'elegance', the correspondent probably did not realise that eleven or twelve storey-blocks with four flats per floor are unlikely to ever look slender. A more complex issue was the actual surface treatment for Bison's concrete exteriors. The firm's elaborate publicity material, dating from before the completion of the first blocks, illustrated a wide variety of treatments in colour and tone, proclaiming 'a complete range of external finishes ... including every type of exposed aggregate, tooled concrete, tiling or brick tiles ...' – the latter only up to twelve storeys. Several kinds of surfaces could occur on one building. In practice, however only few of these possibilities appear to have been taken up. The lively relief on the South Kilburn Redevelopment Area was a late exception. The firm's response to the criticism by *The Times* at the Kidderminster opening was clear: 'external refinement did cost money and the appearance of factory-built flats would reflect the price that local authorities were willing to pay for their construction'. Yet overall the firm insisted that 'there was no reason why factory-built flats would not look as well as flats built by conventional method'.[32] The Bison blocks that were to come usually adhered to the same light, slightly brownish-grey, given by the materials used. One may thus conclude by stating that Bison exteriors, as well as the external surface covering of Wimpey blocks, created a 'natural', not to say an 'Arts and Crafts' look – impossible as this may sound in the context of 'industrialised building'.

All in all, Bison's and Wimpey's systems marked a significant further development, and a greater sophistication of the principal modes of construction of high blocks that had emerged around 1950. What was new was the way in which these firms turned their systems into strong brands: in contrast to others, such as Reema, who stressed the diversity of their designs, Bison and Wimpey insisted on a particular look. Those with a narrow view of architectural creativity tended to bemoan the standardisation and the degree of commercialisation of it all; yet within the history of the wider architectural and building world, branding on such a scale was a strikingly new phenomenon and represented a major enrichment of the contemporary British scene. Overall, we can highlight the dramatic shifts in post-war housing construction by recalling that in 1950, there was only one major choice: brick, or brick plus render. By contrast, the wave of high-flat construction from that date onwards generated a very considerable variety of methods. In that sense prefabrication led not just to 'standardisation' but also to architectural diversity; to a new diversity for bespoke designs and package deal blocks alike.

11 Designing the tower block environment; class and civic symbolism

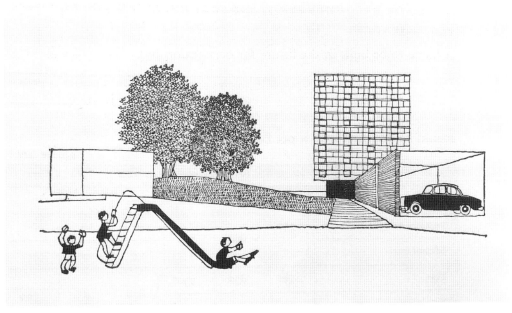

'The Home in its Setting', a section in *Homes for Today and Tomorrow*, the 'Parker Morris Report'. Drawing by Gordon Cullen, 1961.

Services inside the block

The car is parked in the street alongside the pavement; the front entrance to the dwelling is clearly located and there may be an additional access via the back; the internal technical facilities, such as plumbing, electrical systems, and heating can be arranged to suit any individual preferences – including the 'traditional' open fire. The space at the back serves for hanging out the washing, for pets, and for children to play, for putting up a shed or two, for the refuse bins to be tucked into a corner; and finally, of course, most households have an actual garden all to themselves.

Can one imagine a more banal, uncontentious account? When considering a block of flats, however, each and every one of these activities and facilities constitutes a potential problem. As far as the municipality is concerned, council-owned houses, whether terraced or semi-detached may, with some exaggeration, be dubbed 'maintenance-free', or at least, 'problem-free', and the pace of change, if any, is a slow one. But with a council-owned block of flats, all of these uses are the council's concern, the subjects of endless, often highly technical discussions within Housing Committees and among technical experts of all designations. The complexities start with any block of flats, they take a leap onwards with flats above four or five storeys and they can increase exponentially with further floors. Not only are the various demands more complex in themselves, but they can actively interfere with each other; for instance, the

demand for parking spaces may conflict with the desire for quiet areas of grass. 'There never will be a time when all problems have been solved', bemoaned a despairing Housing Manager in 1962.[1] There was, furthermore, a view that the costs of all the facilities and measures required should be borne more directly by the tenants themselves.[2] In a 1959 article, John P. Macey, the long-suffering housing manager of Birmingham Corporation, rounded off a long list of management problems by trying an upbeat tone, by urging tenants to bear in mind the privileges and attractions conferred on them by their life at the 'heart of the town', and not to hanker fruitlessly after an uncomplicated suburban environment, where the only worry would be 'to keep the rabbits from devouring the lettuces'.[3]

The discussion of the complex new methods of construction of high blocks must be followed with an account of some of the internal fittings that went with them. The most important innovations were found at the very centre of the block; as many services as possible were now concentrated in that location. The old British habit of placing the waste pipes on the rear exterior of the building had been bound up with the assumption that the back of a building was architecturally and socially inferior, and that the 'unattractive' pipework could freely be exposed there. From the early 1950s such displays on any part of the outside of a block were increasingly considered architecturally objectionable.[4] Single stack plumbing, as part of a vertical service core at the centre of the block was now the universally agreed solution – not least because, apart from its effect in

99

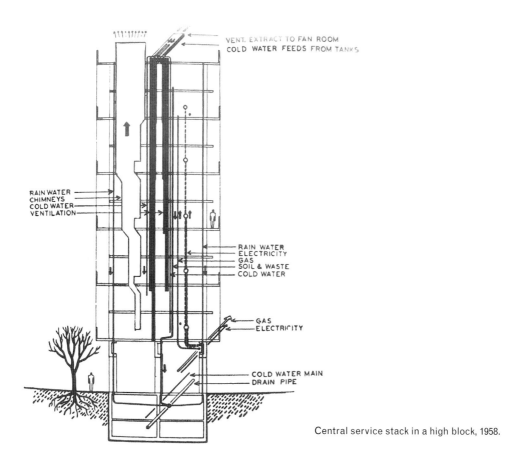

VENT. EXTRACT TO FAN ROOM
COLD WATER FEEDS FROM TANKS

RAIN WATER
CHIMNEYS
COLD WATER
VENTILATION

RAIN WATER
ELECTRICITY
GAS
SOIL & WASTE
COLD WATER

GAS
ELECTRICITY

COLD WATER MAIN
DRAIN PIPE

Central service stack in a high block, 1958.

shortening all pipework, the walls surrounding the service core also contributed to the strengthening of the block as a whole. Related to this was the relocation of the bathroom and toilet into the interior of the new point blocks, an innovation reputedly first introduced in the LCC's Fitzhugh development in Wandsworth by the mid-fifties (cf. p. 63).[5] Here there was an initial need to overcome the entrenched public-health preference for openable windows in these rooms. Against this argument a range of planning advantages were cited, above all that the new internal position allowed deeper and thus squarer layouts, leading to greater economies of construction; it was also argued that placing rooms internally avoided the elevational design problems posed by smaller windows. What had to be provided in compensation was a ventilation system, with or without fans – another element within the service core.

Of all the services inside the block, heating and hot water were the most technically complex. For five-storey blocks the old method, fireplace and back boiler, was still seen as acceptable. Occasionally, high maisonette slab blocks also still used it.[6] But for high point blocks it was out of the question, not least because of the resulting multiplicity of flues. Architecturally, too, the design of the top of a block to incorporate a clump of long projecting flues would have been a difficult proposition. According to Margaret Willis, the LCC's housing sociologist, 80% of the tenants of new blocks approved of the new kinds of heating, while still sentimentally professing their

preference for a coal fire.[7] There were three principal methods of 'central' heating: firstly, hot water central heating, which was referred to as 'district heating' in cases where the boiler was in a separate building at some distance from the blocks – a relatively rare arrangement, seen, for instance, at the Pimlico redevelopment (Churchill Gardens) in Westminster. There was underfloor heating, to be topped up with various mobile heating contraptions in each room, and there was warm air heating. Predictably, all methods were 'appreciably dearer' than the old fireplace system, but there were important collateral advantages, for instance, that the coal no longer had to be transported to the individual flats, which reduced dirt and wear on the lifts.[8]

Refuse removal was another thorny problem. Birmingham's Macey recalled the smelly 'midden' piles in the yards behind early council flats; gradually, these were replaced by chutes fixed on to the block, whereby the rubbish ended on a pile at the bottom; this then led to containers being placed at the bottom of the chute. In London, a 'diversity of systems' of refuse disposal prevailed even in 1951.[9] From the 1930s onwards a new French system, Garchey, was experimentally introduced in a few prestige complexes, such as Quarry Hill in Leeds and later in Park Hill in Sheffield. All rubbish, except the very largest items, was deposited in the sink and swept away with the waste water, to be collected centrally at the bottom. But this system indeed proved calamitously expensive, adding 5–10% to the capital cost of each flat[10] and it was avoided by most large

Left: Central dust chute: London, Iberia House, New Orleans Estate, Hornsey Lane, N6, Islington LBC, 1968.
Right: Dust chute contained within the body of the building: London, Thaxted Court, Fairbank Estate, N1, Hackney LBC, 1968.

Fig. 1. No centre mullion: one casement not bolted, feels insecure.

Fig. 2. Firm mullion to hold on to, left-handed fixed light easy to clean with right arm.

Fig. 3. Added stretch to clean fixed top light.

Fig. 4. Large fixed pane directly over sink.

Fig. 5. Easy clean type hinges with too narrow gap.

Windows in tall blocks that can be cleaned from inside, 1958.

authorities, including the LCC.[11] Instead, the method that was almost universally adopted for high blocks was a more sophisticated version of the chute system. A dozen or so flats share a hopper, situated as far away as possible from their entrance doors. This hopper leads to a pipe of carefully regulated measurements and construction, with moveable bins located at the bottom in a special compartment that was closed off by shutters. The top of the chute can be carried up to the roof of the building, where it is left open for ventilation.

Another municipal housing service was the provision of facilities for clothes washing and drying. A large block would normally contain separate rooms for washing at a ratio of around one for every twenty flats.[12] But then, gradually, during the 1960s, many households acquired their own washing machines. That, however, still left the problem of drying. It was one of the accepted conventions of British housing that washing could not be hung out in locations that could be regarded as 'public', a custom that of course collided with the conviction that drying in fresh air was always best. For a while, some of Birmingham's high blocks provided open drying areas on the roof. There could also be specially designated areas on the ground somewhere close to the block. Another solution was to provide special drying rooms,[13] though these were given up, too, when tenants acquired their own tumble dryers. In Glasgow, there was another, more expensive variant – an additional, fully enclosed 'drying floor' at the top of each block.

Balconies projecting, glass,
maximal openness: Birmingham,
Nechells Green, 1961.

Naturally, where there was a private balcony, this also provided a good solution to the drying quandary. To begin with, it is
important not to confuse terms, to keep apart private balconies
and the semi-public access balcony leading to the dwelling's
front door. According to the Ministry's guidance, all flats 'likely
to house families with young children should have a private
balcony, and this should measure at least 40 square feet (or
3.7 square metres)'.[14] The most careful detailing was required.
Railings should prevent toys from falling though the gaps, yet,
on the other hand, the possibility of seeing through the railings
when sitting down was an advantage. In architectural terms, in
the design of the elevation and in devising its cladding, balconies created many problems.[15] Moreover, general architectural
shifts in opinion also had an effect: from the late 1930 into the
1950s, in the context of the new Modernism's strong desire for
openness, we see boldly projecting balconies with minimal
railings. After 1960, with a new trend towards solid walling,
balconies tended to be at least partly recessed into the block,
to provide protection from the weather as well as to create a
'general sense of enclosure within the building'.[16]

Balconies in all directions: Brighton, Grove Hill,
Albion Hill RD, from 1958.

Balconies recessed: London, Brassett Point, Leather Gardens, Manor Road , Stratford, E15, 1963.

Left: London Great Arthur House, Golden Lane, Estate. (cf. p. 53).
Right 'Top Hamper': London Lewey House, Joseph Street, E3, Stepney MBC, 1964.

More problematic were the design issues newly created by Modernist towers at their extreme top and bottom. With framework construction, there was no longer any need for solid walling on the ground floor, and there was thus a new freedom, leading to a diversity of solutions, decided afresh in every case, with no hard-and-fast rules ever laid down. For instance, the ground floor could be left open, showing only a number of piers or columns, sometimes referred to by architects as 'pilotis' – a bow to the authority of Le Corbusier. But there was also room for any kind of use, for car parking or for groups of sheds, for transformers, or perhaps for a caretaker's flat. A few blocks even included a lavish two-storey open space.

On the other hand, flats could also be accommodated here and these could even be given small private gardens or terraces; yet such ground floor flats were deemed not to be popular because of a lack of privacy.[17] By contrast, the 1960s Wimpey and Bison blocks could not offer much variety or any open spaces because of their mode of construction; not being of the normal framework type, walling had to be solid from the bottom up.

At the top of the blocks, the Modernist desire for square outlines banished the tradition of pitched roofs, helped by the fact that, with the advance of central heating, it was no longer necessary to support or conceal the high chimney flues required by individual fires. Instead, in almost all cases, it was water tanks and lift machinery which projected higher than the main part of the block and it was the architect's decision either to hide these facilities behind some kind of parapet, or to display them openly, either as straightforward boxes – Lord Holford dubbed them 'top hampers'[18] – or as striking decorative features (cf. p. 202).

Left: Balcony at ground level: London, Wimborne Court, Wenlock Barn Estate, Shoreditch MBC, N1, 1955.
Right: Lavish free space at ground and first floor level: London Luxborough Tower, Luxborough Street, Marylebone Road, W1. GLC 1966.

Access: Internal lobby, London, Claremont Estate, Woodgrange Road, West Ham, E7, 1957 (cf. p. 63). An image that appeared very new at the time, epitomising the Modern tower dwelling.

Access

How does one get up to a high flat? Arguably, the single most decisive innovation in the built fabric of council housing was the introduction of lifts. Cleeve Barr saw them as an integral part of the 'sociological progress' of the era.[19] The lift was, of course, an expensive item, adding some 5–10% to the building cost of each flat.[20] The Housing Acts of 1946 duly introduced a special subsidy for this purpose, of £7 per flat – not a large sum, if the overall construction cost of a flat amounted to £3000 or more.[21] In Scotland, the rule was now that lifts were needed for any block of five storeys and more, excluding those where the top two floors were maisonettes; in England the demarcation line was one-storey lower. Many of the massive number of five-storey London blocks that had already been built, and were still being built, were now fitted with lifts; from around 1950, however, because of their relatively uneconomic use of the lift, the number of newly built blocks of that height was dwindling. In blocks of eight floors and more two lifts were normally needed. Naturally, the greater number of flats served by each lift, the greater the savings, a ratio of around 1:50 was seen as a reasonable maximum[22] – still a generous figure when compared with, say, some US public housing blocks of the time. Some savings could be achieved by stopping only on alternate floors. As regards speed, hitherto the maximum for most lifts had been 100–150 feet per minute, but in blocks of 12 to 15 floors, or more, a speed of 250 or 300 was thought essential, costing twice as much;[23] each of the eighteen-storey LCC Brandon Estate towers boasted two of these 'high-speed' lifts.

While, in principle, nothing could now appear more straightforward than the requirements of vertical communication, horizontal communication was always treated as problematic, and thus provided a challenge that stimulated a variety of very different solutions. In England, a heightened sensitivity to all issues of access stemmed from the fact that the vast majority of dwellers were accustomed to having a straightforward, direct entrance into their dwelling from the street. Within multi-storey housing we saw previously that the morphologies of the two major types, point block and slab block, also usually meant two very different modes of access. In some ways, the point block continued, or rather, took up, a mode that was the 'normal' one in Scotland and Continental Europe, where an internal staircase leads to two or a few more flats across a small lobby, on each floor. London designers then created the variants of corridor access described above: the short corridor of the flat-cum-maisonette type and the internal corridor of the 'scissors' type. The internal corridor, or internal lobby access was seen by many now as the preferable solution. In an early tower at the Claremont Estate in West Ham the 'pleasant access ... with enclosed lobbies' was hailed as a 'great advantage'.[24]

Another, very different type of access also occurred very frequently in England, including perhaps half of all blocks in London built during the 1950s, an arrangement which went under a variety of names: 'balcony access', 'gallery access', or 'deck access'. From the mid -19th century onwards, the access to flats in public or charitable working class housing blocks in England was normally via a gallery, situated at the back of the building, at the back of each floor. Before the 1930s all blocks showed a strong contrast between the often quite richly decorated front along the street and the very utilitarian-looking back. The access galleries usually showed quite flimsy metal structures attached to the walkways, with no 'architectural' pretensions at all. In many cases not only the galleries but also the staircases had wide openings to the outside. The main reason for this was, of course, to save costs, but there were also socio-political-moral issues involved. Basically, the 'poor' were not trusted, either to remove dirt, or to avoid 'undesirable acquaintances'.[25]

Then, during the later interwar years a major change occurred in gallery-access planning, with the access ways now built in solid brick, integral with the body of the block, often incorporating curved Art Deco forms. This could also mean a complete reversal of the front-back relationship, with the balcony access usually now at the front of the block, facing the street, and the back facing a relatively secluded and private area; in this context, the traditional concepts of 'front' and 'back' began to lose much of their meaning.

Thus balcony-access, in its 'revised' form, continued in many blocks all over the country, throughout the fifties and into the sixties, although it never quite attained the ubiquity achieved by 'galerijbouw' in post-war Netherlands. A very frequent London combination was the long gallery-access slab with the maisonette type, usually of eleven storeys, but sometimes higher. The major features of these maisonette blocks have already been described, including their repetitiveness, the narrowness of all the spaces, and the varied 'free façade' mode of creating the elevations, with the access ways forming the main feature.

But the shape of the access ways was always a matter of more than just morphology. Traditionally, as has just been stressed, one of the aims of providing openness around the flats was to make the inhabitants feel 'observed', 'supervised'. By the 1950s, however, a new concern had arisen which pointed in the opposite direction: a general desire for more privacy. In the case of the two-roomed flat, it was just the kitchen and the bathroom and toilet which had windows on to the access balcony, but in larger flats it was now seen as a problem that one of the bedrooms also faced on to the balcony.[26] In addition there were problems of vertigo and, not least, there was the weather. Walking along to reach one's maisonette or flat on the 10th floor could feel 'like being on the bridge of a ship in a violent storm at sea,'[27] especially when the balcony faced north.

At the same time, the issue of balcony access was seized upon by the emergent profession of 'housing sociologists'. Preferences were turned around once again: a detailed sociological investigation in 1962 concluded that while balconies 'afford little privacy, they help, however, to promote social contacts'.[28] In 1957 Cleeve Barr's own stated preference was for the lift lobby type of access, and yet, in his own Picton Street blocks he used, like everybody else, the narrow balcony access mode. By then another point of view had emerged: in his book of 1958 Cleeve Barr briefly reflected on images of an idealised past or working class life, of 'tenants from the slums sitting on their doorsteps'.[29] A small faction among designers and critics had indeed been championing a new version of balcony access, based precisely on their idealised view of the past, a version of a much greater width which was now re-labelled 'deck access', 'street deck' or 'streets in the sky'. The aim of Alison and Peter Smithson's Golden Lane Competition entry of 1952 was explicitly the recreation of the pedestrian pavement, as an ideal place for neighbourliness.[30]

In the 1960s a number of factors came together to create an extraordinary architectural episode. Firstly, Modernist architecture demanded external exposure; there was New Brutalism's well known delight in garnering the tops of all kinds of high buildings with prominent lift towers, dubbed 'hammerheads'. Council dwellings' internal shaping was usually standardised and gave little opportunity for striking spatial arrangements. All the more architects took the opportunity for complex spatial displays on the outside. The obvious motif was the staircase, especially with long slab blocks. Often the flights of stairs project daringly from the building, perilously exposing their users to the elements. Another favourite manner was to keep them inside the contours of the block, but expose them to the outside all the same. A council block could thus appear punctuated with large and small holes through which the sky or greenery could be seen.

The greatest challenge was, again, height; it was now increasingly held that life for the occupants high up can feel isolated. To visit a friend in an adjacent high block involved a cumbersome journey, having to go down right to the ground. Thus increasingly bridges were thrown across blocks. Here the balcony access ways were the natural locations from where to lead on to those bridges. An extreme demonstration of this desire for multi-connectivity was the Aylesbury Estate in Southwark. Sometimes bridges occur between medium, even low-to-medium rise blocks, supplemented with ramps which served to go up and down with prams. Portsmouth housing excels with these formations. Some of the very large developments of the 1960s have been mentioned above, dubbed 'conglomerates', whereby towers are complexly bound in with systems of horizontal linkages. Lastly, many of these elevated inner suburban complexes created vast spaces for garages on the ground floor, or even somewhat below, where natural light is often in short supply.

It seemed only natural during the 1960s, during the years when conceptions of the town laid particular stress on 'urban' liveliness, that all those spaces and communication lines were, according to their designers, continuously populated and enjoyed by all their users. Every one of such a large group of dwellings should feel something like a complete town.

LONDON – THE BALCONY ACCESS STORY

Top row: The early development of London balcony access modes,
also in relation to the 'front vs. back' conundrum: The two illustrations top left show a block in Shoreditch, London of ca. the early
1930s with its back[yard} and its street front. The two views on the
right illustrate an adjacent block of 1949 where the balcony access
now shows on the street front while the other side – there is now
no real 'back' any more – gives out to a quiet park-like area. Ground
floor dwellers can even have a private garden.

Middle left: The access balcony of the block top right.

Middle right: Balcony access of the Roehampton Alton West maisonette slab blocks (cf. p. 70).

Bottom left: a 'street deck' in the Park Hill Estate, Sheffield (cf. p. 162).

HOUSING AT PRIMROSE BANK
FOR OLDHAM COUNTY BOROUGH
ARCHITECTS   Peter Dunham, Widdup and Harrison F.F.R.I.B.A.

VARIATIONS ON THE THEME OF ACCESS IN THE 1960S
Oldham, Primrose Bank Project, 1966.

A designers' vision of life in a new medium-rise high-density
complex at Ballymena, Northern Ireland, 1963.

108

Casterbridge and Snowman Houses, Abbey Estate, Belsize Road, NW6, Hampstead, LBC, 1965.

LONDON

Mursell Estate, Portland Grove, SW8, LCC, 1963.

Valois House, St. Saviour's Estate, Grange Walk, SE1 Bermondsey, SE1, MBC, 1959.

LONDON
Multiple entrances: London John Walsh [Tower], Montague Road, E11, Leyton MBC, 1962.

Central exposed liftshaft: Didbin House, Andover Estate, Islington, N7, GLC, 1972–79.

Top: Garages and sheds for Normandie Tower, Norwich, Rouen Road, 1965.
Left: Half-basement under-croft with garages: London Haberdasher Estate,
   N1, Hackney, LBC, 1966.
Above: Garages and sheds: London Barnwood Court, E16, Newham LBC, 1967.

Around the block

The new high blocks, that is the general run of them, differed fundamentally from most earlier kind of walk-up blocks of flats in that they were now surrounded on all sides by free space. There were a number of practical uses claiming that space, seen as the 'logical extension' of the use of the dwellings themselves.[31] The first necessity was for a place to store all those implements which could not be kept inside the flat, in the form of a shed, something that was, after all, found with almost every common row house.[32] Thus, integral groups of small private, lockable sheds can be found adjacent to a great many blocks. A major designated use was pram storage. However, for high blocks this was no longer needed, as the pram could be transported up to the flat via the lift; moreover, families with young children were thought unsuited to accommodation in high flats in the first place. In general, the preoccupation with sheds was on the wane.

Instead, it was cars that proved to be the greatest problem in the planning of housing schemes. There were no widely followed rules for this, no planning models for the placement of garages; what was certain was the tenants' desire to park their car as close as possible to their dwelling, as well as the continuous increase in the numbers of cars. Virtually no provision had been made up to the mid or late forties, but by 1955 the LCC was already adhering to 25%. By 1962 the stipulation was one car for each dwelling, although perhaps fewer in very high density estates. The sixties brought many solutions for garages, such as digging out the grounds around the block to create an under-croft, at great expense. Even Birmingham's Housing Manager Macey, normally so positive in dealing with new challenges, expressed despair when it came to cars: there was 'no immediate solution' in sight.[33]

Playground: London Regent's Park Development, NW1, St. Pancras MBC, 1954.

Far more systematic efforts were taken in the creation of play spaces. The architects Eastwick Field, designers of several council schemes, boasted that 'so many of our estates are positively crawling with children'.[34] A new emphasis on sport-like play-activities had emerged in the interwar period, and children and young adults at play among modern blocks of flats, bathed in sunshine, became an enduring image of the post-war years. Equally familiar was the counter image which showed seemingly unhappy children playing in old decrepit environments. In 1954 it was claimed that five million children were completely without a playground.[35] There was a new idealisation of play conducted on public land, rather than in private gardens, while playing in the street was seen as inappropriate, dirty and unsafe. There was a conviction that the right kind of playground would help shape its users' character and morals. Housing managers, educationalists and architects closely co-operated. A new science of age-specific playing habits developed, requiring differentiated spaces, for the 2–5, the 5–10 and the 9–15 groups.[36] However, by the early 1960s more and more conflicts occurred; such as between playground noise and the desire for privacy and quiet. Later in the 1960s, there was less emphasis on designated play areas and children were assumed to prefer roaming more freely throughout the estate.

Landscaping

There was not only a plethora of proposals for the practical use of the grounds around tall blocks, but also a more general discourse regarding the shaping of the estate's environment, usually under the heading 'landscaping'. In 1956, one commentator coupled boasts that the 'internal standards' in British housing were 'without peer' with laments that standards in the

external 'environment' were far below those of Scandinavia, Switzerland and Holland.[37] When architects and planners travelled to Sweden in the years around 1950, it was landscaping, as much as the point blocks themselves, that impressed them. Nevertheless, the radical new designing of the grounds that developed in post-war Britain was principally based on English, American and German Modernist town planning innovations.

Untitled, London c. 1960s.

Landscaping: London Loughborough Road Estate, Brixton, SW9, planned 1952, LCC.

The proper care of the surroundings of high blocks always demanded 'a fully comprehensive pattern of planning' (Jensen).[38] And according to architectural commentators, that was naturally to be the task of the architectural profession. For Cleeve Barr, it did not seem incongruous to admonish architects to try and meet engineers and builders on the latter's territory, while insisting on the 'wider employment of the public architect' as the prerequisite for progress in landscaping, or, as he put it, in 'total design'[39] – although on occasions, Ministry design guides did recommend additionally the use of a 'landscape specialist'.[40]

The key value from the 1930s or 40s onwards was openness. Openness, first of all, meant greenery. The lack of it was one of the salient characteristics of traditional urban low class districts. But now it was not just a matter of planting a few trees or bushes, somewhere, but all blocks of flats should be completely, or almost completely, surrounded by greenery. Here, once again, we return to the traditional 'front versus back' issue. It now was the task to free the block completely from the line of the 'corridor' street; as already explained in the context of access ways to the flat, the notion of a decorative front versus a purely utilitarian back simply disappeared. The blocks of an estate could now be spread freely over an area, to fulfil the best daylight conditions or any other specified practical requirements. These ideas can be traced back to the English Garden City tradition, they were further developed by the American Radburn system, which replaced the normal street at the front with a communal garden area, traversed by pedestrian paths, while the car access was relegated to the other side, in as restricted a space as possible. As far as roads were concerned, a sharp distinction was now made between local access roads and major through roads. In Berlin, many of the early 1930s radical *Zeilenbau* blocks appeared to be surrounded by the same kind of public green on all sides. One of the most tangible results was the complete separation, wherever possible, of pedestrian ways and roadways. Within an estate tarmacked road access was needed for the collection of garbage, and, as unobtrusively as possible, for the cars to reach their designated space, but all these roads had to be as short as possible.

'People today are very much more space-conscious than they were', wrote planning critics D. Rigby Childs and Jack Whittle. The expression 'space about buildings'[41] was dear to Modernist architectural discourse, referring to interiors as well as to the exterior. It was in this context that the point block came into its own. 'One of the great advantages of the point block is in the creation of park areas surrounding buildings with an absence of any sense of enclosure or restriction', wrote Jensen.[42] It is no surprise to find efforts to anchor the new emphasis of 'space' historically, in the traditions of landscape garden design. Cleeve Barr, for example, underlined the continuity of this art from the 18th century through to Modernism: as a communist, his interpretation laid special stress on the transition from the elite use of parks by the nobility to their availability as an amenity for all.[43] A further model was provided by some late 1930s projects for single high blocks placed on the edge of parks, as a demonstration that the suitability of the tower was not confined to dense urban surroundings. All the more significant were those new developments which were located in an actual, pre-existing park. High blocks could now be justified as serving yet another purpose, namely to help preserve old trees. In his already mentioned mid-fifties work on 'the Englishness of English Art', Nikolaus Pevsner ends his chapter 'Picturesque England' with illustrations of Roehampton and Ackroydon.[44] Roehampton, for

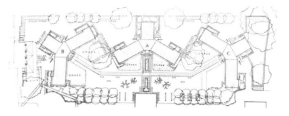

Above: Landscape planning on a small city centre estate: London, Stafford Cripps Estate, 1954 (cf. p. 11).

Left: City centre green, semi-private, adjacent to ground floor maisonettes: City of London, Golden Lane Estate (cf. p. 93).

Below: The turn towards hard surfacing: paved yard at the London Winstanley Estate, Battersea, SW11, 1963–66 (cf. p. 135).

many, marked the apogee of English Modernist council housing design. By contrast, in the densest English urban situations, of, say, 200 p.p.a. or over, greenery did not at first glance appear to make sense, and yet even the City of London's Golden Lane complex succeeded in creating comparatively large green spaces, relatively secluded, and directly accessible from some of the maisonettes.

Moving down from high rhetoric, actual figures could be given for open space requirements: four acres, that is the size of a small football pitch, should be provided for every thousand inhabitants. 'The town dweller needs the relaxation that can be given by the sight of grass and trees'. Such 'amenity greens' were held to guarantee privacy and 'freedom from excessive noise'.[45] However, grassed areas often proved difficult to maintain, and there was the question of how much they should be fenced in.[46] All this must have contributed to a waning in the enthusiasm for expansive green areas after 1960. The high-modernist longing for openness was met head on by the late-modernist counter-tendency towards enclosure. Low walls, changes of levels, a greater diversity of planting and

hard paving were now favoured, tending to create varied environments of intricately small spaces. A new assessment was made in 1967: 'high rise blocks standing among green spaces… make a mistaken attempt to bring the peace of the country into the town', as those spaces are 'too small to serve as public parks', thus argued the landscape architect of the much noted Winstanley estate in south London, which included precisely these more enclosed kinds of spaces.[47] Moreover, a new way of calculating the tower-to-ground space relationship had emerged among some town planners opposed to high building. Termed 'diminishing returns', it turned the optimistic statements of gaining ever more open space on their head: the higher the towers, the less open space would be available, because of ever-growing ancillary fixed-space demands, especially for car parking. By that time the most advanced, conglomerate-planned kinds of high-density medium-rise estate were going up in some London Boroughs, such as Camden or Southwark, with the most intricate plans that included few if any grassed areas – and no high towers either.

1969 visions of tower block environments from a book
by R.P.A. Edward, The *Tower Block*. Illustrations by
Gareth Floyd.

Tower blocks as civic symbols

Municipal tower blocks were often seen as the exact antidote to the low-rise suburban ideal: concentration instead of dispersal, bold architectural gestures instead of timid repetitions of worn-out formulae. However, the first wave of bold Modernism of the 1930s and 40s shared something important with the Garden City concept, namely a hatred of the traditional urban street and the old narrow back yards, and its designers strove to replace them with a homogeneously light, airy and green environment. But by the 1940s Modernism was starting to adopt a critical attitude towards all garden city and garden suburb types of housing. They were 'eating up' up too much of the nation's precious land. In all new developments a much greater density seemed desirable. High blocks could contribute to this and no distinction was made between inner and outer suburban locations; it seemed perfectly acceptable to build high blocks in all low-density suburbs.

The 1950s, however, saw yet another major change in attitudes, with the rise of the 'townscape' movement, and its new aesthetic of the dense and lively urban environment.[48] There were now frequently-repeated admonitions that it was time for the British to learn to value urban life in its own right. These critical discourses strikingly chimed in with the expanding powers of the cities and towns themselves. The planning legislation of 1947 had given urban local authorities extended powers to expropriate, rebuild and change. This included

plans for radically reshaped town centres. Many, if not most cities, and many middling towns, as well as some suburban hubs, began to plan extensive, often hugely ambitious new centres,[49] the one most talked about being in the very centre of London, Piccadilly Circus, famous not least for the fact that nothing ever came of it. During the immediate post-war years, city centre rebuilding efforts had concentrated on grand public buildings and Beaux Arts-inspired layouts, as in Plymouth (cf. p. 53). By 1960 attention was increasingly being directed towards the commercial sectors of town centres. In some 'go-ahead' places, such as Coventry, or New Towns like Stevenage, the perceived hub of a town might be largely identical with its principal shopping centre. Most of the old centres of provincial towns were now perceived as drab, chaotic and completely lacking in a Modern look. One of the major innovations was to devise schemes for the effective separation of vehicular and pedestrian traffic. In stark contrast to the lavishly spacious city-centre layouts of the preceding decades, the new vision of a town centre was one of togetherness and the highest possible density.

Was there a place for public housing, too, in this new concept of the town centre? On the face of it, this would hardly have appeared profitable, nor would it have chimed with the strict Modernist principle of dividing towns into separate zones. Yet for some designers, such as the Cumbernauld New Town

London Lambeth Borough Council, project for centre redevelopment, 1967.

chief architect-planner, Hugh Wilson, it now seemed that there was scope for centrally located flats as well.[50] One more time Sweden seemed to provide a most convincing model, in the town-centre complex at Vällingby, a satellite of Stockholm, completed in the mid-fifties, with a number of point blocks closely surrounding a large indoor shopping centre. It was argued that the use of verticals to enliven horizontal structures would ensure an 'integrated three-dimensional design', and help spread 'urbanity and life' to the wider central area. Already, from the late 1940s onwards, Gibberd had drawn attention to the significant role of public-housing towers in, or adjacent to the centres of towns (cf. p. 156). Clearly, adding a sizeable number of new inhabitants living close-by would also provide a significant commercial stimulus. A new, complex, multi-layered, 'megastructural' way of planning such a centre, pioneered so spectacularly in the early and mid-sixties in Cumbernauld, allowed tower blocks to be built on top, starting several floors up, reducing the cost element.

Here, for once, was a planning and architectural movement that principally happened outside London. Other than in the unique case of the Barbican, which, although City Corporation-owned, was not social housing, there was no way in which a really dominating public housing block could be imagined in the very centre of the capital. Even relatively large public-housing tower interventions, such as the Berwick Street tower in Soho of 1959, nor even the twenty-five-storey tower at the southern tip of the LCC's Elephant and Castle Redevelopment Area, Draper House, could be seen as dominating their surroundings. One has to go further out – for example to Edmonton Green, in Enfield, in outer north-east London – to find a typical group of tall, twenty-six-storey towers atop a large shopping centre and associated giant car parks. Other ambitious London projects, such as Edward Hollamby's 1967 plan for the central redevelopment of Brixton, which was to include towers with well over 30 floors,[51] were unrealised. It is, instead, the larger provincial

cities which excel with their massive 1960s groupings, such as Sunderland, whose market and three nineteen-storey blocks of flats, constitute the real centre of the town. In Cwmbran, the Welsh new town, a twenty-three-storey public housing tower is the only high block, marking a corner of the civic centre, where it 'provides a focal point for the scheme' (cf. p. 171).[52]

The 'positive visual and civic significance'[53] of public housing interventions in city-centre redevelopments was accentuated even more in a succession of set-piece schemes in the great Midland cities. Nottingham's Victoria Centre blocks, Coventry's Mercia House and Birmingham's Stephenson Tower all mark key civic and commercial nodes, as well as counting as the highest, or almost the highest, council housing blocks in the town. Birmingham may be seen as an exception, in the sense that it precisely did not launch plans for a specific city-centre renewal project, but this was not necessary, as the city's numerous high council towers in and near the centre, especially the Sentinels, were already helping to create urban ensembles of this kind.

However, with most of these towers we also reach the tenurial borderlines of public housing. Coventry's Mercia House was to be let to 'professional people'; Nottingham's Victoria Centre blocks excluded applicants from the Council's housing list and in the case of Birmingham's Stephenson Tower, the Council trawled for higher-income tenants after it initially failed to find enough 'normal' council tenants. In Salford, too, the twenty-three-storey tower which forms part of the giant Salford City shopping centre of 1968 was reserved for 'middle income group tenants'.[54] Thus in these cases, the dwellings were council built, but not mainstream public housing. In the end, however, they all remained in the municipal sphere, in terms of their architectural ambitions and as signs of civic valour. In any case, nobody in those cities was to build more tower flats for several decades.

The naming of blocks and estates

The concluding act in the creation of a block, or of a group of blocks, was that of naming, a task that included the fastening of the actual lettering on to the walls. Thereafter the name remained linked to the building's presence. The actual process of naming took hardly any time and incurred no great expense. There is almost no recorded documentation regarding the decision-making, and the councillors who usually chose the names hardly seemed to reflect on it in any general terms. The blocks's designers and the wider architectural world were seemingly not concerned with it at all. And yet it would be hard to imagine dealing with the topic of British council housing, for instance in a book like the present one, without those names. Looking from Britain, one cannot possibly imagine how tower-dwellers in cities as diverse as Berlin, New York City or Singapore were, or are, able to identify their individual blocks, of their homes, by using just street names or block numbers – although there was one significant exception to this 'British' custom, namely Glasgow Corporation, which used a Continental-style street-numbering system for most of its tall blocks. In all cases, at any rate, the primary aim of labelling a block is to help in finding it: in 1963, the LCC Housing Committee heard a complaint that some of the signs were too small.[55] Birmingham adopted unified large signs which are lit from behind. In addition, almost unfailingly, London estates also put up a sign-board, with a plan showing and naming all blocks in a group, together with a 'you are here' pointer. The board provided another name, that for the 'estate', as well as, sometimes, the name and coat of arms of the commissioning municipal authority. In London, with its overlapping and competing 'sovereignties' of the LCC/GLC and the boroughs the sign of the authority constituted a reminder of local politics.[56] In the rest of Britain, however, these boards are somewhat less likely to occur.

To attach a name to a house or a group of houses is something that appears to go back a very long time, and that also, significantly, survived and continued alongside the more modern convention of identifying houses by street numbers. Such a 'tag' almost always consisted of two components. The first component was the more singular and specific one, a name relating to a locality or a person's name, or the name of an organisation, such as Peabody; it could include names which sounded singular, such as 'Ocean Estate' in Stepney, or the 'Shakespeare' towers in Leeds. A special category in council housing was the way in which some blocks, or, more rarely, whole estates were given the name of a long serving councillor. Liverpool, we read in the *Municipal Journal*, has 'the custom of naming blocks after its public servants', even while they were still serving.[57] Part of the city's newest estate in 1958, two multi-storey blocks were named simply 'The Braddocks', or 'J. and E. Braddock', directly referring to two formidable Liverpool Labour politicians, Alderman John Braddock and his wife, Councillor and MP Bessie Braddock, who, at the ceremony, personally declared 'their' estate open. The City's most publicised Block, Cresswell Mount was named after a former deputy chairman of the housing committee (cf. p. 198).

Naming: a rare example of a large sign, date uncertain, London Pitfield Estate, Shoreditch, N1.
The Royal Oak Courts blocks were built in 1952.

Leeds, 'The 3 Shakespeares', Burmantofts, 1969, Wimpey: Shakespeare Towers [sic], Shakespeare Grange, Shakespeare Court. Leeds has the habit of additionally attaching the names in large letters near the top of the block, in this case the blocks' names are truncated, written on the side (cf. p. 215).

By contrast, the second component of the label was chosen from a much narrower range of more general terms. There were two basic parts of the designation, one assigned to the group of buildings as a whole, and one for each block. The label for the group had been a complex matter in England and Wales for a long time, as a number of terms could be used – in contrast to Scotland, where most pre-1939 tenement blocks, both council and private, were normally identified straightforwardly by street numbers. For the earliest, usually small, English blocks of flats in the 19th or early 20th century in the poorer areas, the basic term 'house' almost always appeared sufficient, as, for example, in 'Beechwood House'. Increasingly, from the later 19th century onwards, larger groups of blocks were given a group label. Several were available and these must be seen, first of all, within the system of English terms for dwelling types as a whole. Any term would do, with the exception, of course, of 'terrace' and 'tenement', as these were the types of dwelling to which the new blocks of flats were seen as diametrically opposed. 'Buildings' was a frequent choice, but most important was the term 'dwellings', which could be further qualified as 'working class dwellings' or 'artisans' dwellings'. Those formulations underline the enduring importance of class distinctions in the labelling of housing in England. It was vital to distinguish the lower class block, as a genre, from the blocks for the better-off which were emerging in other parts of London at around the same time; the most frequently used designation for the latter was 'mansions', or 'mansion flats'. And yet it is equally noticeable that 'classy' labels keep descending down the social ladder. The key example in the 19th century had been the term 'terrace', a label first applied to the grandest projects, but which, by the end of the 19th century, could be found tacked on to rows of the meanest and smallest houses. Likewise, these kinds of labels could be the focus of deliberate public 'reform' policies. As we stressed at the beginning of this book, after 1945 the designation 'working class' was officially abolished, and with it the terms 'buildings' and 'dwellings', too.

Above: London South Acton Castles, Bollo Bridge Road,
W3, Ealing LBC; Signboard in c. 1990
Right: The 'Acton Castles': Corfe, Harlech and Beaumaris
Towers, 1968

From the early 20th century, two new terms became dominant in Britain for a group of purpose-built lower-class dwellings. In Scotland, the word 'scheme' (like 'project' in the United States) straightforwardly denoted an orderly, separately-demarcated group of publicly-sponsored dwellings for lower-income citizens, planned in accordance with some regularised spatial formula. In England it was the term 'estate' that became prevalent, a word with a number of meanings, and shifting ones at that. Harking back to its early associations with high class buildings and high class landholdings, it continued to carry general overtones of probity and of order, which increasingly merged with notions of the rigour of Modernist town planning. Gradually estate proved to be a particularly convincing term to signify the togetherness of the group of houses or blocks, visually, on the ground, as well as for the purpose of orientation on the map. It certainly established itself as the key term for large-scale public developments of suburban houses. Again, London's customs were most strongly-pronounced, and authoritative. From 1945 onwards, when redevelopments in the inner suburbs rapidly grew in size, the term 'estate' seemed indispensable. Awareness of an estate name, of the group of houses where one lives, is vital in areas such as Lambeth or Southwark, where one council estate directly adjoins the next. 'Estate' has remained the official designation, and, in fact, its popular use in England and Wales today is now principally tied to a group of council houses.

Class associations were especially prominent in the issue of the naming of the individual block, whether it stood by itself, or formed part of a group, an 'estate' or a 'scheme'. In England, the use of 'House' for an individual block carried on throughout the 20th century, the Barbican and Roehampton being prominent examples. But now about half a dozen more words began to enter general currency. A more specifically architectural term was 'Point', while another, particularly inviting name was 'Gardens'. With the terms 'Dwellings' and 'Buildings' having become 'politically incorrect', we now frequently encounter terms from the opposite end of the social scale, such as 'Court' and 'Grange', or, more rarely, 'Lodge'. Pursuing their etymology further would require a deeper exploration of the history of the law, or of the literary history of the evocative power of those words. In all these cases, however, an ever-present, underlying issue was the class-specificity of labels. The term 'tower' seemed self-explanatory and relatively neutral, but when used in plural form, as 'towers', to designate an individual block, one can detect an echo of prestigious country house names of previous centuries. One is here reminded again of the 19th century naming inconsistencies, when 'singular' terms such as 'Villa' or 'Cottage' were applied to long rows of very basic dwellings. Was this done simply to show off, to increase profits, or was there even an ironic intent? Even if we, today, could personally ask the people who decided on these terms, whether in the 19th or the 20th century, there would probably be no decisive answers. Moreover, all these conventions also had regional or national variations: in Leeds, for example, blocks trumpeted their names, often placed in huge letters near the top of the building. In Scotland, other than in Glasgow, tower block names became an area of relative convergence with English practice, with 'House', 'Tower' and 'Court' the most popular choices. What this all underlines, especially in England, is the persistent appeal of aspirational labels, expressing complex formulae of social distinction and architectural distinctiveness.

PART THREE – TOWERS ACROSS BRITAIN

The fundamental mission, and appeal, of the Welfare State was the provision of its services in like measure for all, without regard to the location of the recipients. As far as public housing was concerned, this certainly applied to everything new that was provided inside the council dwelling. Council housing in Britain was shaped by central government laws, prescriptions and recommendations which were regularly amended.

So far, however, the story we have traced has been almost entirely a London one. This stemmed from the fact that it was principally the London confraternity of architects who initially devised the new types of blocks, who were always in the forefront of building high and thus appear to have set the pace for the country as a whole. Chapter 12 will explore further variations of the principal planning themes in the contributions provided by major London designers from the later 1950s onwards.

The chapters which then follow, 13 and 14, will turn to the regions. In Chapter 4, we reviewed the national patterns of municipal power in the housing field, by underlining common trends in a diversity of places. From this point onwards, by contrast, the stress is on the individuality of each city in turn. First of all, how exactly can one define their relationship with London? It was indeed extremely diverse and any use of the label 'provincial' would be highly misleading. There was of course a natural hierarchy in that the smaller the town, the less likely it was to appear innovative. In the 1960s many medium-sized towns preferred 'package deals', which in London played much less of a role. There could also be in many cases a time-lag. Even some of the largest cities, such as Manchester and Nottingham, hardly thought about building high before 1960. On the whole, Part Three of this book deals with what happened in the 1960s. However, such an approach does not do justice to the diversity of the relationships between London and the other towns, and it also obscures the very significant differences between the towns and regions themselves. Coventry and Sheffield can be assigned leading roles in a national context, noting their direct exchanges with the London architectural world. Birmingham was a match to London in the ways in which it excelled in daring projects from 1943 onward; yet the dynamics of its performance proceeded quite independently from the capital throughout the period – as one could expect from the 'Second City' of England. Liverpool and Leeds were known through their massive contributions in the 1930s: the latter city excelled every other town in Britain, including London, with the

modernity of its giant Quarry Hill blocks. After the War these cities slowed down somewhat, and spent much time with experimenting. Finally Bristol, which joined with innovations a few years after London, went very much its own way until the early 1960s. By the mid to later 1960s differences between all towns were ironed out somewhat by the spread of package deals, although even that process showed many variations.

Lastly, we can refer to the old notion, within England, of the 'North-South divide'. Some towns in the South, but by no means all, joined in with high blocks from the very late 1950s, cultivating some degree of architectural individuality, but on the whole this was very little noticed nationally. It was the Northern cities and conurbations which, during the 1960s, created a distinct group among themselves. This was due to the way in which they vociferously defined themselves as 'working class cities'. In terms of housing this entailed the blanket destruction of what were considered substandard small houses – a campaign which then generated the biggest crops of high blocks in the 1960s. Here one finally reaches a stage where one can speak of a real politicisation, or ideologization, of public housing. Many of the promoters in these cities would have maintained that the merits of quantity production should override any reservations voiced by those insisting on architectural diversity. At that point one may conclude that any one of the major Northern cities, with its double story of tower block experimentation in the 1950s and tower 'mass-production' in the 1960s, provides a more complete and unified picture of British council housing than London, with its diffuse multi-authority set-up.

Alongside all this, Scotland, as we saw earlier, formed a semi-autonomous entity within the British context. Central government housing and planning powers were the responsibility of the Scottish Office in Edinburgh: the resulting policies were usually similar, but hardly ever identical, to those 'south of the border'. Scottish cities and large burghs formed a separate civic and cultural network, with the bipolar 'Central Belt', divided between Edinburgh and Glasgow, playing the role of 'metropolis', and London perceived as a distant, though powerful force – with the sole exception of Glasgow's Gorbals, designed by architects (Matthew and Spence) who were seen as both 'from Edinburgh' and at the same time 'national British' in status. The perceived polarisation between London and the 'provinces' was seen as an English affair, with no direct relevance to Scotland.

12 London variants

London's situation with regard to public housing is unique in many senses of the word. If one begins by remembering that London is an immensely wealthy city in every respect, then what is most striking is the way in which London built, proportionally, as much public housing as any other British city, hardly less than many of the 'poorest' industrial towns. And this not only applied to those districts of the metropolis where old poor housing predominated, such as in the East End, but large complexes of council or other kinds of charitable housing can be found in almost all the other parts, too.

What was it that drove the perceived need for council housing in the capital? Primarily it was because it had mostly been in London that the aims of 'social reform' had first been formulated by writers and politicians from the middle of the 19th century onwards. Under the catchword of 'the housing question', or the 'housing problem', the issues became familiar to many. It all entailed a sense that much of the city's old housing was 'bad', and had to be rebuilt. On top of this, the war destruction of 1940–44 greatly added to the picture of squalor and need, far more than in any other British town.

The actual initiators of the building of housing were the local councils, their housing committee chairs, as mentioned in Chapters 4 and 5. And with London's division into such a large number of authorities, there were a great many officials. From the late 19th century onwards there was also a central authority, the London County Council, but as far as housing was concerned this simply added one more agent – albeit an exceedingly powerful one. Thus the narrative of London council housing was for a long time a two-tiered one, disturbed only by the 1964–65 local-government reorganisation: prior to that, within the area of the County of London there were the powerful London County Council and the relatively weak Metropolitan Boroughs; after that, within the vast expanse of 'Greater London', there were the rather less powerful Greater London Council and the increasingly assertive London Boroughs. In any case, both of them provided public housing largely independently from each other – the only significant overlap being the overriding planning powers exercised by the upper-tier. Very frequently, there was an intense sense of competition. As a result each borough sports housing built by the borough and by the LCC/GLC.

Another obvious manifestation of London's general wealth is the wealth of architectural quality. Architectural wealth is also what distinguishes its public and charitable housing. It can be demonstrated plainly through its high standards in every practical respect, spaciousness, ample fittings, pleasant surroundings. But the principal interest lies in its being almost constantly innovative; often architects of some eminence contributed to it. It goes back to about the middle of the 19th century with the introduction of the block of flats as the principal type of public housing for the inner parts of the city, developing through ever changing variations. Another bold undertaking, by the LCC, just after 1900, was the building of outer suburban low-density cottage estates.

By the late 1930s a certain routine had set in, but this had begun to be broken by a new experimental spirit with which the account in this book began. It first of all marked the entry of the most ambitious avant-garde designers into the field of housing, and of flats in particular, mostly bespoke, but also charitable in some cases. During the war the architectural discourse, often coupled with an intense concern for town planning, firmly allied Continental Modernism with the task of finding new kinds of mass dwellings. Once again, the first five years after the War brought a certain routine by essentially continuing the methods of the interwar years, on the part of the LCC, that is. Now came the high point of borough-sponsored ultra-Modern architecture, especially in Finsbury and Westminster. In Chapter 5, we traced the story of the architectural 'coup' within the LCC, in 1949/50, which led to establishment of the strongest designer power imaginable, creating 'the best architectural office in the world'. Chapters 9 and 10 then explored the innovations in planning and construction that poured out largely from that Department during the 1950s, including the slim 'point' block and the maisonette slab block. To combine the two types provided further exciting challenges.

One of the LCC Architects' Department's central policies was to emphasise teamwork. In this section we deal both with both the LCC/GLC and the boroughs. In the latter, more stress had always been put on the name of the single architect-designer, whether in-house or from a private practice. London's major contribution to multi-storey design from 1950 to 1960 was thus two-fold: the planning innovations generated principally by the LCC's architectural office, and the way in which most of the city's prominent and self-respecting practitioners in private practice, young or established, tried their hands at a showpiece council tower project. The resulting diversity of architectural solutions was without parallel. Some of the most architecturally high-flown of these blocks, by Lasdun, Goldfinger or the Smithsons, are by now considered major London landmarks. In this section the emphasis is also on those towers that are less well known.[1]

CLUSE COURT
St. Peter's Street – Frome Street – Dame Street, Islington, MB, N1, 1954. Two blocks under the same name, with only 28 dwellings each. Early examples of marking out the place of the lifts and staircases leading to the maisonettes, but there is also a conservative stress on continuous walling.

KEELING HOUSE

Claredale Street, Bethnal Green, E2.
First plans for maisonettes 1953/4,
designs 1955, built 1958 to 1959, for
Bethnal Green Borough Council by
Denys Lasdun (initially Fry, Drew,
Drake and Lasdun). Engineers: Ove
Arup and Partners, Contractor:
Wates. 56 two-bedroom maisonettes and eight bedsit flats. Lasdun
contributes his very own and most
unusual solution of the maisonette
type. He completely separates out
the vertical communication cores
and then, instead of providing the
usual access for eight or more flats
along the usual straight access
gallery, he cuts each access into two
parts, each providing access to only
two units. To emphasise the close
grouping of it all, Lasdun speaks of
'cluster', a term that had recently
been foregrounded in the writings
of the Smithsons. The block marks
an important step in the architect's
career; Lasdun had just completed
his Hallfield Estate in Paddington
(cf. p. 87), still in the form of
Lubetkin-inspired slab blocks in
strictly rectangular formation. The
odd angles and the radical separation of the communication cores at
Keeling House look forward to his
major works of the 1960s, e.g. the
University of East Anglia.

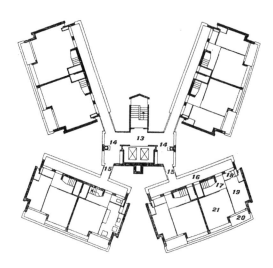

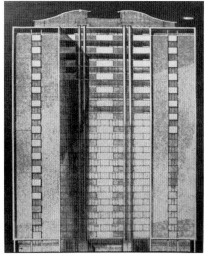

GRAYSON HOUSE

Above: Galway Street, Pleydell Estate, EC 1,1959–61.

Top right: Design of 1958.

Bottom right: Michael Cliffe House, Finsbury Estate, Skinner Street, EC1, 1965–68. By Joseph Emberton, Dr. Carl-Ludwig Franck and Tim Tardrew. Thus another major name in British Inter-war Modernism carried over into the post-war period, indeed, Emberton succeeded Lubetkin in working for the Borough, starting with the Stafford Cripps Estate (cf. p. 11). Emberton himself died in 1956. The firm's further estates culminated in the Finsbury Estate's twenty-five-storey Michael Cliffe House (by Franck and Deeks). In 1968 Islington's twenty-seven-storey Peregrine House in City Road followed in the same vein. A characteristic feature are the mighty pipes which could be mistaken as structural members, but which in fact are the dust chutes. The passages in the centre of Grayson House serve as fire escape passages only.

HIDE PLACE (HIDE TOWER)

Regency Street, Westminster, SW1. Planned from 1957, built 1959–61, for
Westminster Council by Stillman & Eastwick Field (in charge: Ralph Smorczewski).
Engineers: Charles Weiss & Partners; general contractors: John Laing and Son
Ltd. 162 flats of various sizes on 21 regular floors; with a total of 23 floors. Hide
Place was for a time the highest council block in the country, reaching 226 feet (70
metres). The plan type, comprising a number of flat sizes, is 'neither slab nor point'.
The construction combines in situ core parts with a framework of prefabricated
parts, plus prefabricated cladding using concrete panels (cf. p. 86). Hide Place was
the most intensely discussed tower at the time, with the architects given ample
opportunity for self-reflecting presentations. 'To choose to build a tall building is in
itself an aesthetic decision ... but [it] cannot be made in isolation, economic, social
and practical matters are also involved.' The architects cited the client as demanding 'the strictest economy ...' but also as having 'the courage to accept the unconventional. The atmosphere in which we worked was a stimulating one'. Sir William
Holford, on the other hand, called Hide Place 'a typical building which had achieved
more than average results'. He also quoted the Royal Fine Arts Commission's
rather perfunctory words: '... no adverse comment'. Compare some contemporary
and later blocks, e.g. Brandon, Birmingham.

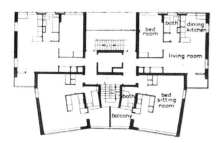

AVONDALE SQUARE

Old Kent Road, Southwark, SE1. West Point, Centre Point, East Point, drawing 1959.
Designed in 1959 for the Corporation of London by Sir Lancelot Keay, Basil Duckett &
Partners (in charge: Norman Rix), with the engineers Ove Arup and Partners; built by
Pauling & Co. Ltd. (Rush & Tompkins) in 1960–62. Each block contains 62 flats. One reason
for the unusual slenderness of the blocks is the small size of the flats, with two one-
bedroom flats at the garden side, the Southern side, and two bedsits at the Northern side,
the entrance side. The non-rectangularity of the plan helps to sharpen the edges, as does
the way in which the floor slabs project very slightly from the wall surface; the infilling /
cladding is in white gault brick.

SIVILL HOUSE
Columbia Road [Square], E2, 1963–64. Skinner Bailey & [Berthold] Lubetkin for Bethnal Green MBC. Here Lubetkin continues his exercises in façade patterning (cf. p. 84). According to John Allan, Lubetkin 'seeks refuge from the real world in the certainties of geometrical order... using a U-shaped cladding figure in permutation to project an abstract image of metamorphosis as the eye progresses up the building' (on the south side only). Inside, the linking part between the two parts of the block shows one of Lubetkin's daring spiralling staircases.

ST. MARY'S TOWER FLATS
Frances Street – Samuel Street, SE15. 1959–62.
Norman and Dawbarn for Woolwich MBC (cf. p. 84). The 'butterfly' design of
the towers will give each flat 'the maximum amount of natural ventilation and
lighting and will ensure privacy for the tenants'.

CLIFTON COURT
Biggerstaff Street, Playford Road, Finsbury Park, N4, Islington LBC, 1965. The bottom of
the block exposes the r.c. frame most clearly, but above the first floor a completely different
concept of design prevails. Strong corner piers surround the zones of the windows which are
clearly marked out as a unified field; the whole is crowned by a strongly projecting cornice. All
this has nothing whatsoever to do with the construction behind, but much with an extremely
late flowering of the Classical design heritage.

WAYMAN COURT
Richmond Road, Hackney, E8, 1964. Harry Moncrieff of Co-operative Planning Ltd. for Hackney
MBC. A design which, although quite similar in size and plan to Clifton Court, in other ways
marks the complete opposite. Although the actual construction is not revealed very directly,
some components of it, especially the stud walls are clearly accentuated, reaching even over
the top of the building.

Edward Armstrong and Frederick McManus, The Combe,
Regents Park Estate, NW1, 1955–60.

Louis de Soissons, project for Stockwell, 1962.

MORE TOWER BLOCKS BY MAJOR PRIVATE ARCHITECTS

Sir William Holford, Kensal New Town, W10, 1959 onwards.

Yorke Rosenberg & Mardall (YRM), Fifty Roman
Road, Bethnal Green, E2. 1965–67.

George / Trew / Dunn, Winstanley Estate, Battersea,
SW11, 1963–66.

Col. Richard Seifert, Surrey Lane Estate,
Wandsworth, SW11, 1969.

(Sir John) Burnet Tait & Lorne, Kelson House,
Samuda Estate, Isle of Dogs, E14, 1964.

Austin Smith / Salmon / Lord, Lulworth House,
Agar Grove, Camden, NW1, 1966.

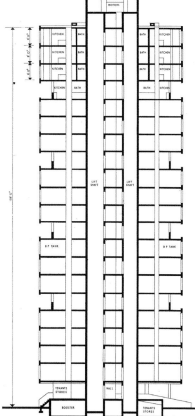

LCC BLOCKS IN SOUTH LONDON

Left page: Canada Estate, Neptune Street, Rotherhithe, Bermondsey, Brandrams Works Site, SE16, 1962.

Right page: Crossmount, Otterburn, Coniston, Kevan Houses, Wyndham and Comber Estate, Wyndham Road, Camberwell, SE5, 1964. Often dubbed 'Canada' blocks, they form a rare example in London of a repeat of a distinctive formula, in four locations. LCC 'Senior Architect' was Colin A. Lucas, Engineer J.H. Humphreys, the contractors Tersons. Part of mixed developments. 80 flats per high block, 4 per floor. There is a clear external expression of the two different flat sizes: the one bedroom ones show at the narrower parts, the two bedroom flats at the wider parts. Constructionally this created an oddity: vertical supports that appear as columns in the middle of the living rooms of the larger flats.

136

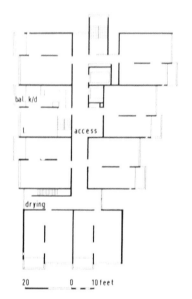

20   0   10 feet

LAMBETH BOROUGH COUNCIL BLOCKS 1966–68.
Top: Ebenezer, Hurley, Fairford Houses, Kennington Lane, SE11.
Above and right: Holland Rise House, Clapham Road, Printers Street, Lett Road, SW9.
Left page: Pinter House, Grantham Road Estate, SW9.

Borough Architect Edward ('Ted') Hollamby (from 1963), previously of the LCC (cf. p. viii) must
be considered the most high-profile designer among the London Borough Architects of that
decade – though the actual designer of the eight maisonette blocks was 'group leader' George
Finch, with Ove Arup as the engineers and Wates as the contractors. There are 80 maisonettes
in each block. The units appear as if they were slotted together, lego-like, marking out the
individual dwellings, each with its strongly projecting balcony and a small sloping roof over
what appear oriel-like projections. More than in other maisonette blocks of the period each
unit appears as a little house.

BEDFORD HOUSE
Above and right: Solon New Road Estate,
  Bedford Road, Lambeth MB, SW4.
  1966–68. Allbetong System.
Far right: Lambeth Council presenting
  its blocks in 1965: 3rd from left Richard
  Crossman, Minister of Housing, first right
  E.E. Hollamby, Borough Architect .

ELLERTON
Mill Lane, West Hampstead, NW6, by Gerd Kaufmann for Camden LBC, 1971.

SHROPSHIRE HOUSE, CHESHIRE HOUSE
(showing also Leicester House, lower maisonette
blocks) Cavendish Road, Angel Road, Enfield,
N18, 1967–68. These blocks are the result of a co-
operation between T. A. Wilkinson, Enfield (formerly
Edmonton) Borough Architect and Planning Officer;
F. E. Ladly, Borough Engineer and Surveyor; the
national Building Research Station (BRS); Fife,
Belcher and Grimsey, Consulting Engineers; the
Enfield Direct Labour Organisation (EDLO) and
others. Most prominent were the four twenty-
three-storey Towers of Enfield's Barbot (Street)
Estate of 1968–70, now demolished. (Left page,
bottom) The Barbot design shows an unusual
degree of regularity. The real determinants are the
external concave concrete panels, battery-cast on
site: the combined two components, wall segment
and window segment, constitute the external walls
and thereby also rigidly determine the positioning
of the internal walls of most rooms.

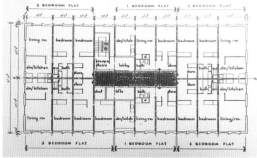

'SF1 BLOCKS'
WINTERTON POINT (HOUSE) AND GELSTON POINT
Watney Market, Shadwell, E1, (1963) 1968, 1966. 'SF 1' was a highly
experimental undertaking of the GLC Architects' Department (no
actual designer mentioned), with general contractor F.G. Minter,
steel designers Redpath, Dorman Long Ltd., Indulex Engineering
Co. Metal-reinforced plastic panels, six of them mounted together,
attached to a slender steel frame. Extensive testing took place
regarding combustibility and weathering in the GLC Depot.

BRENTFORD TOWERS
Waterworks Area, Green Dragon Lane, Hounslow LBC (Wicksteed House in front) (1965) 1967–71 .

145

LANCRESSE COURT
De Beauvoir Estate, De Beauvoir Road, N1,
1967, by Burley Associates for Hackney LBC.

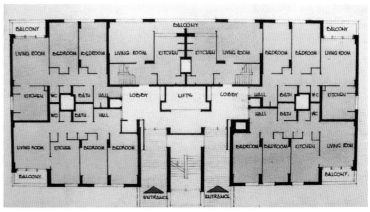

ROZEL COURT
De Beauvoir Estate.

SARNESFIELD, SHENFRITH, PETERCHURCH HOUSES
Camelot Street, Commercial Way, Southwark, SE15, 1968. Taylor Woodrow Anglian (Larsen Nielsen) for GLC.

ALFRED PRIOR HOUSE
Grantham Road, Newham, E12, East Ham BC, 1965.

SARAH LAWRENCE HOUSE
Walton Road, Newham E12, East Ham BC, 1965.

BALFRON TOWER
Rowlett Street, Brownfield Estate, St. Edwards Road, Poplar,
E14, (from early 1960s) 1965–68, with lower CARRADALE HOUSE
1967–70, by Ernö Goldfinger for the LCC/GLC.

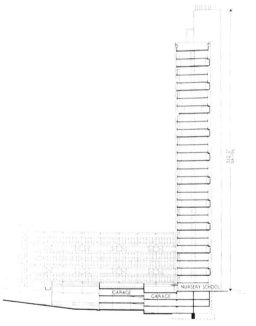

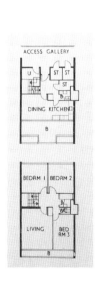

TRELLICK TOWER

Edenham Street Development, W10, 1968–72. Ernö Goldfinger for the GLC. The most noted of all council towers of the 1960s, certainly in London; Trellick being the highest there, counting 31 floors, 98 m, with 175 dwellings. The two towers can be seen as a summing-up of many of the aspirations of the London designers of the 1960s: Blending the slab bloc and the point block types, mixing flats and maisonettes and marking out strongly each kind of dwelling on the exterior, as well as stressing vertical and horizontal communication components, treating them as quasi separate elements. Access is in the traditional way by narrow passages on one side, though these are now completely enclosed. Hence very little light is coming into the flats from that side and thus the other side of the slab is almost completely glazed while the depth of the block is unusually shallow. All this makes the homogeneous constructional framework strongly felt; while the many r. c. external components on and around the blocks also demonstrate the prefabrication process, with a pronounced finish in the bush-hammered mode.

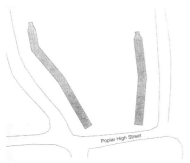

ROBIN HOOD GARDENS [Lane]
Poplar High Street, Tower Hamlets, E15,
1968–72, by Alison and Peter Smithson
for the GLC.

A most idiosyncratic version of the London
high maisonette slab block. The bent shape
of the slabs helps to create an unusually
lavish space between them, and thus the high
density of 142 persons per acre comes as a
surprise. 'The buildings are not organised like
filing cabinets, one after the other [like older
Zeilenbau formations and London maisonette
slabs]'. 'The site has been split like a kipper
... the buildings ... have been organised
to create an area in the centre of the site
protected from noise ...,' indeed, the development is wedged between two major roads.
Further, on the elevations 'the vertical pieces
stop the noise travelling across the face of
the building' (Peter Smithson). The blocks
marked the culmination of the Smithsons'
new conceptualisation of the deck access
type, which they first proposed with their
Golden Lane project in 1952, and which others
then realised at Park Hill Sheffield. The wide
deck access ways are punctuated by tall
open spaces which mark the points where
they meet the lifts and stairs and where one
can see the sky across the building, giving a
feeling of being in a 'traditional street' (Alan
Powers). Lastly, the window-less Northern
ends of the blocks provide an opportunity for
a tower-like formation.

DARTREY TOWER
World's End Estate, Chelsea, SW10, (1965) 1969–77. Eric Lyons for Royal Borough of Kensington and Chelsea.

WORLD'S END ESTATE
Chelsea, SW10. (1965) 1969–77. Eric Lyons for the Royal Borough of Kensington and Chelsea.

THAMESMEAD
Woolwich, Hartslock Drive, South Mere, SE2. Balency System for the GLC, 1967–73.

CRANBROOK ESTATE
Roman Road, Bethnal Green, E2, (1955) 1960–65, by Skinner, Bailey & Lubetkin for Bethnal Green MBC.
Considered Lubetkin's summa and his valedictory project, a mixed development. '... The 'demonstration
of a formative artistic will' ... a 'lifelong pre-occupation with the diagonal line, following Melnikov ...'. The
towers are placed in a complex relationship as if they were 'members of a family group in conversation with
each other' (John Allan).

ENFIELD
View over Durants Park towards Tiverton, Ashcombe, Honiton, Newton Houses, Exeter Road, 1962. Builder
Wates for Enfield BC. In the distance the four 23-storey blocks at Ponders End Alma Road / Scotland
Green Road, 1966–67.

13 English regions and Wales

LANDSCAPE AND BUILDING

Diagrammatic section of an old town and Harlow

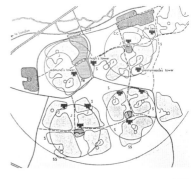

Frederick Gibberd in 1956

HARLOW NEW TOWN
Top left: 'Diagrammatic section of an old town and Harlow [New Town Centre]'.
  Edmund and Hugh Towers are seen flanking the Centre (cf. p. 41).
Top right: Map of planned towers, c. 1960.
Bottom left: Pennymead Tower, by Sir Frederick Gibberd. 1959.
Bottom right: Hugh Tower, 1955.

HARLOW NEW TOWN

If post-WWII London public housing was a realm of architectural privilege, the same also applies to the post-war New
Towns, especially those created in the London orbit; all names
are those of the London planning and design elite. But how
could the English Garden City and 'English Village' ideals which
shaped the plans of these towns allow for towers, except for the
occasional church spire? Yet, most of the New Towns actually
did indulge in multis, even Letchworth Garden City had a plan
for four thirteen-storey towers, in 1961.[1] Of all the new creations
Harlow stood out, not just as regards the numbers of towers,
but also with the concept of their positioning. The town's architect-planner, Frederick Gibberd has already been cited for his
praise of vertical accents per se. 'The intrusion of a "point"
block immediately gives a sharp sense of scale and balance to
the surroundings,' he argued,[2] and that both within their immediate surroundings and for the town as a whole. From the start,

in 1947, Gibberd had envisaged a central multi-storey administration block. The first residential tower, 'The Lawn' at Mark
Hall North, of 1949–51, has already been illustrated as the first
example of a British point block altogether. (cf. p. 63). To find the
block not in an urban but in a low-density garden city environment is not such a surprise when one remembers the numerous
illustrations of high slab block embedded in greenery in the
publications of the 1930s (cf. p. 63). Harlow then built a further
ten more towers; two of them were given some slight decorative accents and were placed on either side of the Civic Centre
complex. However, the eventual reality on the ground came to
differ considerably from Gibberd's new vision. Undeniably, the
towers add picturesque interest at close quarters, but even from
a short way away they may already have disappeared from view;
when moving through the vast green belts between the neighbourhood units, they only very occasionally peep over the tree
tops. With their maximum of fifteen storeys, they are simply not
high enough.

COVENTRY

Tile Hill, Nos 1–187 Ferrers Close, Jardine Crescent, 1953–56. Donald Gibson City Architect with Wimpey (cf. p. 63).

COVENTRY

In recent historical accounts of Coventry, England's most 'go-ahead' post-war city, its public housing profile has received only limited attention. To be sure, the city's innovative town planning was undeniably its foremost achievement – more, it seems, than the actual shapes on the ground.[3] But Coventry's council housing story is one of great innovations, too, and it constitutes an important element within the work of the city's two principal planner-architects, Donald Gibson and Arthur Ling, the latter succeeding the former in 1955. Gibson was one of the country's foremost town planning authorities, while Ling had played a prominent role in the renowned planning groups at the LCC – as well as, more controversially, as the linchpin organiser in Britain's circles of communist architects. These protagonists enjoyed a different status from, say, Herbert Manzoni in next-door Birmingham. The latter, towering figure though he was in his local setting, remained exclusively preoccupied with his city, whereas Gibson and Ling were actors on the national scene.

Coventry differed from all other major industrial cities in the way in which its major growth had come only with the early 20th century. A relatively wealthy town, its slum problems were modest in comparison with those of its neighbours.[4] In fact, the total number of multi-storey blocks is also relatively low, nor do they reach a particularly great height. There was, furthermore, a marked aversion to contractor-led, 'package deal' building of high blocks. Housing architecture in Coventry was unashamedly designer-led, and much of it was experimental to a high degree.

In the first ten years after the war, under Donald Gibson, the city's extensive low-rise peripheral estates had been innovative at least in one principal respect, namely that most of them were built by Wimpey, using their 'no-fines' method.[5] Wimpey then acted as partners in Gibson's first major housing innovation, the three eleven-storey point blocks at Tile Hill, built between 1953 and 1956. With their tripartite or 'T' plan, comprising three flats per floor, they followed the precedent of the slightly earlier LCC Ackroydon blocks (c.f. p. 65). Wimpey was, at that time, already building innovative six and eight-storey flats in Birmingham, but Tile Hill was their first real foray into high-block construction, using their particular combination of no-fines concrete walling with a frame construction, subsequently to be dubbed the 'Wimpey no-fines system'.

Unrealised Arcon Scheme for Brandon Woods, for the Family Health Club Housing Society, 1944–45, partly by Fello Atkinson; the model was clearly the *County of London Plan* of 1943.

COVENTRY
Top: Maisonette slab block, Spongate House, Spon End, Upper Spon Street, 1960, Arthur Ling City Architect.
Left and right: Phoenix House, Hillfields estate, 1959.

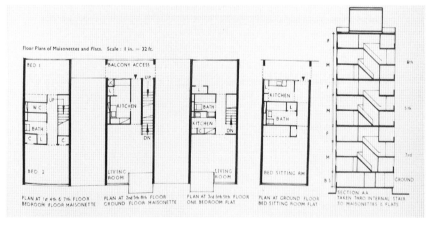

Floor Plans of Maisonettes and Flats. Scale : 1 in. = 32 ft.

PLAN AT 1st 4th & 7th FLOOR BEDROOM FLOOR MAISONETTE

PLAN AT 2nd 5th 8th FLOOR GROUND FLOOR MAISONETTE

PLAN AT 3rd 6th 9th FLOOR ONE BEDROOM FLAT

PLAN AT GROUND FLOOR BED SITTING ROOM FLAT

SECTION AA TAKEN THRO INTERNAL STAIR TO MAISONETTES & FLATS

Wimpey continued with a fair share of Coventry's output, notably with its ten-storey maisonette blocks. But most exceptionally, these blocks had very little to do with the general run of Wimpey's standardised no-fines blocks. Rather, they represent Coventry's second major innovation in multi-storey design, following Tile Hill. The first of these blocks, Phoenix House, part of the Queen Street (Hillfields) redevelopment, was completed in 1960; several more of this type were to be built here and at Spon End. Much shorter than the London maisonette slab blocks, containing only fifty-odd dwellings, their plan was of extreme complexity. Instead of, as in London, just stacking up identical maisonette units, Ling alternated two bedroomed maisonettes with bed/sitting room flats, the flats being accessible from the same balcony access-way used by the maisonettes. Generally speaking, with these planning acrobatics, the blocks are somewhat reminiscent of the contemporary LCC 'scissors' blocks. The structures on the roof, containing water tanks and lift machinery, are also fitted out with bird-like wings, for the blocks 'to be seen from many parts of the city'.[6]

COVENTRY
Above: Hillfields
  Comprehensive
  Redevelopment
  project, 1962. Arthur
  Ling City Architect.
Left: Nauls Mill House,
  Middleborough Road,
  'Liftslab', 1962.
Right; 'Lift slab' con-
  struction in progress.

Coventry's largest urban plan was for the Queen Street (Hillfields) area, a mixed development with a great number of towers, including a block of thirty storeys that was never built.[7] A further contribution, at Queen Street and elsewhere, was a series of seventeen-storey towers, invariably built singly, the first being at Middleborough Road, from 1962. They were extremely wide, containing eight flats on each floor, or a total of 128 flats on 16 floors. It was the 'lift-slab' process of their construction that attracted much attention. The process began with a massive in-situ core of the lift shaft and services, and a spread of steel columns. The floors/ceilings were then cast at the bottom, to be lifted to their respective upper positions. Externally, the blocks were completely surrounded by narrow

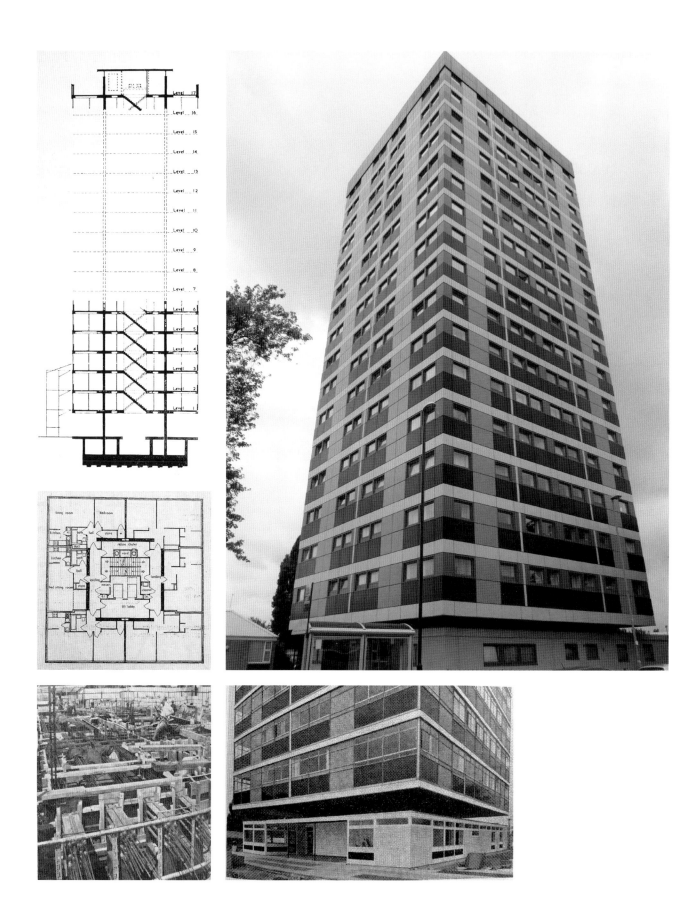

COVENTRY
Alpha House, Barras Green (Heath), Mercer Avenue, 'Jackblock' method, 1961–63. Arthur Ling City Architect with contractor Costain. 'In simple terms, the block starting with the roof, is extended upwards from an assembly plant at ground level, rather like tooth paste from a tube'.

160

COVENTRY
Top: Mercia House, early design, Arthur Ling.
Middle: View towards city centre from Mercia House.
Bottom: Mercia House with Lady Godiva Monument.
Right: Mercia House, Lower Precinct, 1962–67. Arthur
  Ling, City Architect, succeeded by Terence Gregory.

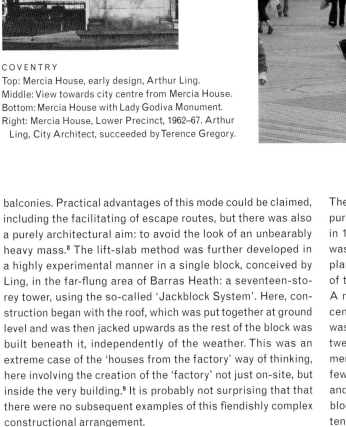

balconies. Practical advantages of this mode could be claimed, including the facilitating of escape routes, but there was also a purely architectural aim: to avoid the look of an unbearably heavy mass.[8] The lift-slab method was further developed in a highly experimental manner in a single block, conceived by Ling, in the far-flung area of Barras Heath: a seventeen-storey tower, using the so-called 'Jackblock System'. Here, construction began with the roof, which was put together at ground level and was then jacked upwards as the rest of the block was built beneath it, independently of the weather. This was an extreme case of the 'houses from the factory' way of thinking, here involving the creation of the 'factory' not just on-site, but inside the very building.[9] It is probably not surprising that that there were no subsequent examples of this fiendishly complex constructional arrangement.

The highest council tower in Coventry fulfilled a very different purpose. Ling's final effort, built only after he had left the city in 1964, by his successor as City Architect, Terence Gregory, was a council tower integrated into the City's famous central plan, in the Lower Precinct, so as to 'form the Western end of the shopping area which extends the cathedral precinct'. A massive block of twenty-three storeys, somewhat reminiscent of the lift-slab blocks, was envisaged at first; but what was eventually built, from 1964, was a much slimmer version of twenty storeys, 'simplified to produce a bold architectural statement'. The three lower storeys are used commercially. As with a few other prestigious 'civic' town centre towers in Nottingham and Birmingham, only part of the flats in Mercia House, as the block was eventually called, were to serve normal council house tenants; 75% were let at an 'economic rent'.[10]

SHEFFIELD
Above: The Hyde Park – Park Hill Complex. City Architect: Lewis Womersley (Hyde Park 1962–67).
Below: Park Hill Project, 1955. City Architect with Jack Lynn, Ivor Smith and others, built 1957–61.

SHEFFIELD

Discussions about housing in Sheffield were markedly different in tone from those in the other large industrial centres. Here the task of clearing slums seemed rather less pressing, although some new projects, notably Park Hill, had certainly been redevelopments. In Sheffield there appeared a greater scope for sociological and aesthetic creeds to exert an influence on council housing strategy, and in that respect, the city can be fitted into a national architectural context. In a flourish of rhetoric in 1963 we read that the city 'could, given national planning and local effort, become a counterweight to the pull of London'.[11]

The beginning of Sheffield's new housing efforts was marked by something completely unexpected. Improbable as it must have sounded to many at the time, the demolition of the old streets went along with a new kind of nostalgia for precisely that kind of street. Conjuring up an image of lower class urban life, designers and critics formulated the 'old/new' concept of a special kind of 'neighbourliness', arguing that 'neighbourliness is the inspiration in Sheffield housing'.[12] The first outcome of this novel concept was Park Hill, perhaps the most architecturally momentous public housing undertaking of the decade. It was designed in 1955 by a team of young architects from outside Sheffield who were heavily influenced by the Smithsons and their sociology of housing and urban design. The Park Hill complex consists of a number of maisonette slab blocks up to a height of thirteen storeys, but height was not what mattered; it was the horizontal connections, the 'walkways', that tied the whole together at all levels; all this implied a denial of the tower and undermined the very idea of an estate consisting of a group of towers.[13] During the 1960s further examples of the high deck access block type were built in Sheffield, including the much higher Park Hill Part Two, or Hyde Park, commenced in 1962; as well as Kelvin and the YDG Broomhall, both of 1967, the latter being Sheffield's contribution to the Yorkshire Development Group programme; eventually almost one third of all new high-rise flats in Sheffield were part of deck-access complexes.

Sheffield's domineering chief designer, City Architect J. Lewis Womersley,[14] and 'his' two successive Housing Committee Chairmen, Albert Smith and Harold Lambert, were fully behind these experiments. But overall these were not their principal concern. Their vision was one that comprised the whole of the city. Sheffield's situation at the centre of a landscape of hills and slopes was to be visually integrated, united, through public housing. As Lambert confidently argued in 1962, the reason for the national and even international interest in the City 'is not difficult to explain'. 'We have envisaged each scheme ... to be carefully integrated with the whole town plan ... because of the geographical characteristics of the city... '.[15] The principal instrument of this visual spectacle was the ubiquitous placing of towers on Sheffield's steep slopes: Lambert recalled in 1987 that 'Like Rome's seven hills, Sheffield's redevelopments were built on three hills'.[16] Over half of Sheffield's towers were located in four major estates, Netherthorpe, Gleadless, Woodside-Burngreave and Norfolk Park. The campaign began,

in 1957, with 26 blocks of four one bedroom flats on 13 floors; this led, from 1960 onwards, to the building of twenty-seven fifteen-storey blocks, followed, finally, by the fifteen seventeen-storey 'twin-towers' of Norfolk Park, a huge estate built in multiple stages in 1963–68 and containing no less than 1,887 multi-storey flats. Quite unusual is the sameness of the towers of Sheffield, all of them sporting corner windows, to counter any disadvantages of facing north. Unusual , too, was the way in which near-neighbour Doncaster copied the Sheffield blocks in its Balby Bridge Redevelopment of 1967.

Sheffield carefully followed the doctrine of mixed development, mostly at a relatively low density of 70 p.p.a. Uppermost were, once again, the overall landscape considerations. For those estates built on new land, the first task was to preserve its woodlands wherever possible. Then 'after an aerial survey a slope analysis was prepared and types of buildings chosen accordingly'.[17] The special design task of the low-rise and

Map of major estates, 1969.

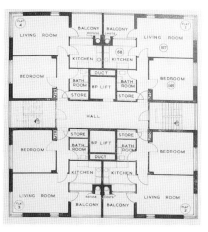

SHEFFIELD
Top left: Hyde Park, view in 1967.
Top right: Wiggen and Keating, Cliff Street, 1963.
Lower right: Plan of a 13-storey block, Gleadless Valley, Herdings Neighbourhood.

medium-rise buildings was that of climbing up the hills, across the contours, which led to multiform solutions for houses and low-to-medium rise six-storey maisonettes. The towers were then distributed mainly along the contours, that is, on the hill tops. Finally Park Hill Part Two (Hyde Park) crowned the Park Hill complex with a tower formation which 'complete[s] the visual composition of the hillside.'[18] With its core of a long nineteen-storey block, two floors higher than the Norfolk Park twin-towers, Hyde Park formed one of Britain's mightiest groupings of high slabs. Councillor Lambert summed it up: 'The building of hill top architectural compositions is gradually creating the fascination of an architectural hill town. It is stimulating, exciting!'[19]

In the 1960s, at precisely the time when package-deal blocks were multiplying elsewhere, Sheffield designers stressed that 'all the schemes ... are the work of the City Architect's Department'.[20] Womersley had left for private practice in 1964 but by then most of the decisive steps in the programme were underway. Another of the City's demonstrations of independence was the strength of its direct labour force, which built, among other estates, Park Hill and Hyde Park. The rest was shared out to a number of big contractors. By 1969 praise for the Sheffield achievement was still running strong: a 'transformation from an old style "industrial town" into a regional centre has been due in no small way to an adventurous housing programme, ... the city so becoming cleaner and greener.'[21] Moreover, Sheffield people 'are prepared to live in something slightly unconventional as long as the requirements of size, amenities and rent are met. There has certainly been no resistance to high-rise blocks and flats.' However, 1969 did mark the end of the towers, now 'no more were envisaged'.[22] – Today, only very few of them are left.

SHEFFIELD
Above: Model of Norfolk Park, from 1963.
Below: Norfolk Park.

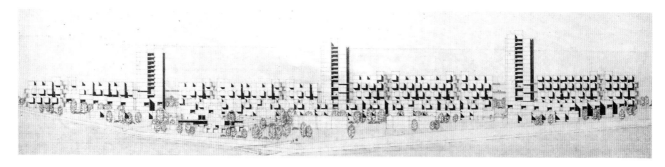

PORTSMOUTH
Portsdown Hill, competition win 1965 by Richard Theakston
and John Duell.

THE SOUTH AND WALES

By contrast with Coventry and Sheffield, the towns of the South,
the South West and Wales cannot be counted as part of the
'design-conscious' London orbit. Often governed by anti-social-
ist ratepayer groupings, they generally lacked the drive of the
LCC or some of the capital's boroughs, let alone that of many
cities in the north. In Portsmouth and Southampton a limited
number of very high blocks played a certain role, but other
towns, such as Reading and Plymouth, appeared exceptionally
unambitious; the first built just seven Wimpey blocks, and the
second, although its population was twice as large, commissioned only six blocks, also mostly by Wimpey, with only three
of them reaching sixteen storeys. Overall, the share claimed
by the national building firms, with their packages, was large.
Bristol alone stands out with its early vigour and architectural
originality. None of these regional developments caught much
attention at a national level.

Council housing in PORTSMOUTH, the largest city on the
South Coast,[23] fell into several distinct phases, which to some
extent paralleled those of the cities of the Midlands and the
North. This was partly due to the fact that space appeared
particularly short, since the city is located on a quasi-is-
land. Initially this caused considerable overspill, but by the
early 1960s that policy began to be doubted: 'keep people in
the city', we now read.[24] At the same time the city's stock of
unfit houses was considered large. For leading councillor
Frank Miles and City Architect F. Mellor, the scene was set
for a burst of housing construction that would considerably
exceed the height of seven to twelve storeys which had prevailed in the city's multi-storey flats since the late 1950s. In
1963 the city's team returned from the Civic Trust Conference
on Industrialised Building, convinced of the need for a new
start. At the same time they remained determined that 'variety
in design can be introduced by ordering a minimum quantity
of more than one type'[25] – not a statement that would have
pleased the package dealers. The first results were two
pairs of eighteen-storey Bison slab blocks, at Park Street
and Somerville Street. Unusually for Bison's products, the
role played by Concrete Ltd's in-house architect, Miall Rhys
Davies, working in conjunction with the City Architect, was
emphasised in the publicity. And, indeed, the blocks show an

Blackwood House, Nelson Road, 1952.

PORTSMOUTH
Above: Somerstown, Leamington House and Atherstone Walk, Earsdon Street, 1967.
   City Architect F. Mellor with Bison's architect Miall-Rhys-Davies, 1967.
Right: Ladywood House, Plymouth Street, 1966. Wimpey.

unusual rhythmic treatment of the windows and their corners and upper edges received a decorative accentuation. Moreover, the high blocks are grouped symmetrically with lower blocks, making scant allusions to a mixed development. A strong contrast to the slabs is provided by three Wimpey blocks of twenty and twenty-four storeys, at Butcher Street and Plymouth Street RDA, striking in their slenderness.

Somewhat like many Midlands and Northern cities, Portsmouth then embarked, from 1964, on two large developments of the kind which, in this book, are dubbed conglomerates – that is, mixed formations of great density in which towers play a subsidiary role or are absent altogether. Much attention was caught by the design for the Portsdown Hill project, far north of the centre, commandingly located on the brow of an escarpment overlooking the Solent, which was won in competition – then an unusual procedure for council housing – by the little-known firm of Richard Theakston and John Duell. Arrays of long medium-rise blocks run along the hill, punctuated by three towers of thirteen, fifteen and seventeen storeys. Built from 1968 onwards, Portsdown Hill, as with most other complexes of this 'conglomerate' kind, only had a very short life. The Henrietta Street RDA (Cannock Lawn) was designed in 1966–1967 by two eminent planner-designers, Hugh Wilson and Lewis Womersley, of Cumbernauld and Sheffield fame respectively. It forms a meandering eight-storey complex with several sets of highly pronounced walkway connections. The latter feature became a Portsmouth speciality, extensively used for four, and even three-storey blocks; in this respect Portsmouth's later 1960s and 1970s housing is somewhat reminiscent of the contemporary work in some London Boroughs, such as Camden or Southwark.

SOUTHAMPTON
International Way, Weston Farm Foreshore, 1964: (from the right) Rotterdam, Copenhagen, Oslo, Havre, Hampton Towers; Wimpey.

Weston Foreshore, Canberra Towers, 1964.

INTERNATIONAL WAY

Above: Weston Foreshore in 1966.
Left and far left: Castle House, Castle Way, from both sides, 1960. Eric Lyons for the Corporation

SOUTHAMPTON's record is equally distinguished, but in quite a different way. Blocks are fewer but generally higher, and there was greater scope for architectural diversity. By comparison with Portsmouth, the clearance issue here appeared less pressing. The city hardly bothered with lower kinds of blocks, but went quite early for sixteen storeys, with Millbank House in the Northam scheme, built in 1959–60, designed by the Borough Engineer, F L Wooldridge and built by Wimpey. That year also saw the commencement of the construction of Castle House, a very rare case of a block in the provinces designed by a major London architect, Eric Lyons.[26] This maisonette slab block is thirteen/fourteen storeys high, and is thus taller than the common London type. In 1963–65 Reema built a

sixteen-storey split-level or 'scissors' type of block at Bevois Street. In 1964–65 the city started its largest undertaking, the serried row of four fifteen-storey blocks and one of twenty-five storeys at Weston Farm. This group was 'branded' as a prestigious undertaking in quite a singular way: under the collective title of the 'International Flats', each block ('Towers') was given the name of a major trading partner of the city and their inaugurations in 1966 and 1967 were conducted in the presence of representatives of those cities. The high-point of Weston Farm, literally, was the enormous, T – shaped, Canberra Towers block. Situated along the eastern waterfront, this row of towers 'can be considered an imposing first sight of the city to overseas visitors on the many liners which regularly call on the Port ....'[27]

BRIGHTON
Above: Theobald House, Blackman Street RDA, 1964. P. Billington, Borough Architect.

SOUTHEND ON SEA
Top left: Chiltern and Malvern, Prittlewell RDA, 1965, Laing.
Left: Grampian, Balmoral Road RDA, 1969. Wates.

BRIGHTON has a comparatively large number of high council towers, many located in clearance areas on steeply-graded sites, Initiator in many cases was the forceful Conservative Councillor S. W. Theobald, the 'King of Brighton'. An early group was Albion Hill Stage 1, comprising four twelve-storey blocks, from 1958, (cf. p. 102) and later on came the higher towers of the Somerset Street Redevelopment Area: with its demonstratively symmetrical plan and elevation Wiltshire House harks back to an earlier decade. Theobalds House, in the Blackman Street Redevelopment (1964), nearer the centre, the highest council block in the town, soars upwards from a two-storey podium with garages and other facilities. Brighton built an unusually large number of private tower blocks, too, and in some cases the architectural distinction between council and private can appear somewhat blurred. A large number of small flats were also built in SOUTHEND ON SEA to cater for the 'comparatively large number of retired people ... on small incomes'.[28]

BRIGHTON
Wiltshire House, Essex Street, Somerset Street CDA, 1965.

CARDIFF
Nelson House and Loudon House, Loudoun
Square, Bute-Town RDA, 1962. Wimpey.

CWMBRAN
Town Centre with The Tower, 1965, Gordon Redfern, Corporation Chief Architect.

WALES

Comparatively fewer towers were built in Wales. Considering its size, Cardiff built very few indeed, although its highest blocks, the two sixteen-storey slabs in Bute Town in 1962, containing a total of 195 flats, are among the larger examples of their kind. The Labour stronghold of Swansea stood out with a burst of high flat contracts in 1961, awarded under Housing Chairman Councillor T. S. Harris, for thirteen blocks in four developments, most of them shared out to national firms, Laing, Wimpey and Reema; but their height did not exceed 14 floors.[29]

The ambitious Central Area Redevelopment in the small town of Flint was marked in 1966 and 1970 by two Bison towers, the first of eighteen and the second of fifteen storeys. The great exception in Wales is the single twenty-two-storey block in the New Town of Cwmbran, planned from 1963 by Gordon Redfern. It is a major example of the 1960s genre of town-centre civic accents, providing, according to a commentary (presumably the architect's), 'the logical termination of the pedestrian system already provided'.

BRISTOL
St.Mary Redcliffe Comprehensive
Redevelopment Area, planned
from the early 1950s, view in 1958;
J.Nelson Meredith City Architect,
followed by Albert H. Clarke;
L.W. Francis, Principal Housing
Architect; builders: John Laing
& Sons, Tersons and others.

Canynge House, Redcliffe Way,
1954–55. City Architect.

BRISTOL

Bristol was a city of fluctuating political control but it also showed a strong planning and council housing tradition. The city embarked on its post-war building campaign with much vigour, and with reputedly rather high levels of rent, too. It opted for a high flats policy during the same years as the LCC and Birmingham, in the early 1950s. This was done quite systematically, but the architectural outcomes resembled neither Manzoni's theatrical gestures in Birmingham, nor the theoretical ways of the LCC – there was initially no mixed development in Bristol. Bristol's formula was its own version of the high slab block with narrow balcony access-ways, containing maisonettes and flats. All these early blocks, built between the mid 1950s and the early 1960s, with a height of up to thirteen storeys, convey a look of solidity and of size, both height-wise and length-wise, which was helped also by the way each block stands out individually, marking the very opposite to the regular *Zeilenbau* formation one can see in London and elsewhere. As Bryan Little, that astute observer of the Bristol architectural scene, noted in his overall discussion of the city's post-war rebuilding, '... it is the multi-storey residential block which

emerges most noticeably'.[30] The blocks' originator was the City Architect John Nelson Meredith, and, from 1957, his successor, Albert H. Clarke.

A beginning was made in a large inner urban clearance area, south of St. Mary Redcliffe, from 1953. At its very centre one meets the first block, Canynge House, Redcliffe Way – a most curious concoction of flats and maisonettes sporting five completely different elevations, and stepping up from four storeys at the ends to six at the centre. Was this meant as an initial demonstration of 'designer power'? Thereafter brick and plaster is abandoned in favour of reinforced concrete frames, but here the 'framework' means an open network of imposing columns and beams, and a solid look is given even to the balconies. One cannot help remembering Bristol's tradition of solid stone work generally. In other developments the same kind of ten-storey slab block cheekily hides its frame behind a flattish cladding. In most cases great play is made of the fact that the upper floor of each maisonette differs from its lower part.

BRISTOL
Waring House and Francombe House, Redcliffe Area, 1957.
Balcony access for Underdown House, Redcliffe Area, 1957.

An example of the ubiquitous late 19th century Bristol way of strongly accentuating a kind of framework in free-stone, contrasting with a rougher kind of 'infilling'.

BRISTOL
Eccleston House, Barton Hill, 1961.

BRISTOL
Glendare House, Barton Hill, 1957.

Brandon House, Jacob's Well's Road, 1957.

Plan of 3 bedroom maisonette, Redcliffe Area.

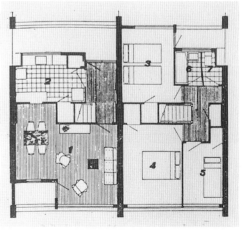

The year 1960 saw a drastic shift in the city's housing policy, from general-needs to slum-clearance, under the anti-social-ist 'Citizen Party', and a five-year burst of multi-storey rede-velopment duly followed, with high flats soaring from 34% of total council-housing approvals in 1959 to 99% in 1962. Over the period 1959–1965, 60% of new council dwellings were located higher than the seventh floor.[31] Hot on the heels of Redcliffe came the Barton Hill Redevelopment Area. Here the slabs are dominated by the fifteen-storey Barton House, a T-shaped com-bined slab and point block, containing flats only. When it was completed in early 1958 it was almost the highest block in the country. Another ambitious project, continuing the Bristol high slab mode but adding to it a late Corbusieran/Brutalist blocky detailing, was proposed in 1960 for a site in Hotwells Road, aiming at the civic enhancement of a major entrance into the city. It caught much attention but was never built.

BRISTOL
Above: Barton House, Barton Hill, 1954–58,
City Architect.

Below: Hotwells Road Proposal,1959, by the Royal West of England
Academy School of Architecture.

BRISTOL
Left top: Emra, Trinnell, Rawnsley Houses, Easton 1966–67, Wimpey.
Left middle: Ashmead House, Barton Hill, 1965.
Left bottom: Walker Close, link to Croydon House.
Right: Croydon House, Croydon Street, Easton Way, 1966–67.

But by 1961, significant shifts in the city's housing designs were already underway. The long high slab was largely given up in favour of the point block. It was easier to erect on uneven terrain and it did away with the narrow external access balconies which were now increasingly criticised. The city eagerly launched into package-deals, or near-package-deals, from the big firms, above all Laing and Wimpey. In Barton Hill, the eleven-storey Ashmead House of 1965 contains only flats which are now accessible from inside, even though it is still a lengthy slab. Out of favour for a time went Bristol's rugged concrete framework and its complex infilling. Elevations were now extremely flat and uniform, as with the seventeen-storey Croydon House at Leadhouse Road, Easton, built by Laing in 1966–67. Mixed development was still not much favoured, but there is a four-storey complex of maisonettes next to Croydon House, linked to it via a short bridge. In the end, the maximum height of Bristol's blocks was only 18 floors, as with Northfield House in Catherine Mead Street, Bedminster, of 1969.

BRISTOL
Above: Kingsdown Redevelopment Area, 1965.
Left: City Architect Albert H Clarke.

The last major redevelopment, and a kind of summing up of Bristol's programme, was Kingsdown, built from 1965 onwards. It consists principally of three fourteen-storey slab blocks, arranged in quasi *Zeilenbau* formation, mighty, but 'yet not obtruding aggressively against the skyline'.[32] The area, close to the city centre, is densely built up as well as hilly, which makes for complex ground formations. All in all the complex appears carefully embedded into the fabric of an old district. Between the three high blocks there are numerous ancillary ground-level facilities, as well as six-storey blocks set at right angles, which are accessed by balcony passages. As elsewhere in Bristol these lower blocks are linked via short bridges to the main blocks. Thus Kingsdown can be counted in some respects as part of the 'conglomerate' movement of the mid-1960s. Overall, it was a project the city was 'specially proud of'.[33] Can it, with its predecessors, be recognised as yet another witness of Bristol's long-standing *genius loci* of good building? Nearby Bath's pioneering Berkeley House has already been shown among the earliest towers (cf. p. 63).

BIRMINGHAM

BIRMINGHAM
A short guide to Birmingham, published by the City of Birmingham Information Department, c. 1972. Council tower blocks are seldom out of view from the city centre, here they appear next to the Civic Centre (Brindley Drive, cf. p. 189).

BIRMINGHAM

'Heart of England', 'Second City'- in the context of public housing, some of Birmingham's sobriquets amount to more than endearing eulogies. Indeed, Birmingham's fame was second to none when it came to the image, and the reality, of a caring and active municipality. It could be claimed that no British city is better suited to studying the central tenets of post 1945 flat-building than Birmingham.

The city was by far the largest local authority in England acting as a single unified body, and in that sense it was far more powerful than London with its divided, multi-level municipal structure. Birmingham's municipal culture in all matters of architecture can furthermore be shown in the way in which its designer power was exercised by outstanding individuals from the 1940s to the 1970s, by Sir Herbert Manzoni, A.G. Sheppard Fidler and J. Alan Maudsley; London, again, offers no direct parallel.

Left: The city planner and the city architect: Sir Herbert Manzoni (left) and A.G. Shepard Fidler, c. 1955.
Right: John P. Macey, Birmingham Corporation Housing Manager, 1954–63.

The crux of the Birmingham story, however, was that council flats were not just a matter of simple provision by a benevolent council but the subject of a long-running debate. Especially in the early days, in the early 1950s, when multi-storey building had begun, there was the constant refrain: 'Birmingham is not flat-minded'.[34] Before 1939, and even during the immediate post-war years, the city's efforts in that field had been miniscule in comparison with London or Liverpool. And yet, Birmingham was the provincial city that appeared to need flats more than any other, not just because of its size, with its 1.1 million inhabitants, or the length of its waiting list, but because of the need to rehouse residents from the largest 'slum' areas in the country. In 1945 it was claimed that 100,000 dwellings were 'unfit for human habitation', more than one third of the city's total housing stock.[35] By the end of the 1960s the city had demolished 45,000 and built 68,000 dwellings of all kinds, of which over 24,000 were blocks of flats of six storeys and above, that is 22%, a proportion that was higher than London's 20%, and lower only than Glasgow's 26.5%.[36]

The great majority of Birmingham's multi-storey blocks, though, were of six to thirteen storeys, although as elsewhere, there was a constant rise in the average height, with the two Sentinels of the early 1970s and their thirty-two storeys as the crowning effort, the highest social housing blocks in Britain altogether. However, so far historians, such as Sutcliffe and Dunleavy, have concentrated narrowly on the politics of Birmingham housing, while as regards its architectural characteristics the city has tended to be talked down, even sometimes by 'local' voices themselves, including Birmingham-born writer Lynsey Hanley.[37]

In actual fact, the story of the beginning of high blocks in Birmingham was a dramatic one, and especially so in architectural terms. It was directed by the city's municipal engineer,

Herbert J. Manzoni (from 1954 Sir Herbert). As so many other English cities, until the early 1950s Birmingham did not have the position of a municipal architect, nor that of a town planner. All these tasks were dealt with in the office of Manzoni, who was widely credited as one of Britain's most powerful municipal officers, standing at the helm of his Department from 1935 until 1963. The city's Inner Ring Road, constructed in the 1960s and 70s, is his most enduring legacy.

To what extent Manzoni might be called an architectural designer as well is not clear, but there was, certainly at times, an immense architectural ambition. A longing for grandiose schemes had suddenly broken out during the war, in a series of illustrations, published in 1944. Manzoni joined the wartime anticipation of post-war planning efforts and in line with Abercrombie's visions in his *London Plan* of 1943, he proposed sets of large high slab blocks embedded in lavish greenery. But in an adjacent area Manzoni envisaged a much denser development, alongside an almost ceremonial, 'arterial' road which was to be lined with a series of fifteen-storey blocks, destined for 'hostel accommodation for single people', ending in an even higher central building.[38]

The inspiration here was clearly not Gropius's International Modern Style, as in Abercrombie's case, but the 'Gratteciel' area at the Villeurbanne district in Lyons, built in the 1930s; Manzoni faithfully followed even many of its details, such as the stepped tops of the blocks. Of course, there cannot have been much hope of ever realising such a scheme, nor did Birmingham build many long slab blocks, the type with which London began to excel with. Apart from some further bold plans nothing happened for many years. Manzoni's grand project had actually been destined not for the city centre but for one of the downtrodden inner suburban areas, Duddeston (Nechells). In 1950/51 he resumed his ambitions in the same area and started a series

BIRMINGHAM
Duddeston and Nechells Area [Nechells Green], Redevelopment
proposals, Herbert J. Manzoni, City Engineer and Surveyor, 1943.

Villeurbanne, Lyon, Gratte-ciel Area, 1930s.

BIRMINGHAM
Top: Home Tower, Duddeston and Nechells Area Redevelopment,
 1950–1954. S.N.Cooke and Partners for Birmingham Council.
Right: Duddeston and Nechells, view, c. 1953.

of blocks of the most extraordinary kind. The design stemmed from S.N. Cooke and Partners, Birmingham's premier firm of the interwar period, authors of many commercial structures as well as of the Neo-Classical Hall of Memory in the new Civic Centre Square. With their twelve storeys the Duddeston blocks were the highest in Britain for some years. But with their plan shape, a curiously flattened cross, they did not come under the point block definition, nor that of the 'slab'. With their many curves and odd angles one may call them Art Deco, remotely reminiscent of some private and public blocks of flats in London of the preceding decades. A distant comparison also may be drawn with the five-winged Farragut Houses in New York of 1950–52, though the American city's rigid economy in public housing was not something shared by Manzoni at this point. At Duddeston

the construction is in steel frame, which is completely hidden by solid brick walls. There are six flats per floor, which are extraordinarily lavishly appointed, complete with private balconies and the expensive Garchey refuse system, accessible through seven staircases and four express lifts. No wonder the building cost per flat amounted to £4,300, almost three times of that of a house. The first block, named Queens Tower, was opened in February 1954 in the presence of the Minister of Housing, Harold Macmillan. Three more blocks were completed eventually.[39] Also initiated under Manzoni was the Holte Estate, close to the Aston Reservoir, with four Y-shaped twelve-storey blocks, now in reinforced concrete construction, again designed not in-house, but by Harry W. Weedon, of 1930s cinema architecture fame.[40]

One of four blocks of
Duddeston & Nechells Multi-storey
Flats.
Architects
S. N. Cooke & Partners, F.R.I.B.A.
Consulting Engineer
H. J. Manzoni, C.B.E.,
Chartered Civil Engineer.

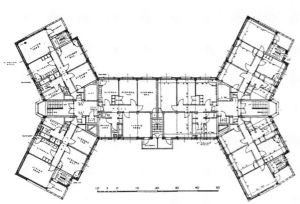

BIRMINGHAM
Top left: Duddeston and Nechells, steel construction,
  Contractor Laing.
Left: Duddeston and Nechells, plan of block.
Top right: Tile Cross, Marston Lane 1951, Wimpey No-Fines.
Above: Aston Hall / Aston Reservoir, 1952. Harry W. Weedon
  for Birmingham Council, 1952.

Was it one of the aims of building these luxury dwellings to convince Birmingham citizens that a flat could be a good place to live? That would certainly not have been said openly. But altogether it appeared obvious to many that the block of flats of some height was the type of dwelling that was now the most needed. Perhaps more clearly than anywhere else, discussions in Birmingham around 1950 laid out the basic propositions for building such blocks, both practical and visual-architectural. Sorely needed was a rise in general output, yet the land available within the city boundaries appeared practically exhausted. The blame for this was now put on the inflexible traditional desire for low-density, space-devouring swathes of two-storeyed houses (cf. p. 55), following the Garden-City movement, of which, in actual fact, Birmingham had been one of the pioneers. From 1950, a consensus grew that the building of such estates should not be favoured any more, and already by 1957 three-quarters of council dwellings were being built as flats.

The principal rationale for flats was set out by Manzoni and the House Building Committee in 1950: 'to help utilise the existing land to the fullest advantage and to increase the overall density of population without destroying the open character of the area'.[41] Thus the straightforward numerical demand for more dwellings was tied in with a very specific spatial-architectural conception: 'open planning' at high densities, whereby 'open' meant the strong preference of public open spaces over fenced-in private gardens. Groups of flats now began to arise in all parts of the city, including the outer suburban edge, with most of them surrounded by ample open space.[42]

Of course, the tenants of new Birmingham council homes, especially of flats, were all expected to pay considerably higher rents than in their previous old dwellings: the proportion of rent to income might rise from one-twentieth to one-sixth. But then, on the whole, Birmingham was a well-off city, at least until the early 1970s. At the same time one could not continue with the profligacy of the Duddesdon-Nechells blocks. Manzoni's other solution from the early 1950s was Y-shaped 'point flats', at first with six storeys and soon with eight. Contractually this coincided with mounting alarm at local building industry overstretch, which led to a decision to call in national firms, in this case principally Wimpey with their 'no-fines' technique.

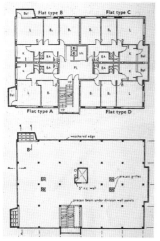

There was another aspect in which Birmingham could not stay behind: the municipality had to appoint a proper Municipal Architect whose tasks differed clearly from those of the City Engineer and City Surveyor. The choice fell upon A. G. (Alwyn Gwilyn) Sheppard Fidler, who had been making a name for himself as the architect of Crawley New Town. He was appointed in 1952, but his office was given its own separate status only in 1954. In order to bolster the architectural image of Birmingham and no doubt also to demonstrate his independent professionality, Sheppard Fidler became a very frequent speaker in national conferences on housing. There was one other major participant in these campaigns, John A. Macey, the City's Housing Manager, who saw it as his particular task to administer the new types of blocks and to help dwellers to come to terms with all the unusual features they contained. Like Sheppard Fidler, Macey occupied an important position in the national forum of his profession.[43]

In later years, Sheppard Fidler was critical of the architecture of Manzoni's blocks of flats, branding them 'mud pies,'[44] though one also needs to stress the continuity with Manzoni's basic aims, to build high flats in all parts of the city and to employ national building firms. Wherever he could, Sheppard Fidler departed from the older kinds of heavy brick walling and adopted the latest Modernist trends of glazed fronts; he also strove to replace the serried ranks of blocks preferred by Manzoni with looser ways of grouping. Along with Cleeve Barr, Sheppard Fidler argued for 'integrating the architectural department's designs with the builders' structural knowledge' (cf. p. 181).[45] His pronouncements with regard to the primacy of construction have already been cited. An extreme case, not as to height, but as regards structural boldness, was that of his much-publicised four blocks at Millpool Hill Estate. Rarely was the structural frame exposed so prominently on the outside of a block, with the walls treated as 'mere' infill of the lightest kind. To the apparent lightness of the architecture was added the openness and neatness of the surrounding grounds.

The same sense of lightness is conveyed by the designs for a new type of short slab with six flats on each floor, planned from 1958/9, and comprising either eleven or sixteen storeys, as at Lyndhurst and at Nechells Green. Here the elevation is strongly divided, asymmetrically, into two sections, with the staircase marking this division. The vertical and horizontal edges, as well as the vertical lines flanking the staircase, received a strong, added accentuation. Many of the blocks show a kind of open pergola at the top, to be used for hanging out the washing. A much lower density is conveyed by Chamberlain Gardens, on the 'better', south-west side of the city centre, a relaxed group of widely spaced nine-storey blocks, amid extensive lawns and carefully preserved old trees.

So far, we have dealt with design and layout details of estates which could be located anywhere within the conurbation; yet Birmingham's overwhelming problem was how to replace what were seen as the vast blighted areas of small nineteenth century houses. They seemed to stretch much further out from the centre than in most other towns. Apart from Duddeston Nechells, four further huge Redevelopment Areas had been marked out. Manzoni himself had helped with the national planning legislation, in 1947, which enabled municipalities to compulsorily acquire the land and demolish

the properties. Each area, it was now agreed, needed not just new housing but also all other facilities so as to create proper 'neighbourhoods'. The immediate formula available for the architect to use in this task was, of course, 'mixed development'. Sheppard Fidler and Manzoni before him had paid lip service to the concept, but in the early fifties it was flats above all that they wanted to introduce; after all, the city possessed enough houses in all locations. But in the cleared inner areas it seemed vital to provide houses as well as flats. It so happened that MHLG's influential housing design-guide, *Flats and Houses 1958*, took as a case study a district in Birmingham, Upper Highfields, for which it proposed a set of the most complex mixed development solutions, already cited above in Chapter 9. While what was built hardly looked like the drawings in the book, the principle of a mix of houses, low-rise flats and high flats was adhered to. The city then returned to the mixed development idea in the outer areas as well, and with it came again the building of much larger numbers of houses. In tune with a practice that also prevailed elsewhere, such as in Hull or Nottingham, the large and much praised Primrose Hill district, planned from 1962, showed a sharp contrast between the centrally placed seventeen-storey point/slab block and the surrounding lower kinds of houses.

In Birmingham, as elsewhere, the years around 1960 marked a low level of output. By 1962/3 this was felt to be an intolerable state of affairs, while slum clearance was accelerating and the general housing waiting list kept growing. A gigantic building campaign was set in motion, firstly on new land at the eastern edge, resulting in two totally new peripheral 'townships'. The first, Castle Bromwich (Castle Vale) comprised 5,000 dwellings of which almost 2,100 were in high flats, that is, in 35 tower blocks. One twenty-storey block marked the main access point. Eight sixteen-storey blocks formed a group, as did a larger number of the eleven-storey ones, forming a regimented array that had no parallel in the British Isles. In a much larger settlement just outside the city boundaries, Chelmsley Wood, the number of towers was even greater, but because of their generally lower height and more scattered location they make far less of a visual impact than the Castle Bromwich blocks.[46] A different kind of impression is created by a large group of thirteen-storey blocks at Druids Heath, now rather loosely sprinkled over a hilly terrain.

In the years 1965 to 1968, Birmingham's output grew enormously again and with it the proportion of high flats, the latter peaking in 1965 at 88.1% of all newly built dwellings.[47] As in most other large municipalities the much lamented low level of output in the early '60s had coincided with severe shortages in the building industry. To overcome those problems, during 1962 and 1963 Birmingham, too, searched for the 'right' system and for a contractor who could promise efficient delivery. Sheppard Fidler pleaded for Camus but the Council chose Concrete Ltd and its Bison system, with the local builder Bryant acting as the contractor; eventually 89 Bison blocks were built, and in addition, to complicate matters, Bryant also built many 'non-systems' high flats as well. Alongside this, Wimpey also continued to build many blocks in the city. In 1967 the proportion of 'systems' in the City's programme soon reached a maximum of 83%,[48] a figure which also covered low-rise construction, mostly of two-storeyed houses. Importantly, the majority of these high blocks, whether 'system' or 'traditionally' built, were largely based on designs produced by the City Architect's department, and thus the term 'package deal' cannot be taken as absolute here.

BIRMINGHAM
Above: Canterbury Tower, Summer Hill Street, 1965, City Architect with Wimpey.

Opposite page, top left: Castle Vale Scheme on the Castle Bromwich Airport Site, from 1964, Bryant.
Top right: 'Before and After in Unett Street, New Town', 1966
Bottom left: Castle Vale, seen in c. 1990.
Bottom right: Druid's Heath Alcester Road South, 1965. Bryant (Bison).

BIRMINGHAM
Left to right: Canterbury Tower, 1965, Wimpey; Durham Tower, 1968, DLO;
  Salisbury Tower, King Edward Street 1965, Wimpey.

Lee Bank RDA, Cregoe Street, 1962. City Architects and Wimpey.

Shortly later, in 1964, Sheppard Fidler left for private practice, a step that was interpreted by some as a flight from the 'output-orientated' housing procedures adopted at the instigation of the Council. Reminiscing twenty-five years later, the architect attributed the decisions taken over system-building to the manipulation of greedy councillors by contractors, not least through lavish site trips and parties:[49] It certainly seemed apposite that the next City Architect, Sheridan-Shedden, greatly favoured systems, as did his successor, Alan Maudsley, from 1968. Maudsley outlined Birmingham's ethos as follows: 'The confidence and support of the House Building Committee and the disciplined enthusiasm of the department (which spread to every contractor, public utility and statutory authority involved) enabled the entire programme to be tackled on big business lines ....'[50] The amount of work given to local contractor Bryant, however, appeared out of all proportion, building, as they did, most of Castle Vale and Chelmsley Wood – and a corruption scandal duly surfaced in the 1970s.

Top right: Prime Minister Harold Wilson with Council Leader Harry Watton in 1966 at the opening of Charlecote Tower, Cregoe Street.
Right: Alan Maudsley, Birmingham City Architect 1966–74, here seen in 1976.

188

Maudsley, like Sheppard Fidler, was also explicit about 'aesthetics', pointing to 'the availability, within a given system, of a variety of equally valid elevational treatments. This is an important means of avoiding monotony'.[51] Here the City Architect's statement is perhaps slightly misleading: the Birmingham Bison blocks of eleven to fourteen storeys look essentially the same, marked especially by the long slit that opens the balustrade of the balconies on the main facade, whether they are found in Castle Vale, in Druids Heath or among the Bromford blocks, or for that matter, in other towns as well. At the same time Birmingham also adhered to a kind of hierarchy: those Bison blocks are found only in the suburbs and hardly ever further inwards, in the proximity of the city centre. For the latter areas, a new kind of block of twenty storeys was introduced. Its shape appears to go back to 1962, when Sheppard Fidler's staff planned the seventeen-storey block for Primrose Hill. All those blocks show the same elevational formula, with bands comprising windows and balconies, but a measure of individuality was introduced by varying the sequence of windows and balconies. The first twenty-storey block came in 1963 in Cregoe Street, in the Lee Bank Redevelopment Area, close to the city centre, and was built by Wimpey. The twenty-storey contracts were shared out in five ways: to Bryant, using in-situ construction, to Bryant, using Bison, to Wimpey, to Wates, and to the City's Direct Labour Organisation.

To these towers, most of them sited within clear view of the city centre, three especially significant developments must be added, which are located in the closest proximity to key points of the city – a situation to which there is hardly a parallel anywhere else in Britain. The first group was at the Civic Centre Site at Brindley Drive: a line of fifteen and sixteen-storey towers, built in 1966–70, standing right behind the Concert Hall, and now also behind the new Library. In Birmingham's protracted saga of the planning of this new civic centre, Sheppard

BIRMINGHAM
Galton, Norton, Crescent, Cambridge Towers, Civic Centre Site, Brindley Drive ('Little Venice'), City Architect with Bryant, 1966/1968.

Plans for Civic Centre, by City Architect (Sheppard Fidler ?), c. 1964.

BIRMINGHAM
Left: 'The Sentinels of Holloway Head', early design
  by J.R. Sheridan Shedden [?], 1967/8.
Right: Air view of City Centre: In the middle ground,
  next to New Street Station, is Stevenson Tower, 1965

Fidler had envisaged, in proposals of 1958, four office slabs on the site, providing strong vertical accents for the generally horizontal look of the centre.[52] By 1965 it had been decided to build council flats instead. It formed part of a much broader new urban ideal which had entered city planning policies. For the all-powerful Leader of the Council, socialist Alderman Harry Watton, the straightforward aim was 'to bring ... living accommodation into the heart of the city';[53] '...to bring life back into the city centre', as he expressed it when he inaugurated Stephenson Tower, at the New Street Station Site, built from 1965, which, to distinguish it from all the other towers, rose to a height of twenty-one storeys.[54]

All these manifestations were outdone by a pair of blocks of quite unprecedented height, the 'Sentinels'. In 1965, Sheridan-Shedden had broached the possibility of a thirty-storey project at Holloway Circus with the House Building Committee, couching the proposal in a very tentative manner. Maudsley then developed the project after Sheridan-Shedden's death, in the process also consulting James Roberts, Birmingham's most up-to-date private practitioner. It was all to be linked to a commercial development, with shops and parking, but this never came to fruition. At an early stage it was instead decided to enlarge the towers to a height of thirty-two storeys. A published view during this design stage shows quite extravagantly glazed elevations. There was even a mention of Goldberg's strikingly circular towers in Chicago as a source of inspiration. Yet on the other hand, it was stipulated in 1967 that 'the finish of these flats would be comparable with normal Corporation standards'. Indeed, as built, the Sentinels' elevations hardly differ from those of the twenty-storey towers, as

any other architectural treatment would, one must assume, have been far too costly. Each Sentinel block contains 244 flats, eight on each floor. Construction – by Bryant, unsurprisingly – comprises an in-situ concrete frame with precast exterior 'wall units'. In the event, costs per flat amounted to £4,000 and there were hints that they would be unaffordable for many. Most decisively, the blocks were meant to mark 'an entrance to the City Centre', hence their name, which was attached to them very early on. Their completion happened at much the same time as when the Queen opened the Inner Ring Road, in April 1971. And yet, in the end, like the Stevenson Tower, the Sentinels received no attention at all at a national level. Even the regional journal, *Architecture West Midlands,* gave them only perfunctory praise, conceding that 'a great deal of effort was put into ensuring simplicity of line and form'.[55]

By then the storm-clouds of popular and media revulsion against high flats were spreading nationally; in the city the Conservatives had enjoyed an electoral triumph in 1968; it all contributed to a scaling-down flat-building altogether. At the same time, there appeared to be a moment of general contentment: 'Birmingham's housing problem all but solved, census shows'.[56] A persistent Birmingham sentiment came to the surface again, notably in the comments of Alderman Anthony Beaumont Dark, the newly-elected Conservative Chairman of the City's House Building Committee, in the *Birmingham Mail* in 1969: 'Birmingham people don't like flats, and frankly neither do I'. Beaumont Dark's conclusion was that 'ultimately he hoped that only 10 per cent of the city's total units of accommodation would be in the form of flats'.[57]

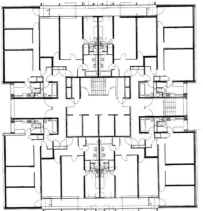

The Sentinals, Left Cleveland Tower, right Clydesdale Tower, City Architect with Bryant.

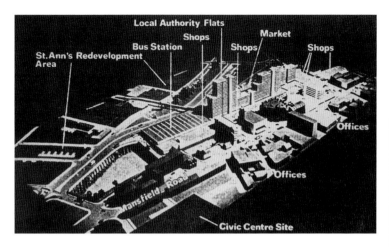

NOTTINGHAM
Victoria Centre, Arthur Swift & Partners for Nottingham Corporation,
(1964) 1968–72.

OTHER MIDLAND TOWNS

By comparison with Birmingham's precocious efforts, some other Midland cities must be called laggards in high-rise construction. NOTTINGHAM's contribution only started in 1960, with an eleven-storey maisonette slab block, Highurst Court. Traditionally housing had enjoyed cross-party support, but after 1961 a more competitive climate developed over slum-clearance and housing output. In the five years from 1963 onwards, Nottingham took to multi-storey flats wholeheartedly and rapidly. Height shot up immediately, with 21 blocks (a third of the city's total) at between sixteen and twenty-one storeys. Significantly, too, all of those 21 blocks were built by the two mightiest multi-storey contractors, Wimpey and Bison, which perhaps marks a record in 'package deal' power among larger British cities. Nottingham had been particularly slow in establishing a City Architect's Department, with David Jenkin appointed to the new post only in 1964: the Wimpey package-deals were largely negotiated with the city's Estates Surveyor and Valuer, E.W.S. Martin.[58] This state of affairs was noticed as early as mid-1964 by the national architectural establishment, i.e. the London architectural press, which contended that Nottingham's blocks were not placed in 'the right kind of spot'; soon critics saw nothing but a city 'plagued by a rash of towers'.[59] The city's towers were, nevertheless, highly diverse in their appearance and contexts, from the unusually variegated twenty-storey Wimpey tower enlivening the vast area of 1950s low-density spread of Clifton and the clump of five stark Bison towers in a denser suburban redevelopment area at Willoughby Road.

NOTTINGHAM
Southchurch Court, Farnborough
Road, Clifton,1967. Wimpey.

NOTTINGHAM
Willoughby Court, Lenton Towers,
Willoughby Street, 1965, Bison.

To set a very different and more 'market-friendly' accent, the council, Conservative-controlled from 1967 onwards, created the multifunctional Victoria Centre, 'a city centre in the true sense of the word', according to the architects, the little-known private firm of Arthur Swift & Partners, busy designers of office buildings. Approved in 1968, the complex was crowned by 500 local authority flats, twenty-two storeys high, surpassing by one floor the other Nottingham blocks. But all this was not shaped in the form of one single tower, or a series of towers, as with some other contemporary civic centres, but as a pile of sections of very different height, seemingly built up randomly. One of the blocks contains London-type 'scissor', or 'split-level' maisonettes. As one might expect in this context, these flats were not used for applicants on the Council's housing waiting list. Finally, Nottingham's largest housing undertaking, the Balloon Wood complex, started in 1966, marked the city's participation in the YDG (Yorkshire Development Group) consortium; along with Bison's inner-urban Hyson Green deck-access redevelopment of the same years, it signalled the end of point block building for Nottingham.[60]

LEICESTER
Top: Southgate RDA Proposals, 1965.
Left: Rowlatts Hill, Stephen George, City Architect with Bison, 1964.
Right: Goscote House, Single Persons' Residences, 1971, City
   Architect with Department of the Environment.

LEICESTER lagged even further behind, as pressures for rede-velopment had been considerably lower than in other cities of its size. The appointment of the Polish-born Konrad Smigielski as its first City Planning Officer in 1962 marked a new and radical modernising era, promoted by the Conservative chair of the Town Planning Committee, Kenneth Bowder. Very soon, in 1963, Smigielski was joined by a new City Architect, Stephen George, and a greatly expanded team of designers and researchers. In strong contrast to Nottingham's haphazard spread of diverse blocks, Leicester's officers produced a string of major projects, each presented as a complete entity. There was Rowlatts Hill, St Matthews, Highfields and the unbuilt Southgate project, to be situated close to the city centre, and finally the outlying

Beaumont Leys complex. 'I thought, "That's my city!" – because there were possibilities', were Smigielski's retrospective words.[61] These groups spoke the language of early 1960s plan-ning, that is, a combination of the mixed development concept with clearly marked-out complex 'urban' centres, which also appeared the ideal location for a number of closely grouped high towers – totalling some twenty overall. Some of their ele-vational detailing was to be unusually vigorous. In the event the city built only ten towers, half of them reaching more than twenty storeys; their builders were Wimpey, Laing and Bison. A rather different and quite exceptional approach was tried with Goscote House, a single-persons block in Highfields, where the elevation sharply accentuates each individual bedsit.[62]

WOLVERHAMPTON
Heath Town, Brockfield House,1967–70, Borough Architect
A Chapman. A spectacular example of a 1960s 'conglomerate' (cf. p. 79), just outside the town, mainly consisting
of long horizontal blocks which are linked by an elaborate
system of walkways; plus a component of four towers.
The contractor was Wates, the Black Country's leading
multi-storey builder.

WALSALL
Above: Bywater, Preston, Brooks Houses and
others, Union Street, Paddock RDA, 1966, Wates.

WEST BROMWICH
Below: Greenford, Lissimore, Mountford, Kenrick
Houses, Glover Street, Kenrick Way, 1964. Wates.

LIVERPOOL
Above: Coronation Court, Eaglehill Road,
  Lower Lane, Fazakerley, design of 1952.
Right: Coronation Court, 1954–56, Ronald
  Bradbury, City Architect.

LIVERPOOL

In post-war discussions of the 'housing problem', the protagonists in the major cities almost prided themselves that theirs was 'the worst'. Liverpool population figure was 800,000, compared with Birmingham's 1.1 million, but the number of its 'unfit dwellings' came close to Birmingham's, as did its early post-war output figures, 47,000 (1945 to 1965). Even though, by 1965 an astonishing 78,000 'slum houses' were still waiting to be dealt with, far more than in the other metropolis. Thus there may have been some substance to Liverpool's claims to be the 'worst' case in England. And yet the stresses and strains of planning and housing reform in Liverpool appeared somehow less divisive. The post-war 'out-county' satellite town of Kirkby was always considered a relative success story.[63]

Liverpool's urban landscape was characterised by a strong contrast between the spread-out suburban areas and the dense dwellings in the centre. Liverpool's 19th-century mass housing, especially the tenement zone close to the docks, had been much more compact than the sprawl of Birmingham's small houses. From there, it was perhaps not such a giant step towards Liverpool's massive blocks of council flats in the first period of slum-clearance in the 1930s, blocks which were given a monumental look by City Architect Lancelot Keay. In 1948 Keay was followed by Ronald Bradbury, to be more precise, by Dr. Ronald Bradbury, Ph. D., F.R.I.B.A, M.T.P.I, City Architect and Director of Housing. Bradbury had previously, as Glasgow's Director of Housing, designed that city's first high blocks. He had studied at Manchester University, like other major figures in reformist design, such as Leslie Martin and Donald Gibson; Bradbury, too, became a national authority in all matters of municipal housing, and was known for his frequent abrasiveness. To begin with, the Liverpool story parallels London's in the way Keay's monumental blocks were now becoming strongly disliked. In its new housing the city took to building medium-height blocks of flats grouped in low density formations.

LIVERPOOL
Top left: Elizabeth ('Bessie') Braddock at the 1958 opening of 'The Braddocks', with Alderman Jack Braddock (centre) and Labour Leader Hugh Gaitskell (right).
Top right: Councillor Braddock, 'finding out for herself in Everton Ward slum', 1950s.
Left: Cresswell Mount block, Everton Heights RDA, City Architect with Wimpey.

The massed building of blocks which then followed, from the mid-fifties, had few parallels. By 1981 half of Liverpool's council dwellings were flats, a very high proportion for England. The decision to build high-rises came in the early 1950s. In 1954 a Council deputation went to the USA, where they were impressed by New York's systematised public housing, but found some of its high-density estates 'rather frightening' and 'alien' in character.[64] In 1955 Bradbury also reported in detail on New York's new mass housing at the RIBA Symposium on High Flats.[65] But already in 1952 the City had started the plans for an exceedingly ambitious ten-storey experimental slab block, 'Coronation Court', curiously situated rather on the suburban edge. The design of its elevations changed greatly by the time construction began in 1954, and the façade relief provided by its complex RC frame construction was enlivened with short access balconies, all clearly designed as a contrast to the brick solidity of the City's 1930s style blocks. From 1955, Liverpool began its little-noticed contribution to the eleven-storey point block theme with the squat-looking Medea Tower at Mitylene Street.[66] In a far more prominent position, at Boyd Street on the Everton escarpment, a ten-storey maisonette block, Cresswell Mount, was begun slightly earlier, in 1954, forming part of an emerging mixed development area at the Anthony Street RDA. A far cry from London's Le Corbusier inspired maisonette slabs on stilts, Cresswell Mount, brick-faced, stood firmly on the ground. It was soon followed, from 1955, by two further blocks at Anthony Street, the 'Braddocks', completed in 1958, showing a more pronounced RC framework. Much publicity was given to their inauguration by the very councillors whose name they commemorated, John and Elizabeth Braddock, while Cresswell Mount bore the name of the late Deputy Chairman of the Housing Committee.[67]

Above: 'A 21-storey block is shown against the Liver Building', 1957.

LIVERPOOL
Above: Cresswell Mount, 1954–57.

Right: Everton Heights. To the left, Cresswell Mount; in the foreground the two 10-storey 'The Braddocks – J. and E. Blocks', 1955–58 (cf. p. 258).

With the attention that these Everton developments attracted, as bright splashes in a sea of unrelieved greyness, the Council now wanted to sound enthusiastic about going higher.[68] Now the usual arguments were marshalled in support: lack of land, proximity to the workplace and a long housing waiting list. Local newspapers advocated higher blocks, even of 21 floors, arguing in 1957 that this would be 'two storeys greater than even the highest in use in London' and they compared the twenty-storey dividing-line with the 'barrier in the world of aeronautics'.[69] In fact, any height would be acceptable in Liverpool, as long as it remained below that of the Royal Liver Building. Alderman David Nickson, Chairman of the Housing Committee, was more cautious in his advocacy: 'these buildings will not be a sore finger ... on the landscape. We are quite sure in our minds that the living accommodation is good ... what worries us is the people ... they will be working class, they have always been

used to the more ordinary types of dwelling ... if we can persuade the people to accept this type of building as a reasonable home, then we will have achieved something worthwhile.'[70]

By the early 1960s Liverpool had completed a total of eight blocks of ten and eleven storeys, hardly an achievement compared with Birmingham, let alone with the LCC in London. The journey from verbal publicity to realisation was a long one. It did not help that the political factions in the council were at loggerheads, with Maxwell Entwistle's Conservative administration pushing for bold gestures and Labour here being on the cautious side. 1961 was as anxious a year in Liverpool as elsewhere: output had fallen to 1,517, compared with 2,408 in 1958. Now the decision was taken to set an annual target of 5,000 completions, and 1961 saw the start of 24 blocks, still of no more than eleven storeys in height, though the upper limit

LIVERPOOL
Right: Entwistle Heights, 1961–65.
Bottom: Entwistle Heights and
Milner House, Harding Street,
Parliament Street; Ronald
Bradbury, City Architect, as
presented at the London Royal
Academy 1960 (cf. p. 42).

went up to 14 and 16 in the following years. In terms of publicity,
all this was outshone by Entwistle Heights, a twenty-two-storey
block at Harding Street, whose drawings were proudly exhib-
ited in London at the 1960 Royal Academy Exhibition, though it
was only competed in 1965. As regards the number of flats, 168
on 21 floors, i.e. 8 flats per floor, this was easily the largest sin-
gle-block project of its date anywhere. Construction comprised
in-situ r.c. frame with brick and concrete panel infilling, so that
a quite delicate-looking framework is clearly evident. While it
was still under construction, however, attention had already
turned towards Liverpool's next major undertaking.

**LIVERPOOL'S NEXT FLATS WILL
BE 22 STOREYS HIGH**

LIVERPOOL
'Pilot Maisonettes', Classic Road, 1963. Camus 'in conjunction with Dr. R. Bradbury'.

Ground floor of the Camus block, Sheil Road.

Sheil Road, from 1964, Camus System. view c. 1990.

In 1962 a Liverpool delegation went to Paris, where they were duly impressed by the busiest of the French 'systems' firms, Camus. In early 1963 a massive contract was announced, for 2,486 dwellings in twenty-two and fifteen-storey blocks, plus 1,206 garages. In contrast to Camus's partnerships with vast state building combines in the USSR, here the usual British arrangement of licensing by a local firm would apply – in this case the well-regarded Unit Construction Company Ltd. A factory was erected by Unit on land leased from the Corporation. To demonstrate the system's capabilities, a small block of maisonettes was built quickly in Classic Road in 1963, whereupon Bradbury and Camus devised their 'standard' twenty-two-storey Camus tower – which in plan and overall shape essentially continued the Harding Street block. Among the 'package' firms Camus had a good reputation for straightforwardness as well as flexibility. The construction was described, in Camus's own words, as one that 'entirely eliminated a

structural frame in the traditional sense, the walls and floor slabs when grouted together forming the equivalent of a monolithic structure'.[71] The first six twenty-two-storey blocks were begun in 1964, mostly on small gap sites to maximise dwelling gain. Logan Tower at Boundary Street was the first to be completed in 1966; altogether ten such blocks were built by the end of the 1960s.

Taken together, Liverpool towers featured a wide spectrum of differing elevations. There was a strong contrast between, on the one hand, the flat and extremely repetitive elevations of the Camus towers, in all their concrete whiteness, with dwellings right down to the bottom, and, on the other hand, many of the fourteen to seventeen-storey blocks, which were clad in red brick or had red brick infill, with a more elaborate roof line and varied uses of the ground floor, all of which suggested a somewhat higher level of comfort. These blocks occur in most parts

LIVERPOOL
Hartsbourne Avenue,
Childwall, 1963–64. Wimpey.

Belem Tower, Aigburth Drive, Princes Park. 1958.
Ronald Bradbury, City Architect.

Ullet Road, Sefton Park. 1963.

of the city. But it was still a very bold move, in socio-political terms, to put a line of them on the edge of Sefton Park in one of the 'best' districts of the city, embedded in greenery, at the Croxteth Drive development of 1963–5. However, a precedent had already been set in 1958 with the placing of the eleven-storey Belem Tower at Aigburth Drive, at the very entrance of Sefton Park, an extraordinary position for a council tower block, in a location where one would normally expect a picturesque gatehouse.

Taking stock nearer the end of the 1960s, the number of blocks dotted all over the urban landscape had grown rapidly. Liverpool excelled with its fourteen to sixteen-storey towers, 81 of them, against Birmingham's 55 blocks of that height. As in Leeds the building scene was largely contractor-led, with Wimpey taking a large share. All this proceeded relatively unaffected by the radical changes in the City's government during 1963. Alderman Jack Braddock had died in that year. Bradbury remained 'City Architect', but was divested of his responsibility for housing,

LIVERPOOL
Above: View 146, Blocks A and B, Great Homer Street, 1963.
Right: Northwood, Liverpool/Kirkby, 1964.

which was taken over by the architect J.W. Boddy, now the 'Director of Housing'. More important appeared the fact that a glaring gap was now being filled: so far there had been no Town Planning Department; this was instituted in 1962, with Walter Bor as the City's first Planning Officer; it meant that a younger generation of planners was now trying to establish a power-base. Bor was highly sceptical about many aspects of the existing policy on tower blocks, especially their ubiquitous and dispersed siting, and, with his colleague Graeme

Shankland, immediately proposed, in 1962–3, a most ambitious city centre renewal project, the so-called 'Strand Paradise', which included a concentrated group of five very high blocks, but which remained on paper.[72] Theirs was also the outer suburban development at Netherley, built from 1967, containing 16 eight-storey deck blocks with over 1,300 dwellings. It was one of the many conglomerates of those years, in this case no longer featuring any towers at all.

BOOTLE
Strand House, Washington Parade, 1965, in c.1990 and in 2014

BIRKENHEAD
Central Area Redevelopment, Eldon Place, Oak Street, from 1956. T.A. Brittain,
Borough Architect with Arup Engineers and Prometo construction system.

MANCHESTER
Heywood, Argyle Street, Darn Hill, 1962–63, V. Austen Bent, Director of Housing with Laing and Sectra system.

MANCHESTER REGION AND BEYOND

For the many corporations that make up this region, one of the ways in which they could express their identities was with their particular outlook regarding multi-storey blocks. The City of MANCHESTER itself appeared as one of the most reluctant, tower-averse of all English municipalities,[73] while only a few yards away, Salford was classed the most enthusiastic in the whole of England. Among the most vehement slum-clearance apostles had been the Mancunians Sir Ernest Simon and Lady Simon, but they linked this entirely with a fervent advocacy of garden suburbs, trumpeting their satellite township of Wythenshawe as a shining example. By the early sixties, general output in Manchester, as in most other cities, considered low, though vigorous plans were also in train for demolition of some 68,000 'unfit' dwellings. Manchester's problem was not land shortage but a lack of urge to build. Pressure to step up building came principally from the Medical Officer of Health and, unusually, directly from the Ministry of Housing. By 1959–60, finally, the first plans for blocks of sixteen storeys emerged, but only blocks of eight storeys were built, Manchester being by now some ten years behind London and Birmingham. From 1961 onwards Wimpey and Laing began building twelve-storey blocks; it was the latter firm that made the running from here onwards. Manchester's high blocks attracted national attention

only once, when, after abortive negotiations with Camus, Laing built its first four thirteen-storey Sectra blocks in an 'out-county' estate at Heywood; along with Taylor Woodrow in London and Camus in Liverpool, this marked the important step of the country-wide acceptance of foreign 'systems'.[74] From 1962 onwards, the thirteen-storey type of block became the Manchester staple, 61 of them being completed. In overall numbers of high blocks, Manchester gradually caught up with many other cities, but their size remained relatively modest, with seventeen storeys being the maximum. In the context of the City's other mighty buildings, especially its city centre offices, council towers made no great impression at all, in contrast to, say, the way in which high blocks impacted on the centres of Newcastle or Birmingham. Manchester Council's particular aversion to height also helped to fuel another sharp twist in housing architecture, towards medium-height, deck-access 'conglomerate' complexes in Hulme, from 1966, and in Longsight and elsewhere, which rarely exceeded ten storeys in height. Among the designers was Chief Assistant City Architect Robert Stones, a sworn enemy of towers.[75] Overall this paralleled what happened in Leeds, Sheffield and elsewhere, whereby the perceived failure of the Manchester complexes appeared more severe than in those cities.

Just across the road, SALFORD's policies were the diametric opposite of Manchester's. In total contrast to Manchester – though somewhat like Glasgow, Salford saw itself as a city under threat from overspill pressure, from Manchester's expansionism as well as from a shortage of land – and thus massed multi-storey building appeared the obvious response. The city's performance was in line with the most ambitious towns, beginning with an eight-storey block in 1954, then proceeding to eleven and twelve storeys from 1958 and to fifteen storeys from 1960, finally reaching twenty-three storeys by the end of the decade. The city then shot into national prominence with a major development formed out of two adjacent redevelopment areas, Ellor Street and High Street, right in the centre, organised from 1960 by the ambitious City Engineer, G. Alexander McWilliam and his chief architect J.H. Earle. Fundamental here was a total adversity to overspill. The aim was to completely replace all the old dwellings with well over 2,400 modern ones on the same 89-acre site: there were to be fourteen fifteen-storey slabs and assorted twelve and four-storey blocks, with plenty of open space in between. At one end of the area the plan envisaged a vehicle-free shopping district.

When, after building three fourteen-storey slab blocks, the project began to suffer long delays, the Ministry of Housing's architects exploited the situation to try to bring it under architectural control, somewhat as a provincial echo of the famous 1949/50 LCC coup.[76] In a withering critique of McWilliam's layout, Cleeve Barr argued that the 'architectural arrangement of most of the blocks of housing appears accidental and based mainly on a theoretical north – south axis. The spaces around buildings would be architecturally unpleasant and the views would be ... haphazard to the extreme'.[77] These comments by somebody who would normally be expected to pass judgment primarily on organisational matters indicate the rapid and widely shared changes of architectural preferences in those years. McWilliam's slabs and flowing spaces would have seemed ideal in the late 1940s, but by 1960 a generally much denser look was preferred. To rectify matters, an external academic consultant was brought in: none other than the mastermind of '1949', ex-LCC chief architect Robert Matthew himself, together with his Edinburgh University 'Architectural Research Unit' and his planning colleague Percy Johnson-Marshall, who was in effect to be chief design co-ordinator; finally there was Arup, as the engineer. All this constituted a rare example of a national intervention in municipal affairs.

The no-overspill principle of the project was retained, to be recast to reflect the denser and more complex architectural ideas of the time. It now comprised three distinct areas, a high density residential area (185 p.p.a), a large shopping and commercial centre, and a fully-fledged civic centre. The housing would consist of meandering ranges of maisonettes up to eight storeys high, as well as eleven identical towers of twenty-three storeys. Five of them were built. The plan still envisaged green spaces, all strictly pedestrianised, and tightly enclosed by the long ranges of the maisonettes. However, progress was still extremely slow. The civic centre plans were abandoned on cost grounds, typically for the period, and the shopping centre was

treated as a separate entity, including a tower to be let at cost rent. Building took until the early 1970s, now with much more heterogeneous sets of high blocks, but still dominated by the twenty-three-storey towers. Contractors included Salford's Direct Labour force and local pre-casting company Fram, which, somewhat quirkily, collaborated with the Edinburgh Architectural Research Unit to devise its own 'system' for the seventeen-storey blocks. The result was a notable design solution in the way the edges of each external panel are clearly marked. As eventually completed, the Ellor Street/Church Street redevelopment was a veritable English *grand ensemble.* Ironically, though, with its reliance on serried ranks of slab blocks, as well as its relatively wide open spaces, the development in many ways returned to McWilliam's concept of 1960. All in all, however, Salford's policy to retain all its inhabitants within its boundaries resulted in one major distinction, namely of achieving the highest capita output of public housing of any English city.

SALFORD
Ellor Street Area, old and new in 1966.

SALFORD
Top: Ellor Street Area, view from the East
Above left: Ellor Street Project 1960, Salford City Architect.
Above right: Ellor Street, the Robert Matthew – Johnson-
  Marshall project, from 1964.
Right: Ellor Street, the 1972 view includes Salford Shopping
  City and its tower.

STRETFORD
Stretford House, Chapel Lane 1965, the highest block in the Manchester
conurbation, nicknamed 'Perry's Folly' after a former Borough Engineer.

ROCHDALE
Top: College Bank, College Road, Falinge
   Area B , begun 1964, view from the town centre.
Middle: A preliminary study, 1964.
Bottom: View from the South.

As a set-piece of council towers dominating the centre of a middling town, it would be hard to match ROCHDALE's College Bank group, with its proud array of blocks of 17 and 21 storeys. A run-down area happened to lie close to the town centre as well as being situated on a ridge. The towers were grouped with the utmost care in spacing and height when seen from the centre. The group soon received a nickname,

the 'Seven Sentinels' and was indeed 'regarded as part of the town centre development rather than of the normal housing programme'; 'rents [in its 750 flats] are a good deal higher than the usual Corporation dwellings'. Applicants had to be of 'good standard'.[78] According to the contractors it was 'designed by Wimpey to the requirements of H.G. Mercer, Borough Engineer'.

PRESTON
Sandown Court, Avenham Lane, 1963.
Building Design Partnership (BDP).
Oxford Street, Development from 1959 to
1967, BDP and Lyons, Israel & Ellis.

The housing in PRESTON's principal re-development area, Avenham, close to the town centre, has the extremely rare distinction of being designed by several nationally renowned (meaning: London) architects, resulting in the even rarer distinction, for public housing, of being mentioned in Pevsner's original *Buildings of England* series.[79] From 1963 onwards, Lyons, Israel & Ellis designed eleven-storey blocks and James Stirling and James Gowan contributed distinctive high-density-medium-rise groups. The Building Design Partnership, whose principal, (Sir) Grenfell Baines came from Preston and who kept a branch office there, designed the two tall towers. Unusually, they are fitted out with maisonettes on the top floor; comments stressed that 'the normal [Bison] finish of the panels has been enhanced by the use of three types of exposed aggregate which give strong contrast ... a unique character.'[80]

Leeds's claim to 'fame' with regard to bad housing lay with its 'back-to-backs', a term which primarily signified not the bad state of old housing, but a 'bad' *type* of housing, in fact the 'worst' of all of English housing types. The first council-housing reaction against that world of small crowded dwellings in the inner suburbs, with their dense street networks, was one of a most unusual grandeur: the Quarry Hill complex, begun in 1934. Forming not just a series of individual buildings, as was normal with 1930s housing, the estate consisted mainly of enormous continuous, rounded blocks, up to eight storeys high. Its construction comprised a new French kind of steel frame, clad with pre-cast concrete panels, and it boasted numerous advanced services. After the war, however, it experienced escalating problems and was entirely demolished in 1978.[81] The architect of the estate, R.A.H. Livett (designated City Architect from 1948), helped shape the city's council housing with a succession of major projects until and beyond his death in 1959. His second major undertaking, of 500 dwellings, was Saxton Gardens,

planned before the war, but built during the later 1950s. This time Livett chose a series of high slab blocks. But instead of adhering to the model of the newly-completed Churchill Gardens in Pimlico, with its regular *Zeilenbau* formation of rows of identical blocks, the seven slab blocks at Saxton Gardens present a kind of crescendo, with the first row of blocks being of five storeys, the next ones seven and nine, and the culmination coming with a centre part of ten storeys.

Livett's next ambitious project was a totally different proposition. The city's rulers, notably Housing Committee Chairman, Alderman Karl Cohen, embarked, uniquely in the mid-1950s, on a large-scale rehabilitation programme of older houses; but this improvement drive was strictly balanced with large-scale new construction, including high blocks on gap sites and larger peripheral developments. From 1957, Livett responded to this demand by means of the new orthodoxies of mixed development, including point blocks and slab blocks, and planned

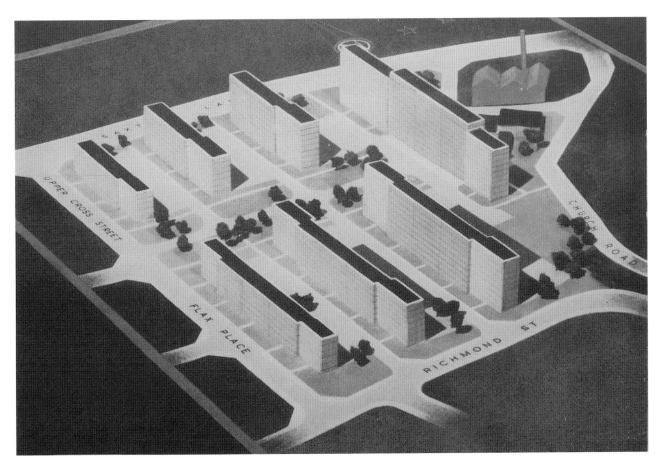

LEEDS
Saxton Gardens, Flax Place (1939) 1955–57, R.A.H. Livett City Architect.

LEEDS
'Design for ten-storey "point blocks" to be erected on several sites, in the inner and outer suburbs'; City Architect R.A.H. Livett 1956.

Map of part of New Town area, 1962.

Four builders following Livett's scheme: Sims, Reema, Shepherd, Wimpey.

more than a dozen schemes in several locations, totalling almost 3,000 flats. There are houses and four-storey maisonettes, as well as a large number of eight, nine and, predominantly, ten-storey blocks. For these high blocks, Livett devised two prototypes, a T-shaped point block and a short slab block, comprising a detailed plan and a generic elevation. In a variant on the negotiated-contractor formula, newly practiced by the LCC, six builders, local and national, namely Myton, Shepherd, Townson, Simms, Reema, Wimpey, were each allocated a number of blocks and invited to 'adapt' the design 'to suit their own constructions'.[82] Architecturally, the experiment in Leeds brought mainly a number of variations of detail, such as at the

rooflines, or the shape of the balconies. The large Yorkshire builder, Shepherd & Son Ltd., was bold enough to announce that its blocks were 'designed and built by Shepherd'. The largest share fell to Reema, which was by that time advertising itself as a 'specialist in concrete building'; its main contribution was the prefabrication of most elements, including external slabs. Until years later the firm put stress on both the originality and the quantity output of its 'system' in Leeds. Indeed, Reema had come out with the cheapest construction – and Wimpey the most expensive. And yet it was Wimpey which was to take the lion's share of housing in Leeds in the 1960s.

LEEDS

Top: Lincoln Towers, Lindsey Mount Towers, Ferriby Towers, Granville Road, Lincoln Road New Town, from 1958.

Right: 'Proposed 23-storey flats', J.R. Sheridan-Shedden, City Architect, 1960.

Leeds's council housing in the 1960s was a very different story. Like Liverpool, Leeds now laid stress on a sudden leap upwards. In 1960, Livett's successor as City Architect, J.R. Sheridan-Shedden, caught the limelight with an announcement of 'twenty-three-storey blocks in Leeds housing plans', one floor higher than the recently announced Liverpool block.[83] A few years later, in his City Architect position in Birmingham, Sheridan-Shedden was to propose the highest Council Towers in the land, the thirty-two-storey Sentinels. The Leeds design, in the way it is drawn, makes a pronounced departure from the solid-wall effect of the Livett groups, by sharply exposing the thinnest kinds of stilts at the ground and first floor levels and by featuring a light elevational pattern above. Secondly, as everywhere else in the early sixties, the demand in Leeds was for quantity, and thus the 1960 announcement stressed numbers, promising 35 blocks of multi-storey flats on seven different estates throughout the city, including a number of seventeen-storey blocks. The first set of twelve-storey towers, the widely publicised Wellington Hill (Barncroft Drive),[84] shown at the Royal Academy, was begun in 1961. With its exposed ground floor stilts, the design follows Sheridan-Shedden's twenty-three-storey project to some extent. But with the higher blocks during the following years the design contribution by the City Architect's office, now headed by

LEEDS
Clyde Court, Clyde Grange, Wellington Road, Wortley, 1965, Builder: Costain

E. W. Stanley, tended to merge with the constructional neces-
sities of the package dealers. An elevation that essentially
presented hole-in-the-wall pattern could hardly accommodate
the delicate rhythmic variations of Sheridan-Shedden's model
block. Essentially the Leeds housebuilding scene was, during
the later 1960s, in the hands of the builders, operating under
repeat negotiated contracts. Altogether there were nine firms,
though half of all multi-storey contracts went to Wimpey, totalling 55 blocks: in 1969 the firm could look back proudly to 'seventeen busy years' in the city.[85]

As the 1960s wore on, the housing scene in Leeds, just as in
Liverpool, became increasingly divided. While the contractors
held sway, quantitatively, a counter-movement was also taking
hold, as local-authority architects organised designer-controlled 'consortia' for system-building. The Leek Street development of 1966–68 was the first major outcome of the Yorkshire
Development Group's undertaking, which was dominated by a
preference for 'conglomerate' designs and an implicit or explicit
dislike of high flats. The YDG's chief designer, ex-LCC architect
Martin Richardson, was on record as a trenchant opponent of

LEEDS
Torre Road, Ebor Gardens, Burmantofts, 1966. Wimpey (cf. p. 118).

Ald. I. N. Bellow, Chairman of Leeds Housing and Property Management Committee, outside the 25-storey Cottingley Heights flats, which he opened yesterday.

No more tall flats for Leeds-Alderman

LEEDS
Cottingley Heights / Towers 1970, Wimpey.

The Yorkshire Evening Post, 1972.

tower blocks.[86] By the end of the 1960s came the national policy switch towards 'rehab' of old houses – already well-established in Leeds – as well as a new trend towards more intimate kinds of new housing, dubbed 'village districts'. For council towers in Leeds, there only remained one final fling in 1970, in the form of a pair of soaring twenty-five-storey Wimpey blocks on a hill in outer-suburban Cottingley. As a mixed development, this estate also represented an extreme solution, its other component being just a carpet of diminutive-looking houses. Yet as with so many other massive last-gasp projects in towns up and down the country, Leeds's most striking contribution to post-war tower block housing received no professional publicity at all.

ROTHERHAM
Beaversleigh, Clifton
RDA, 1968–70.

HALIFAX
Shaw Lodge, Shaw Hill, 1967–70, J.L. Berbiers, Borough Architect wtih Wimpey;
  avoiding North-facing windows for living rooms.
Westbrook, Blenheim and Cobden Courts, Richmond Road RDA, 1969.

An altogether more relaxed ambience could be found in KINGSTON UPON HULL. Here, land was more plentiful and the 19th-century mass housing appeared far less dense and threatening. The late 1950s saw small groups of nine-storey balcony access slabs and the early 1960s a number of fifteen-storey blocks. In 1963, City Architect David Jenkin began the planning of Orchard Park, three miles north of the centre, ultimately comprising around 3,500 dwellings in successive 'villages'. Bransholme, even further out, speaks the same language with the flatness of swathes of lawns and curved streets, lined by smallish-looking houses, all bristling with innovation. In 1965–7, Orchard Park was augmented by eleven gap-site towers of considerable height, including four of 20 and 22 storeys, creating the most striking contrast. A similarly placed pair of seventeen-storey blocks was added to Bransholme. The dominant tower contractor in Hull was Truscon, but the Orchard Park blocks are by Wimpey; their unusually complex outline is reminiscent of their contemporary blocks at Clifton in Nottingham, but at Hull the high blocks were added not as an afterthought but as part of a comprehensive strategy. In the later 1960s, Hull's story, too, ends with two YDG undertakings, the conglomerates at Bransholme and Linnaes Street.

SUNDERLAND, a Labour stronghold, maintained a high output of public housing throughout. From 1964 a systems-minded Borough Architect, Harvey Bishop, began to judiciously enlist many of the top national firms to participate in the housing drive. Gilley Law, a large complex situated just outside the town, including seven seventeen-storey towers, was the second major Taylor-Woodrow/Larsen-Nielsen commission in the country, following on from the LCC's Morris Walk. Hahnemann Street, 1964, was a relatively early seven-storey deck access complex, allowing Laing to adapt their Sectra system for this building type, a modification which would later be reproduced in several more controversial schemes for the Northern Ireland Housing Trust. Wimpey began its Sunderland blocks in 1963 and Bison followed in 1964. For good measure there were also several blocks built directly by Direct Labour. Most innovative in planning terms was the Town Central Area development of 1967–70, built by Gilbert-Ash and combining a commercial centre and multi-storey car park, crowned by three nineteen-storey council towers; a rare built example of this type, at a time when so many similar schemes remained on paper. In this case the designers were prominent architects from outside, something more likely to happen with undertakings that were more than just council housing.

HULL

Above: Dodsthorpe and Milldane, Orchard Park, 1965–67, Wimpey.
Below: Padstow House, Bransholme, 1968.

SUNDERLAND
Above: Gilley Law, North Moor
  Lane, 1964. Builder Taylor
  Woodrow Anglian / Larsen-
  Nielsen system.
Right: Gilley Law, early view.
Below: Central Development,
  Harvey C. Bishop Borough
  Architect with Joint Architects
  Ian Fraser and Associates
  and Llewellyn-Davies, Weeks,
  Forestier-Walker and Bor.
  (1961) 1967–69.

GATESHEAD
Teams Redevelopment Area, Redheugh and Eslington Court, 1966.

THORNABY ON TEES (TEESSIDE)
Anson and Hudson Houses, Wheeldale Crescent, 1962, Shepherd Spacemaker System.

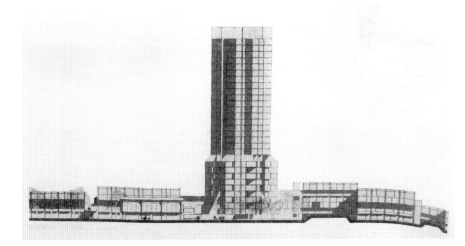

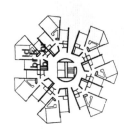

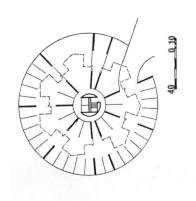

WHICKHAM
Derwent Tower at Dunston, Ravensworth Road RDA (1966) 1967–69, The Owen Luder Partnership.

Rearing up out of the peri-urban Tyneside sprawl, there stood (until its 2012 demolition) one of the very rare cases of a prominent private London architect designing large-scale multi-storey housing in the English provinces – the thirty-storey Derwent Tower by Owen Luder, built in 1967–69, in this case even more incongruously, for the small urban district council of WHICKHAM. In a way, this tower could also be counted among the London extravaganzas pictured at the beginning of this section – although we should note that almost all of Luder's prominent work actually was in the provinces. The tower was part of a mixed development, or rather a 1960s conglomerate-type of a group of dwellings, containing three and five-storey housing, all linked by walkways. The tower's most exceptional shape and construction consisted of a slender, stepped shaft ringed by polygonal extrusions; it stemmed from the decision not to use piles for the foundation but a 'Lorenz Fehlmann' caisson, that is, a tub-shaped structure which had to be both wide for stability, and round so as to help with the even distribution of forces; at the same time the space inside the caisson could be used as a large car park. The broader lower part of the tower, containing two bedroom flats, was partly supported by leaning buttresses. The narrower top part contained one-bedroomed flats. Most of Luder's works featured daring displays of boldly curved or oddly-angled concrete, and thus he may be called a 'Brutalist', though he did not belong exactly to the Goldfinger, Smithson, or Lasdun camps. The plan of the tower does, however, evoke the latter's Bethnal Green cluster block of the decade before – a project with which this section began.

NEWCASTLE UPON TYNE
Cruddas Park, Park Road, Scotswood Development,
with Cruddas Park House, 1960–62
George Kenyon, City Architect with Wimpey.
Cruddas Park seen from bridge (see next page).

NEWCASTLE UPON TYNE

The public housing of Newcastle can be seen as a kind of median of all that has been reported about English towns so far. The number of unfit dwellings was somewhat lower than elsewhere, but their clearance was still given much emphasis. Tentative beginnings towards height came during the early to mid-fifties, with a quickening of the pace and a jump to new formulae at the end of that decade. A spate of fifteen-storey blocks followed in the early and mid-1960s, along with a few twenty-storey point blocks, culminating in slim twenty-six and twenty-eight-storey towers in 1966–68; in the wider Newcastle conurbation, too, the tower block story ends with two massive tower-less conglomerates.

Within Newcastle's post-war housing programme, the driving political leadership provided by the Housing Committee Chairman (1958–62) and, later, Council Leader, T. Dan Smith, complemented the consistent design leadership of the City Architect, George Kenyon. In one major respect, Newcastle council housing, especially high flats, differed markedly from most of the major English towns, namely in the relative strength of the local building firms, above all Stanley Miller, and the weakness of 'national' contractors and package dealers; Wimpey's and Laing's share was comparatively small.

Architecturally, Kenyon turned away from the uniformly brick-clad and window-as-hole mode to one that emphasised the building's skeleton, leading to sharp outlines and regular horizontal and vertical bands. Wall segments are clearly shown to be inserts. This remained Newcastle's formula for most blocks

and its first manifestation came in a group of five fifteen-storey towers included in a redevelopment at Scotswood Road/ Cruddas Park, from 1960. This group acted as the introductory showpiece of Newcastle's new housing, to signal the arrival of T. Dan Smith's new 'Modern Newcastle' above the city's celebrated riverfront,[87] especially when the giant twenty-storey slab of the Cruddas Park Neighbourhood Centre was added to it. A further mark on the skyline above the river is provided by the three twenty-storey hillside towers of Westgate Road of 1961–63, displaying 'a bold and simple silhouette on this very prominent site'.[88] The Shieldfield group followed, very close to the city centre, its fifteen-storey blocks being complemented by one slender twenty-six-storey block. At Jesmond Vale (from 1966), the same type was extended up to twenty-eight storeys, though this height is somewhat negated by the development's location in a valley – one comment on its completion hailed it as 'well sited both in prospect and aspect ...without being oppressive'. In 1967, while the Jesmond Vale tower was still being built, the LONGBENTON Urban District Council, just north of the city, started its Killingworth Township as a vast exurban conglomerate of deck blocks up to ten storeys high, dominating its ultra-low-density surroundings like a glowering citadel, rather than a 'rocket'. Within Newcastle proper, in 1971 the council finally began with a truly exceptional design, the Byker development, this time designed by an internationally renowned architect, Ralph Erskine. With its most sophisticated quirky kind of randomness it could not have been further from the sharp rectangularity of Kenyon's Modernist discipline; the straight verticality of a slim tower had now become something unthinkable.

NEWCASTLE
Cruddas Park House, Scotswood Road Development, Westmoreland Road, with shopping centre, 1965.

NEWCASTLE
Todds Nook, Westgate Court, Vallum Court in Westgate Road
1961, City Architect George Kenyon, with builder Stanley Miller.

NEWCASTLE
Vale House, Jesmond Vale, 1966–68, Douglass Wise
& Partners with builder Stanley Miller, builder.

NEWCASTLE
Above: Shielfield Area, from 1959;
  the central tower, Shielfield House,
  1967; builder Stanley Miller.
Left: Byker Development, Ralph
  Erskine, 1968–84.

Ravenswood 1, Cumbernauld NewTown, built 1965–66, Cumbernauld Development Corporation architects (Northside Group, Roy Hunter group leader) with Concrete Scotland Ltd. The design-led development process at Cumbernauld contrasted strongly, and intentionally, with the production-led approach of Glasgow Corporation - whose vast programme dominates much of this chapter. The CDC architects' integrated planning and landscape concept for the town's housing zone was based on a site-specific scheme of low-rise high-density terraces, punctuated by a landmark line of point blocks along the 'Northside' escarpment. The blocks were designed in a customised variant of Bison Wall-Frame and let to higher-income 'executive' tenants.

14 Scotland

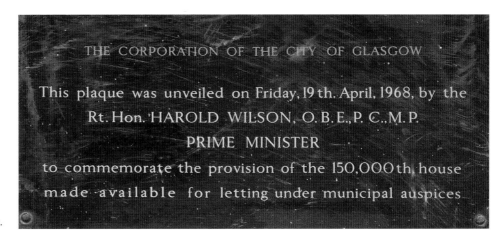

THE CORPORATION OF THE CITY OF GLASGOW

This plaque was unveiled on Friday, 19th April, 1968, by the
Rt. Hon. HAROLD WILSON, O. B. E., P. C., M. P.
PRIME MINISTER
to commemorate the provision of the 150,000th house
made available for letting under municipal auspices

Springburn CDA Area B – com-
memorative plaque in the lobby
of one of the 26-storey blocks
(198 Balgrayhill Road, see p. 230).

We saw in Chapter 4 that the uniquely British national system of 'council housing' took a uniquely exaggerated form in postwar Scotland, in a self-reinforcing, circular interaction of local political power and pressure, low rents and high output – and that the unchallenged focus of this system was the general-needs building programme of Glasgow Corporation, led with uncompromising force by the city's Housing Committee – a programme that also encompassed local employment in the prominent role of the city's 'direct labour' building force, the Housing and Works Department (HWD), which accounted for two-thirds of the city's mid-1950s housing output of around 4,000 or 5,000 dwellings per year. Architecturally, Scottish council housing had differed quite strongly from its English and Welsh equivalents up to the late 1950s, in the dominance of low-rise flats (as opposed to cottages, or 'houses' in the English sense) in all urban settings. In villages and small towns, the dominant Scottish form was the so-called 'four in a block', a two-storey block of four flats, whereas in the four cities (Glasgow, Edinburgh, Dundee and Aberdeen) and the larger Clydeside towns, three or four-storey tenement blocks predominated, built of bricks or blockwork and similar in their staircase-access plan-form to the middle-class tenements of 19th-century Scotland, but laid out in open patterns, in and around expansive courtyards, more like the slightly later, 'sectional' planned low-rise blocks of Khrushchev's USSR. But from the late 1950s, these low-rise tenements started to be drastically reduced in numbers, and instead there was an upsurge in building of multi-storey tower blocks, quite similar in some respects to the towers in many English and Welsh provincial cities.

To some extent, it could be argued, this move from tenements to towers amounted to a diminution of Scottish 'architectural distinctiveness' in housing architecture, although there were still some subtle and strong differences: the Scottish towers tended to be rather taller in height, and were frequently used on their own, as part of high-density infill developments. In addition, in Scotland there were relatively fewer deck-access developments, probably because of the lack of any earlier tradition

of gallery-access workers' flats – although the programmes of the Glasgow and Dundee city councils in the late 60s and 70s briefly featured a considerable output of deck blocks. But this shift towards very high blocks also formed part of a Britain-wide development: by the late 1950s, as Chapter 4 highlighted, the escalating conflict in many cities over slum-clearance and land strategy, between municipal 'housers' and reformist regional planners, had begun to provoke many councils into building multi-storey flats, often in a rather haphazard manner, to defend themselves from losing population and revenue through population 'overspill', by retaining decanted slum-cleared populations within their own boundaries at high density. That pattern applied as much in the city of Birmingham as in Glasgow, but the scale of the tower blocks, and their relative prominence within the new cityscape, was much smaller in the English city.

GLASGOW

However, many of the respects in which Scottish towers appeared to be 'different' from those in England, including the built-form aspects mentioned above, as well as a somewhat greater emphasis on 'package-deal' contractor-designed projects as opposed to schemes designed by local-authority or private architects, were in fact distinctive features not so much of Scotland as a whole, as of the City of Glasgow in particular. This was hardly surprising, as it was in Glasgow that the battle between housers and planners reached its all-time climax, and land supply and housing location became the focus of uniquely bitter confrontations – reflecting the dominance of the 'Glasgow housing problem' within Scottish national housing and planning circles – a dominance not equalled by any city in England, other than London itself.[1] The eventual result of this was an extreme production emphasis, focused, as we will see shortly, on very high towers in package-deal schemes – an approach not found to the same extent in any other city in Britain, Scottish or English.

Glasgow, Woodside CDA Area A, from 1964, Concrete Ltd (Bison) with City Architect A G Jury.

Springburn CDA, Area B, Phases 1 and 2, Balgrayhill Road, 1964–68, four 26-storey towers designed and built by Reema Scotland.

Initially, during the 1940s and early/mid 1950s, Glasgow had not seemed a likely focus for large-scale tower-building: in contrast for instance to 'anti-flat' Birmingham, the continuing predominance of 3 and 4-storey tenements within Glasgow Corporation's housing programme had been sufficient to maintain annual output at around 4,000 or 5,000 flats, mainly on peripheral sites like Drumchapel and Easterhouse. In 1944–49, the Housing Department had devised its own system of concrete large-panel precasting, using 'foamslag' aggregate from power station waste, and had built an ambitious precasting factory at Amulree Street, Tollcross, but the panels were only suitable for low-rise dwellings, and after a prototype two-storey block of flats had been built at Penilee, followed by several hundred production dwellings, the programme was phased out.[2] The typical four-storey tenements of the 1950s were instead built in terrazzo-faced or roughcast brick or blockwork, some in crosswall construction, and all in enormous negotiated contracts with local firms such as Lawrence and Stuart, or with the city's direct labour organization. With high-density tenements accounting for around 95% of the Corporation's output, only a few experimental multi-storey blocks were attempted, including the asymmetrical, 8-storey, balcony-access Crathie Court

(built in 1946–49 as a single women's hostel, with central government encouragement) and the 10-storey hilltop slab blocks of Moss Heights (1950–54). During the mid 1950s, however, the powerful regional-planning alliance within the Department of Health for Scotland and Glasgow Corporation devoted huge efforts to stopping the city's Housing Committee from carrying on with these peripheral schemes, through an unprecedentedly aggressive new towns and green belt strategy – first set out in Patrick Abercrombie and Robert Matthew's 1946–49 Clyde Valley Regional Plan, and set in train in 1947 when the government designated the first Scottish new town, East Kilbride, at the same time cancelling much of the land allocation for Corporation peripheral schemes. This strategy culminated in 1957, when the city planners issued a far-reaching 'Report on the Clearance of Slum Houses, Redevelopment and Overspill'.[3] The report proposed to squeeze the Housing Committee's programme in a pincer movement: firstly, a vast redevelopment programme of 'comprehensive development areas' (CDAs) under close planning control, and a maximum density of 165 persons per acre; and secondly, sweeping overspill provisions to take away the decanted population resulting from these density curbs.

Above: View of Glasgow's 'Council Towers' from the north-east in 2011
Below: Glasgow, Hutchesontown-Gorbals Area C, 1960–66, Basil
  Spence & Partners: royal foundation-laying in 1960 (Housing
  Convener David Gibson second from left, City Architect
  A G Jury third from right, turning round).

The first of these CDAs, Hutchesontown-Gorbals, an area of dilapidated and overcrowded tenements, was widely seen as the symbolic epicentre of the city's 'slum housing problem'. In 1954, the recently-appointed City Architect and Planning Officer, Archibald Jury, drew up an initial proposal for redevelopment with a densely rectilinear carpet of fairly even-height towers and slabs, together with four-storey flats and maisonettes. But by 1957 this had been replaced by a more variegated and phased development plan, still at 165 p.p.a., but dominated by two very different multi-storey designs – Area B by Robert Matthew and Johnson-Marshall (1958–64) and Area C by Basil Spence (1960–66; demolished 1993).[4] The involvement of Robert Matthew and Basil Spence in the project, as the only Scottish Modernist architects of truly international standing, reflected the central position of Glasgow within the housing-planning debate. Both chose solutions dominated by tall blocks. Spence's section was built in the form of two monumental slab blocks in in-situ concrete, supported by massive slanting columns and featuring inset upper-floor communal balconies, or 'garden slabs', romantically intended to evoke tenement drying-greens, or 'garden slabs', and adjoined by a multi-level commercial centre at right angles. Matthew's layout was a rectilinear grid of 18-storey

Top: Glasgow, Hutchesontown-Gorbals redevelopment, unexecuted 1954 redevelopment
  proposal by the planning staff of City Architect Archibald Jury.
Bottom: Glasgow, Hutchesontown-Gorbals redevelopment, 1966 aerial view during construction:
  at right, Area B, 1958–64, Robert Matthew Johnson-Marshall; at centre, Area C, 1960–66, Basil
  Spence; at bottom left, Area D, 1963–69, by Harold Buteux, SSHA Technical Director.

towers and lower blocks aligned, typically of CIAM practice, on a north-south axis (to optimise daylight and sunlight exposure), disregarding the existing street alignments. Internally, the towers (originally designed for the Leith Fort competition in Edinburgh, 1957 – see below) were planned by project architect Ian Arnott with an ingenious staggered cross section inspired by a tower built at the 1957 Interbau in Berlin, by J H van den Broek and J B Bakema. Externally, Matthew insisted on a strong contrast with Spence's extravagant concrete modelling: Arnott recalled that his 'philosophy was to keep things simple – he didn't like filigree details and individualistic touches.' Later phases of Hutchesontown-Gorbals included the towers and low-rise blocks of the SSHA's Area D (1963 onwards), the 'Tracoba' Area E towers and deck blocks (from 1968) or the Laurieston-Gorbals CDA extension development of 1970 onwards, including four tall, dark grey 24-storey Crudens slab blocks in in-situ construction.[5]

Left: Glasgow, Hutchesontown-Gorbals Area C, 1960–66, maisonette slab blocks by Basil Spence & Partners, seen newly completed in 1967.
Right: Glasgow, Hutchesontown-Gorbals Area B, 1958–64, maisonette tower blocks by Robert Matthew Johnson-Marshall & Partners.

The later phases of the CDA programme were concentrated in a swathe of land immediately surrounding the city centre, required for construction of the motorway-standard Inner Ring Road proposed in the city Highway Plan of 1965, but only a few of these were developed all at once to a coordinated architectural plan at significantly reduced densities in the same way as Hutchesontown-Gorbals: notable among these were Anderston Cross (from 1964), laid out in a masterplan by a joint Scottish Office/SSHA housing development unit with a fairly dense grid of low and medium-rise blocks clustered round a central 18-storey tower, and built initially in a modified version of Bison Wall-Frame; and the suburban-situated Pollokshaws, developed from 1962 with some of the first realized Bison towers in the country, with pinkish-red tinted precast panels subtly echoing c.1900 Glasgow tenements.[6]

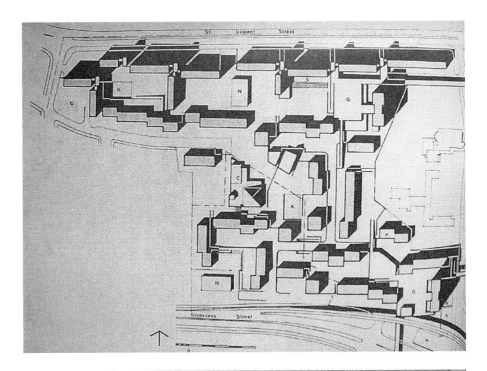

Top and bottom: Glasgow, Anderston Cross CDA development, 1965–70: pioneering medium-rise complex with one tower, designed by SSHA/SDD Housing Development Unit (Phase 1 in collaboration with Concrete Ltd).

234

Glasgow, Laurieston-Gorbals development, 1970–74, designed and built by Crudens.

But by 1965, seven years into the plan's programme period, the predominant form and location of the city's new housing was very different in character from the planner-led formula of the early CDAs, and especially from the extreme individualism of the Spence and Matthew Gorbals schemes. Beyond the CDA zone, wave upon wave of colossal multi-storey towers was rising – twenty, twenty-five, thirty or more storeys high. These were not located in planned redevelopments, integrated with lower blocks, but were thrown haphazardly on suburban gap-sites and pockets of waste-ground. Nowhere else in Britain, so early, were so many large, high blocks completed or under construction at once – a tremendous forest of multi-storey blocks that openly defied the planners' prescriptions in its form and its effect. The 1957 Report had recommended the building of 40,000 new dwellings in Glasgow and 60,000 overspill houses by 1980: but, by 1972, no less than 48,000 new dwellings would in fact be built within the city boundaries, while a mere 25,000 planned overspill dwellings would be provided.[7]

What was the cause of this reversal to the 1957 report's pincer strategy – a reversal which prevented the scattering of the city's population into an array of garden suburbs or New Towns? The recovery of momentum by the Housing Committee resulted, in the first instance, from the initiative of one individual: David Gibson, its Convener from 1961 to 1964, and, as a longstanding former member of the Independent Labour Party, an inheritor of the ILP's impassioned yet homespun socialism. In Glasgow, Patrick Abercrombie's grand framework of planned modernization ran directly up against the implacable opposition of Gibson and many Housing Committee members. They opposed the 1957 Report's redevelopment and overspill programme, because they believed that it would not only fail to rehouse slum-dwellers directly into new houses, but would also prevent the Housing Committee from doing so. To Gibson, wholesale planned overspill seemed a fantasy dreamt up by a dirigiste elite: 'There is enough land in Glasgow to build all the houses we need – if only we can find it!' Exploiting the municipal autonomy guaranteed by Britain's system of 'Council Powers', Gibson's rise to ascendancy within the Housing Committee was meteoric, and by 1961, he had built up a formidable redoubt from which he could launch a stunning blow against the planners. As Sir Robert Grieve later recalled, 'Gibson was the man we regarded as 'the frightening one – a white-faced, intense, driving idealist, absolutely fanatical and sincere, of a kind you couldn't help admiring in a way. He was white with passion about the housing problem – one knew he was a man in a hurry! He saw only the one thing – how to get as many houses up as possible, how to get as many of his beloved fellow working-class working-class citizens decently housed as possible. We all agreed, but the question was where, how, and at what speed!'[8]

The interim response to the 1957 planning report had been a compromise: the planners were promised immediate designation of numbers of further CDAs, but the 'housers' were also appeased by the promise of a new drive to exploit every available gap-site. In that quest, the obvious place to look was outside the planner-controlled CDAs. Here, there were no blanket density zones, of the kind that most famously applied

in London, but merely ineffective 'cartograms' expressing notional population figures for entire districts, including existing housing. Gibson intuitively grasped that, if the multi-storey blocks proposed by the planners for mixed development use in the CDAs were instead built by the Committee outside those areas on gap sites, much higher blocks would be possible, unfettered by planning restrictions and acquisition delays. This would allow a cycle of decanting within the city, bypassing overspill. An entire tranche of such gap-sites was promptly generated in 1959, through a new policy of rezoning of some public open spaces such as golf-courses, and the demolition of the city's large estates of 'prefabs': the sites released would be developed as intensively as possible with high blocks. This reasoning had been encouraged by the prolific schemes of a maverick Glasgow architect, Sam Bunton, who had energetically helped organize the wartime rebuilding of the town of Clydebank following 1941 bombing, and from the 1950s kept up a one-man campaign for the high-density, multi-storey redevelopment of Glasgow in a way that would cut overspill by 50%, using polygonal or pentagonal blocks of up to 20 storeys, in their planning somewhat reminiscent of the dense 1940s 'alphabet' blocks of the New York City Housing Authority.[9]

Bunton's schemes remained unrealized during the 1950s, but by 1960, Gibson's argument had also been boosted by a vivid, but more conventionally-planned demonstration of the potential of point blocks in rapid piecemeal development: Wimpey's erection of the structure of three slim, 20-storey blocks in no-fines concrete at Royston, Area A, in just eight months. Now Gibson could unleash the most concentrated multi-storey drive experienced by any city in the UK. An increasing number of specific 'multi-storey sites' was designated: their 'yield' would be maximised by use of 100% high flats, between 20 and 31 storeys in height, and objections by council planners on grounds of density or zoning regulations would be ruthlessly crushed. Far more of Glasgow's multi-storey flats were in very large and high blocks than elsewhere: the proportion in blocks over 20 storeys high was three times that of London and 18 times that of Birmingham. Glasgow eventually accounted for over a quarter of the UK total of these very tall blocks.[10]

One potential obstacle stemmed from the city's grave building capacity shortfall, but luckily the Convener had available to him the services of Lewis Cross, a senior engineer in the Architecture and Planning Department who oversaw all housing sites and contracts. His inexorable pursuit of site 'yield' laid the groundwork for the City's great surge in Modern housing production, at the same time as his hard-headed negotiation of 'package-deal' (design-and-build) contracts ensured that these sites were filled with dwellings as rapidly as possible. He dealt with each firm personally and in isolation, and kept them all in ignorance of his land bank, feeding large jobs to them stage-by-stage, to keep as much negotiating leverage as possible. Wimpey's Principal Scottish Architect at the time, Tom Smyth, recollected that 'we never discussed any overall programme. Each site came out of the blue, was almost a job by that stage. Cross would ring up: "We've got a site, there's going to be multi-storeys on it, can you do it?" He would never tell you he was

Top: Glasgow, Royston A development, 1959–60, construction
view; designed and built by
G Wimpey.
Bottom: Glasgow, Sighthill
development initial proposal
being inspected by Housing
Convener David Gibson in
his home in Cardowan Road,
Glasgow, in 1961.

Glasgow, Sighthill development, 1961–69, designed by Crudens Ltd and built by Crudens/Truscon.

negotiating with someone else about a job. Management would hit the roof and say, "Someone else has got that big multi-storey job! How did that happen – you're in touch with Lewis Cross!" I'd say, "He's the last person to tell me!"[11] A large, yet typical instance of this approach was Crudens's Sighthill development, a majestic array of ten 20-storey slab blocks, built in 1961–69 in reinforced concrete frame construction in conjunction with Truscon, in the stark setting of a reclaimed chemical wasteground, grouped with 5-storey walk-up blocks at right-angles. This job arrived from Cross in the usual precipitate manner. George Bowie, Crudens's former Chief Architect, recollected that 'my Managing Director came along one day with a piece of tracing paper, with what turned out to be the final shape of Sighthill on it, and a scale – it was ridiculous! – and he said, "How many dwellings can you put on this site?" I replied, "You've got access roads, daylight and sunlight to consider!" He said: "Just put multis on it and some low rise." So in a day I

knocked together some thoughts, and then he asked, "Could you make a model?" I said, "There's nothing to make a model of!" But we put together this thing with matchboxes, and he went away with it. A few days later, he took me over to Sighthill in his Jag, and asked, "What do you think?" I said, "Jesus Christ!!"[12] It would be difficult to think of an approach more different from that of the LCC, with its combination of individual architectural design of each project and competitively-tendered contracting coordinated and controlled by the same local-authority (or sometimes private-practice) architects.

One substantial area of contracting policy, however, eluded Cross's control: the activity of the Corporation's powerful direct-building organization, the Housing and Works Department – a department notorious for its inefficiency and featherbedding practices. Here the turn to multi-storey building was to have dramatic and unexpected results. The Housing

238

Glasgow, Red Road development, 1962–69, Sam Bunton, architect: 1967 advertisement showing construction.

and Works Manager, George Campbell, was worried that Gibson's turn to multi-storey building might lead to large-scale redundancy among bricklayers, and undermine his department's patronage and power base. Impressed, but also frightened by the 'literally fantastic' progress of Wimpey's Royston 'A', Campbell pleaded with Gibson that he should be allowed to devise a 'package-deal' of his own, using modest crosswall blocks to be developed by none other than Sam Bunton. The prototype scheme for this 'package deal', Red Road, soon took on a spectacular life of its own. In 1962, it was discovered that poor site conditions had reduced the area suitable for building. The local steel industry was jostling to enter the housing market, and Bunton saw an opportunity to import the New York skyscraper to Glasgow and 'build the highest blocks in Europe'. Unglamorous crosswall proposals were jettisoned in favour of a mighty outcrop of stark, steel-framed towers, clad in asbestos panels. The complex comprised two enormously

massive slab blocks of 27 storeys, with a repetitive 'section' plan of repeating staircase units, and six slender towers of 31 storeys and central lift/service core (41 storeys having at first been proposed); a small commercial centre and nursery school completed the ensemble, which was adjoined by a development of three 18-storey Reema towers at Coll Street (1967–8), all in a stark and un-landscaped setting bisected by railway lines. Gibson at first tried to keep control of Red Road, but the autonomous status of the HWD stopped anyone from bringing Campbell to heel as calamitous overspending and chaos mounted – stemming not only from Red Road's grandiose scale and untried construction methods, but also from the fact that it was made into a scapegoat to conceal more general HWD disorganization, as one ex-supervisor recalled: 'The millions of feet of copper pipe that disappeared off that job... we know that materials arrived at our site on a lorry, were signed for, and went straight out of the gate at the other side to another site!'.[13]

239

Glasgow, Red Road development, 1962–69, Sam Bunton, architect: 2011 view of one of the two
slab blocks prior to demolition, with the steel skeleton partly revealed by removal of cladding.

Glasgow, Red Road development, 1962–69, Sam Bunton, architect.

But Red Road was in many ways the exception that proved the rule – for Gibson and Cross were elsewhere, by 1962, experiencing significant success in launching the building of very high blocks across the city. Gibson devoted every possible moment to his mission: 'I spend my weekends looking round the city for gap-sites and any odd bit of land that we can put a house up on. My idea of fulfilment is to draw up the car and see the lights of Knightswood or some other [multi-storey] scheme shining out and think of all the families translated from gloom to happiness!'[14] He relentlessly forced through scheme after scheme, against often strong opposition – for instance overriding vehement planning protests in 1963 against a large multi-storey development at Toryglen North, immediately adjacent to railway sidings, clay workings and a refuse destructor: 'The Convener emphasized that... Glasgow in its present shortage of sites could not afford the luxury of avoiding the development of places like Toryglen North. Glaswegians had been accustomed to living within walking distance of industry and would tolerate similar conditions in their new houses. While he appreciated the ideals motivating the criticism of the site, he said that as a practical man, he must bear in mind that conditions there, if not ideal, were infinitely better than those being endured by the families living in slums'. In that single year, contracts for 3,783 flats in blocks of 20 or more storeys were let – well over half the cumulative total of dwellings in such blocks, built or authorised to that date in the whole UK![15] By this stage, the planners' CDA concept was also beginning to be turned against them, as gap sites in CDAs started being developed haphazardly with towers, in the same way as the non-CDA sites. Key redevelopment areas were starting to become indistinguishable from outer-suburban gap sites as isolated towers sprouted within them: for example in the Woodside CDA (with grey-tinted Bison repeats of the Pollokshaws slabs, from 1964); the Springburn CDA (from 1966, including slender Reema point blocks and lower deck-access blocks); Phase A of the Gallowgate CDA (from 1963) with two 31-storey reinforced-concrete-frame point blocks, equalling Red Road as the city's tallest and featuring all-round balconies; or the Townhead CDA (including in-situ blocks in Area A, from 1961, and 25-storey Wimpey no-fines slabs from 1967 in Area B). Overall, by the early 1960s, Glasgow was becoming established as Britain's 'shock city' of very high tower-building – a status that it would keep for the rest of the multi-storey boom, until at least 1970.[16]

241

Glasgow, Townhead CDA Area B, 1967–69, designed and built by G Wimpey.

Glasgow, Gallowgate CDA Area A, 1963–65, architects Harvey & Scott.

Glasgow, Cowcaddens CDA, 1968–75, architects Walter Underwood & Partners.

As early as 1963, however, with Glasgow's multi-storey programme well established, Gibson's restless mind was already beginning to range further afield, with the aspiration of spreading the Glasgow formula of massed tower-building across Scotland. His first aim, exploiting the city's dominance within West Central Scotland, was to encourage and orchestrate higher production throughout CLYDESIDE, in alliance with a handful of other key local politicians. One of the most enterprising of these was Hutchison Sneddon, Motherwell's Council Leader and Housing Convener from 1960. Explicitly inspired by Gibson, Sneddon pushed through a house-by-house survey of the entire Burgh, followed by redevelopment of a swathe of land south of the town centre. To get a self-contained cycle of slum decanting underway, a 1,344-dwelling scheme, including seven 18-storey point-blocks, was built in 1963–66 by Wimpey at Muirhouse, the Burgh's last virgin site. As a result, 'we could pull people out from the tenements and immediately demolish and rebuild on site!' The Motherwell programme also included a distinctive 17-storey slab block at Parkhead Street (from 1963) in a similar steel-framed construction to Red Road, this time with Crudens as main contractor. By the mid-1960s, not just Motherwell but a wide range of Clydeside authorities was duly queuing up in Glasgow's wake, and commencing large multi-storey programmes – and Scotland's overall per-capita rate of high building had almost caught up with that of London.[17] However, nowhere else was as extreme as Glasgow in its devotion to very high blocks used piecemeal, or to package deal building.

Initially, the role of central government in all this remained a very subsidiary one. During the long period of Tory government between 1951 and 1964, the central government Scottish Office was in a weak and reactive position vis-à-vis not just Glasgow but local authorities in general. However, that position changed significantly in 1964, following two developments: the sudden death of Gibson on 27 March following a heart attack brought on by chain-smoking and overwork, and the accession to power of a Labour government in Westminster later in the year – as a result of which Dr. J. Dickson Mabon was appointed Joint Parliamentary Under-Secretary of State, with responsibility for housing and planning. Mabon won the admiration of housing conveners of all political persuasions up and down the country, not only for his infectious enthusiasm but also because, unusually among postwar Scottish housing Ministers, he had devised a coherent housing strategy, based on active collaboration with the 'Council Powers', and was determined to put it into effect. Mabon's plan was to harness and redirect slightly the efforts of the cities, to accommodate the planners' objections, but at the same time to broaden the 'Gibson campaign' beyond Glasgow and the central belt to give an immediate 20% increase across Scotland, and, by 1970, an annual level of no less than 50,000 completions.[18]

Within Glasgow, Mabon conceded the planners some influence over housing location, and authorised studies into a further expansion of overspill. But undiminished, even increased multi-storey building was allowed in less sensitive locations, such as the suburban Knightswood (a favoured site for Wimpey towers since 1962, where a line of 24-storey Wimpey towers was inserted from 1965 into a left-over site at Kirkton Avenue, despite fierce objections from Scottish Office planners and architects), as well as on yet more piecemeal cleared sites in CDAs – the latter supposedly to be balanced by the lower density of later stages, often destined never to be built! By the later 1960s, the proportion of Glasgow high-flat approvals in CDA locations jumped to 82%, from only 43% earlier in the decade. In Glasgow, Mabon had with great ceremony begun easing shut the stable door, just as the last horses stampeded past to freedom. Across the country as a whole, he had not only ended the idea that housing could be taken from local authorities, but had elevated an urban municipal campaign into a nationwide movement, imbuing county councils and small burghs across the land with Gibson's campaigning ideals.[19]

Outside Glasgow, Mabon encouraged expanded building by almost all categories and sizes of local authorities – much of which resulted in the building of high flats, albeit not on anything like the scale or intensiveness of Glasgow. In the case of small burghs, Mabon was quite happy within reason to allow isolated prestige schemes, in the belief that this might be a valuable competitive spur – as in the case of Saltcoats Burgh, whose Town Council successfully pleaded with him at least to sanction a 'wee multi-storey' (two 12-storey Bison towers built at the Glebelands scheme from 1962). In the rural areas, the fact that public housing was the responsibility of the powerful County Councils allowed isolated instances of tower-building even here, as in the case of Lanark County Council, under Housing Convener (from 1958) Hugh Brannan, which built a significant multi-storey programme in 1963–69 in the town of Cambuslang.[20] Also embedded in the county areas were, of course, the New Towns. Largely exempt from local housing pressures, these were much more influenced than the municipalities by professional groups, especially architects. Four of them – East Kilbride, Cumbernauld, Glenrothes and Livingston – built on a substantial scale in the 1960s, and the first two of these constructed a significant number of high flats. In East Kilbride, these mostly comprised scattered groups of Wimpey point-blocks for higher-rent letting, built in 1965–70 (mostly by Wimpey – at Calderwood 5–16, The Murray 8–9, and Westwood 2). In Cumbernauld, high flats were envisaged from the start: groups of Bison point-blocks (commencing 1964 at Seafar 3) were picturesquely located as landmarks on an escarpment along the north-west edge of the town, and 6 and 7-storey slab blocks were incorporated into other areas. Geoffrey Copcutt's megastructural tour-de-force, the Town Centre Phase One (built 1963–6), at first included penthouse flats. Most of the rest of Cumbernauld's housing was made up of dense clusters of two-storey terraces with pitched roofs.[21]

Mabon's 'national-local' housing drive was also increasingly abetted by the other three Scottish cities, Edinburgh, Aberdeen and Dundee. However, owing to their geographical and cultural separation from the Clydeside housing world, and from the dominance there of the 'Glasgow housing problem', with its urgent pressures for slum clearance and mass overspill, the urgency and force of the building drive, and the scale of the towers, was much less extreme. In Edinburgh, where anti-socialist 'Progressives' had traditionally dominated the town council, a multi-storey crash drive directly inspired by Gibson's work in Glasgow had only got underway as late as 1962. In that year, as a result of a politically-deadlocked Town Council, the housing chair passed for the first time to a Labour member, Councillor Pat Rogan, a bricklayer who was intoxicated by the boldness of the Red Road project: 'I thought that was really something – terrific!'[22] The Corporation's somewhat meagre previous output, which had repeatedly dropped below 1,000 annual completions, had left Edinburgh a substantial legacy of 18th and 19th-century slums in Leith and elsewhere: the waiting list had risen rapidly, from 6,000 in 1958 to a peak of 11,000 in 1964. In opposition, Rogan had harried the Corporation's Progressive administration to extend slum clearance beyond the restricted, somewhat Geddes-like 'conservative surgery' of the Citadel and Central Leith Redevelopment Area, where highly individual blocks were squeezed into pocket sites such as Cables Wynd Phase 1, 1963–65, a 10-storey deck-access slab block which, bizarrely, was planned on a curved alignment so as to fit round a retained tenement block, Couper Street (two 20-storey towers of split-level maisonettes, from 1961), or the more outlandish Leith Fort, a combination of industrial-aesthetic towers with Kahn-like jutting service towers, brick deck blocks and low-rise courtyard patio houses (1957–66) stemming from a competition win by young architects Shaw-Stewart, Baikie and Perry.[23]

Once in office, Pat Rogan found that the Progressives' financial cautiousness had left scope for the substantial rises in rate-fund contributions necessary to support a sudden acceleration in the housing drive. There was not much of a land problem, as Edinburgh had the largest 'prefab' estates in the country. Accordingly, 3,616 bungalows were demolished and replaced by 9,272 permanent houses, many in high blocks, by 1967: most of these were built by local contractors such as Miller or Smart in in-situ construction, with only a handful of Bison, Wimpey or other package deal blocks. Accordingly, in his single term of office, ending in 1965, Rogan was able almost to treble the City's programme: dwellings under contract soared from 700 in 1961 to 2,700 in 1962, and completions from 960 to 2363 by the

following year. After 1965, Labour lost the housing chair once again, but Rogan's policies were continued virtually unaltered by his Progressive successor, Adolf Theurer, who enthusiastically supported Mabon's programme in a range of large-scale peripheral projects, including the enormous Wester Hailes scheme of 1967–74, with its 4,800 staircase-access flats in slab and tenement blocks up to ten storeys high, located as an autonomous 'township' on the upland south-western edge of the capital.[24]

Like Edinburgh, both Aberdeen and Dundee were free of overspill pressures; both Tayside and the North-East were regarded by the planners as 'growth' areas during the 1960s, so both cities' populations could expand slightly in the early postwar years, to just under 200,000, and neither suffered from significant land shortage. Yet both pursued energetic multi-storey building during the 1960s and later, highlighting again the now 'routine' status of high flats. In Aberdeen the negotiating skills of the formidable City Architect, George McI. Keith, and the financial acumen and 'sea-green incorruptibility' of Councillor Robert Lennox, the longstanding City Treasurer, provided an exceptionally sound basis for the city's programme. Although Aberdeen had no overcrowding or slum problem on the scale of Clydeside or Dundee, its Housing Committee, generally Labour-controlled but every so often led by the popular Tory 'Battling Baillie' Frank Magee, had set their hearts on a major multi-storey drive after visits to Roehampton and Glasgow in 1959. Aberdeen's high flats, almost all designed by Keith's staff rather than contractors, and built by local firms, fell into two distinct categories: suburban point blocks, and slab blocks in inner clearance areas.[25] The former commenced in 1959–61 with the isolated schemes at Ashgrove VIII and Mastrick 1, building up with Mabon's encouragement to larger mixed developments of point blocks and low flats at Hazlehead I (from 1962, explicitly modelled on Roehampton), Cornhill-Stockethill (from 1966), and Tillydrone-Hayton (from 1965); it culminated at Seaton (1969–74; including 1,247 high flats). Aberdeen's clearance schemes began with Chapel Street/Skene Street in 1961 and built up to the massive blocks (up to 19 storeys) of the Gallowgate and Castlehill redevelopments (1964 and 1966), provided with lavish communal facilities, and their gable walls clad with distinctive pebble-faced slabs. The city's low-rise housing also reflected the North-East Scottish regional fascination with multi-coloured precast ('Fyfestone') facing blockwork. Aberdeen's only real 'housing problem' was its waiting list: the multi-storey programme halved this to 3,700 in 1971. Even so, the Committee's most 'crusading' Convener, Councillor Jock Greig, would still often accost the Deputy City Architect: 'Here's a bit of ground, how about a multi-storey here?'[26]

Left: Edinburgh, Martello Court, Muirhouse Phase
II, 1962–65, Rowand Anderson Kininmonth & Paul:
at 23 storeys, the capital's tallest Council Tower.
Bottom: Edinburgh, Leith Fort project, 1960–63,
Shaw-Stewart, Baikie & Perry.

The City of Dundee was, arguably, the only other Scottish urban centre that in some ways echoed the Glasgow drive for extreme output solutions and package-deal building – although involving mostly much lower blocks. Like Glasgow, Dundee was a city that was highly separate from its rural hinterland. The city's separateness also owed much to its colourful reputation for municipal corruption: a former Scottish Office administrator quipped that 'you always took a witness when you went to Dundee!' Allegations concerning the allocation of contracts and sub-contracts for public building projects – the so-called 'Dundee Dossier' – culminated in a much-publicised court case of 1980. But, at the same time, the city's Modern housing drive was proportionally by far the largest per head of population in Britain, exceeding its nearest urban challenger (Salford) in the 'sixties by 44%: Salford's total 1966–70 output per 1,000 population was 33.8, Dundee's 52.4.[27] The story of Dundee's Modern housing is an unparalleled example of the way in which multi-storey blocks, originally introduced to high-output use in the 1950s by land-starved authorities, above all by Gibson in Glasgow, were then exploited by cities with no such problems, purely in order to raise production further.

Dundee's 'turbulent' municipal life featured an even balance between Labour and (non-Socialist) 'Moderates'. Labour held power from the mid-1950s until 1967, years dominated by three exceptionally forceful Housing Conveners, Bailie Harry Dickson, Bailie James Stewart, and Councillor Tom Moore. The executive power wielded by these members equated to a combination of Gibson and Cross. Between the wars, and in the 1950s, a high output in Dundee had been maintained merely through suburban tenements and cottages on the city's plentiful land. In the late 'fifties, however, with the complexity of slum-clearance on the horizon, Dundee's Labour triumvirate began to consider multi-storey building. During the convenerships of Stewart and Moore (1962–66), a series of dramatic projects was undertaken, which would treble the City's building rate from well below 1,000. Large schemes were started on CDA gap sites, such as the grandiose, 23-storey slab blocks of Maxwelltown (from 1965) and Derby Street (from 1967; by Camus), monumentally crowning the city's skyline as seen from the Tay. In the suburbs, several large multi-storey schemes were awarded to Crudens – culminating in the six mighty 17-storey *Zeilenbau* blocks of Ardler Phase I (from 1964), located on a redeveloped golf course and each containing 298 flats.[28]

The City's most prodigious housing project was not, however, a development chiefly comprising towers, but a vast Crudens scheme of Skarne deck blocks, interspersed with two conventionally-built slabs, at Whitfield, on the north-east edge of the city. The Skarne contract, built in 1968–72, comprised no less than 130 deck-access blocks of 4, 5 and 6 storeys (containing 2,459 dwellings), arranged in an extraordinary and relentless honeycomb of hexagonal courtyards, and dramatically juxtaposed with the stark, open country to its north. Because of this, Dundee's output surged to a tremendous peak of 2,794 in 1970: 88% higher, proportionally, than even Maudsley's best in Birmingham.[29]

Dundee, Whitfield industrialised contract, from 1968, designed and built by Crudens (Skarne): 1967 Crudens perspective.

Dundee, Derby Street CDA, 1967–69, designed by Camus with Dundee City Architect.

Top: Aberdeen, Castlehill development,
1966–68, by City Architect's Department.
Right: Aberdeen, Gallowgate CDA, 1964–66,
by City Architect's Department.

Top and bottom: Aberdeen, Hutcheon Street redevelopment, 1973–75, designed by City Architect
and built by local contractor A. Hall: the city's last inner-area slab redevelopment.

BRITAIN'S LAST TOWERS

It was only appropriate, and to be expected, that Scotland's multi-storey housing drive proved to be unusually resilient: it not only significantly outlasted that of England and Wales, but also even enjoyed a modest revival around 1970, when an absolute maximum in Scottish public housing output was reached, with just under 35,000 public-sector completions. Thereafter completions declined to 13,016 in 1974 and 9,119 in 1977.[30]

Multi-storey towers also featured prominently in this Indian summer of Scottish council housing. After an initial panicky dip after Ronan Point, high building gathered pace again, from 12.7% of approvals in 1968 to 21.8% in 1970, and only finally declined in the mid-1970s. Overall, relatively little deck-access housing, with its connotations of English 'traditional' terraces, was built in Scotland – although the later phases of Glasgow's Woodside CDA (Area B Phase 3, 1970–72) included red-brick deck-access blocks whose canted 'bay windows' calculatedly echoed Glasgow tenements in an almost Postmodernist manner.[31]

More usually, there was a fairly undramatic continuity in the municipal support for the continued building of conventional point and slab blocks. Here a final, surprising twist to Scotland's multi-storey building drive came in the 1970s and 80s in the city of Aberdeen, where the North Sea oil boom had counterbalanced the depressive effects of the 1970s' economic crises, and successive multi-storey projects carried on being built from the 1970s onwards. These included a continuation of the city's pebble-clad redevelopment slabs (15/19 storeys at Hutcheon Street, 1973–76), as well as a unique programme of 'sheltered' point blocks for elderly residents, complete with integral community centres. This programme continued until as late as 1985, when its final project, the Jasmine Terrace development, or 'St Clement's Court', was completed by Wimpey, a year after its foundation-stone had been laid, with typically Aberdonian civic pride, by Lord Provost Alexander Collie.[32]

St Clement's Court was also, appropriately, the last Council Tower built in Britain. From that time on, Aberdeen exclusively applied its municipal ethos of prudent care and civic order to the blocks it already possessed, treating them as assets to be husbanded rather than liabilities to be squandered – unlike cities like Dundee, Liverpool or Manchester, which by the 1980s were already busy with massed demolitions. As a result, by the early 21st century, Aberdeen's Council Towers, and its council-housing stock in general, had become, by default, a 'museum' of little-altered modernist housing, almost unique in Britain – but that, of course, is another story!

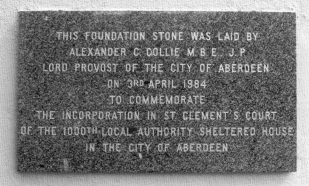

Left and right: Aberdeen, Jasmine Place development (St Clement's Court), 1983–85, City Architect's Department.

Glasgow, Woodside CDA: on the left, Area A, from 1964, 23-storey Bison towers,
designed by Concrete Ltd/City Architect (end walls re-clad in postmodernist
colours 1990); on the right, Area B Phase 3, 1970–74, by Boswell Mitchell & Johnston
(project architect Nori Toffolo).

15 A global perspective

For more than a hundred years, from the 19th well into the 20th century, Britain had provided the Western world with a compelling model for the principal environment for urban habitation, the suburb. This model was based on the picturesque architectural aesthetic of the small(ish) house embedded in greenery, in combination with the planning concept of the 'garden city'. Many modern town planners, indeed, looked on the garden city as the foundation of their discipline as a whole. But that pattern of influence went into sharp reverse from around 1930 onwards. Now, it was Britain that was at the receiving end, adopting from the Continent the doctrine of International Modernist architecture in its entirety, with especial emphasis on certain forms of mass housing, such as the *Zeilenbau* concept from Germany and the *punkthus* from Sweden. During the 1950s, the image of Le Corbusier's Unité d'habitation in Marseilles loomed large over London designers in particular. In the 1960s British housing architects became greatly enthusiastic for a time about large panel construction from France and Scandinavia. So comprehensive seemed this architectural climate of admiration for things Continental, that when the sharp disillusionment with Modern housing began to set in by the late 1960s, a new generation of architectural critics directed much of the blame precisely at the 'un-Englishness' of all those imports.

From a purely socio-political-economic point of view, however, this kind of architectural language of national identity seems merely incidental. From that socio-political perspective the fundamental aim of the great mid/late 20th-century wave of modern mass-housing sponsored publicly was, almost by definition, everywhere the same: to defend the fundamental interests of the state in the 'domestic' realm, including especially the promotion of social cohesion, political stability and economic development. It was also an almost immutable rule that, given the scale and cost of commitment typically required in mass housing programmes, usually only 'developed' states could afford to undertake them. But the position of individual countries or regions of the world on these issues varied hugely, and the organisational and ideological diversity of the subsequent mass housing programmes was consequently great.

In north-western Europe, for example, the post-war hegemony of the idealistic welfare-state model led to an inclusive mass-housing formula of 'good homes for all': the formula of a fully self-contained dwelling for every household; fully equipped with sanitary facilities; surrounded by light, fresh air and, wherever possible, greenery; and built economically through a mixture of social and capitalist agencies. In the state socialist (Soviet) bloc much of the same approach applied, but with almost no 'private sector' element, with more economical standards and on a far larger and more standardised scale, and bound up with strong ideological propaganda; whereas in the United States, the assumed primacy of the private sector in housing and the stern legislative restriction of most public housing to the 'urban poor' compelled a strongly utilitarian approach to both organisation and design. In other slightly less developed countries, for example in Latin America and Southern Europe, the role of the state was typically more indirect and limited, and focused on building for middle-class or 'client' groups, for home-ownership rather than rental. More recently, the emergence in Eastern Asia of a new state configuration – the 'developmental' state, dedicated to the fostering of rapid capitalist growth through radical public intervention and infrastructure planning – gave rise to a new model of mass housing, employing many of the planning technologies of the welfare-state West but within a fundamentally corporate capitalist-led economy. All of these 'regional' approaches had innumerable sub-variations in organisation, including choices between permutations of rental or sale, building by governmental or arms-length authorities, or according to the categories and income levels of inhabitants.

How was this global diversity of mass housing expressed in architectural terms? Within most developed countries outside Latin America and Southern Europe, mass housing certainly involved the prominent, and mostly the predominant use of blocks of flats. In a few locations, especially New York City, large numbers of public housing blocks of around 14–15 storeys were already under construction by the late 1940s, but in Europe heights crept up much more gradually. Only from around 1950 onwards did many blocks of flats begin to exceed the hitherto normal height of five storeys, and by the 1960s blocks with ten or more storeys had become common. But these rules-of-thumb concealed a considerable diversity in architectural solutions. Most 'anglophone' countries, including England as well as Australia, New Zealand, but also some others such as Belgium, continued with their tradition of low building of individual suburban houses, which, in England, accounted for two-thirds of post-war public housing. But in England, from the late 50s, this went alongside a tendency to build high blocks in relatively tall and slender tower form; thus in Britain as a whole the proportion of blocks over 20 storeys is higher than else-where in Western Europe: Sweden, for instance, even though it 'invented' the point block, never went higher than sixteen storeys. This fact alone makes high blocks stand out more: in Scotland, especially Glasgow, the contrast was accentuated by the uniquely high proportion of 25-storey towers, which maintained an effective contrast with the country's traditional four and five-storey tenements, and indeed, by 1970, Glasgow Corporation claimed to have built the highest social housing blocks in all Europe. The tendency of high flats in Britain to take the form of clusters of slender towers was accentuated by the stress, typical of all 'Anglophone' countries, on a strong association between mass housing and inner-city slum-clearance, which meant that many sites were small and densely confined – in sharp contrast to Continental 'grands ensembles' on the city peripheries, and above all the vast and spacious urbanism typical of the Soviet bloc, with its endless arrays of 9 and 13-storey slab blocks, offset by relatively few higher blocks. In Britain, just as in Australia or Canada, towers tended to stand out particularly prominently because of their overwhelmingly very low-rise surroundings, and the desire for prominence was further accentuated by the intense local-political dynamics of the council-housing system, under which relatively small groups of municipal councillors and their attendant architects or 'package-deal' building contractors would eagerly pursue the 'landmark' prestige conferred by tall towers.

If we were to confine ourselves to a strictly utilitarian definition of architecture, under which only strictly practical considerations are seen as admissible, none of these differences should really matter and it would be pointless to try and stress any kinds of national architectural characteristics. But post-1945 publicly-financed building did not proceed quite in that way, and the sharp differences in governmental motives concerning mass housing that we noted above had a clear, albeit indirect impact on built form. The 'Existenzminimum' frame of mind may have been present as a doctrine at some time before 1939 on the Continent and may then have applied to some of the starkest blocks in Britain in the years after the war (cf. p. 112), but from the mid-1950s, this idea was largely banished from western Europe. Instead, minimalism became first bound up, in the later 1950s, with Khrushchev's championing of strictly utilitarian, 'industrial' mass repetition, aimed squarely against Stalinist Classically ornamented façades. With the 1960s to 1980s came some Soviet attempts at variety, focusing on conglomerate planning and more freely-designed 'monolithic' in-situ towers. In the United States a different kind of utilitarianism, combined increasingly with severe racial stigmatisation, was expressed in the massive, ultra-economically-planned red-brick rental towers of the cities' 'housing authorities'.

In western Europe the growing acceptance of the Welfare-State political and social ideal after 1945 meant that something more than pure utility was taken for granted in new mass housing architecture: the growing general wealth made it doubly unacceptable to offer 'minimal' dwellings. Instead, the new type of tower block dwelling, still a great rarity by the mid-fifties, was usually the result of intense architectural planning, often by eminent names; one particularly influential showpiece was the veritable 'architectural zoo' of blocks designed by world-famous architects at the Berlin Internationale Bauausstellung (Interbau / Hansaviertel, cf. p. 61) of 1957. During the late 1950s and 1960s, the interaction between political-organisational structures and architectural design began to generate significant national or regional tendencies or even 'traditions' in mass housing design. In some cases, the imprint of national politics was immediate and obvious, especially in the sharp contrasts between 'Christian Democrat' and 'socialist' policies and housing architectures in some Catholic countries – for example in Italy, where the 'INA-Casa' programme of 1949–63 expressed Christian Democratic 'family' values in its picturesquely-designed 'vernacular' complexes, but was abruptly jettisoned in 1963 for the 'industrially-planned' GESCAL programme after the Social Democrats took over national power. Similarly, in Belgium, there was a strong polarisation between the home-ownership cottages promoted by the Catholic 'De Taeye' law and the rental flats funded by the socialist 'Brunfaut' law. In general, countries where government controls over land were relatively weak, such as Japan, Belgium or West Germany, tended to build modernist mass housing on a somewhat more limited scale than those where they were strong – above all in the state socialist bloc. But in other cases, strong 'traditions' and contrasts in built forms cannot straightforwardly be pinned down and linked to particular non-architectural contextual influences. For example, in the Netherlands, gallery-access layouts (galerijbouw) became overwhelmingly dominant in high-rise and medium-rise post-war social housing, whereas in the state socialist bloc, the so-called 'sectional' (sektsya) plan, with linear slab blocks and repetitive internal staircases flanked by 2–4 flats on each floor, enjoyed a similarly prominent status – but to pin down precisely the cause of these differences is more difficult.

The ideal of an enhanced architectural splendour and inventiveness came to the fore especially strongly in some of the Parisian 'grands ensembles' of the 1960s, combining the traditional 'French' grandeur of scale with a new concern to avoid any kind of ordinary regularity, for instance through curved block plans and highly unusual, sometimes even quirky external features, applied to flats of all heights. The complexity of these French city-periphery schemes of the 1960s – some of almost town-like scale, as with Toulouse-le-Mirail – was paralleled by the somewhat similar complex formations of England's inner-city, slum-clearance medium-rise 'conglomerates' of those years, as well as in a small number of London towers, such as Goldfinger's, with their elaborate access-ways. But applying quirky external features would not have been something that many British architects would have approved of, and one can assume that on cost grounds, their clients, the municipal councillors, would have forbidden it in any case. The diversity of elevations in Britain shown in this book can be taken to have resulted principally from the variety of constructional methods chosen by the architects, in collaboration with their engineer colleagues.

Following the decline and even 'fall' of mass housing in both the West and the socialist bloc, many of the Western ideas and built forms enjoyed a significant 'after-life' in the renewed explosion of mass social housing construction in the 'developmental states' of Eastern Asia from around 1980 onwards. Here, the oblique relationship between socio-political-economic constraints and diverse architectural outcomes applied, too. In late-colonial Hong Kong, for example, the extreme shortage of land and established tradition of high building generated a British-style 'government housing authority' system with both low-rental and middle-income housing programmes, which exploited the British 'point block' system in an extreme form, with standard 41-storey blocks (the 'Harmony' series) containing up to 800 small flats in each block; whereas in decolonised Singapore, with its easier land supply and authoritarian political system, the Government Housing and Development Board placed a greater emphasis on medium-height gallery-access home-ownership complexes, designed to encourage social mixing of the country's diverse ethnic groups. In rapidly-modernising South Korea, by contrast, the interventions of the government were more indirect, and focused on land and finance supply to the powerful executive 'chaebol' corporations – and the built form outcome was different again, in the massed building of tall, repetitive slabs of gallery or staircase-access home-ownership 'apatu-tanji'.

Overall, however, discourses of mass housing architecture were probably more complicated in Britain than anywhere else. Alongside the highly individualistic designs of the most celebrated single blocks or estates, there was also a complex backdrop of other projects with very different characteristics – namely those supplied by the 'package dealers', and built in all parts of the country. Here giving the names of the designers was purposely avoided; instead there was a heavy stress on the industrial pre-production of a 'system' of components, which could be applied in any location: the principal message of the external appearance, especially of Bison-Wall Frame blocks, was precisely that of a building as an assemblage of pre-fabricated parts. Some architects by the mid-1960s had begun to focus negatively on this movement, by contrasting so-called 'open' and 'closed' systems (the latter a 'kit of parts' suitable for architect-controlled design, the latter controlled by contractors, and thus supposedly to be condemned), arguing that the latter amounted to a revival of old-style 'minimal' design – by the mid-1960s an unambiguous bogeyman to anyone involved in British public housing architecture. Among 'progressive' architectural commentators in those years, opposition to 'minimal' housing was exemplified in the new trend, codified in the famous 'Parker Morris Report' of 1961, to analyse dwellings according to their individual functioning elements. These elements could then, in turn, be applied to any type of dwelling, allowing the abandonment of any primary rigid classification into house, flat, high or low block, etc. Yet alongside this, in Britain, there was a new, strong perception of the differences between dwelling types on the part of the 'general public', the drastic results of which became clear in the sharp reaction against tall blocks around 1970. More generally, those many overlapping concepts and arguments reflected a long standing complexity of discourses on housing architecture in Britain: its effects will be indicated in the last chapter.[1]

16 Afterword

There cannot be many countries in the developed world which did not build multi-storey public or social housing at some stage during the last seventy years. But there is probably no other country which presents as clear a narrative as the tower blocks of Britain. Clear, that is, with regard to the story's end: notwithstanding a few stragglers in Scotland and a handful of places in England, from the early 1970s the building of high blocks stopped completely. It meant that every chapter of this book concluded on one or another aspect of the high blocks' demise. The younger sociologists of the 1960s had become sceptical of the claims of Modernist town planners and housing architects that they could create happy communities. Our chapter on the detailed planning of towers ended with the widespread rejection of great height and a reversion to medium height blocks and even 'high-density-low-rise' formations. Purely visual architectural preferences turned away from the tower as a free-standing building towards multiform, interlinked conglomerates, which increasingly excluded towers. Likewise, designers and engineers of the later 1960s ceased their quest for ingenious framework solutions and often returned to heavy brick walling. Moreover, by the later 1960s all those concerned with financing public housing had become convinced that tower blocks represented an exceptionally and unnecessarily expensive way of trying to solve the 'housing problem'. And in each individual city, as we saw repeatedly in Chapter 13, the local story of post-war mass housing almost invariably ended with a major example of the new conglomerate pattern of housing development, abandoning soaring verticality and instead emphasising complex horizontality. Altogether, the quarter-century or so of British multi-storey block building constituted an astonishingly short episode.

Of course, many other countries, especially in the West, were also becoming dissatisfied in those years with some of their Modernist mass housing. But no country appears to have reacted with the violence that characterised Britain. By 1970 the journals that had so fervently advocated high blocks in the 1950s now condemned the Modernist estates outright. In a retrospective article, the Architectural Press's leading journal editor, J.M. Richards, whose enthusiasm we cited at the very beginning

of this book, put it plainly: 'we failed to create the utopia we imagined'.[1] What complicated this story greatly, however, was the way the 'for' and 'against' phases overlapped for such a long time. Adversity to towers can be traced as far back as the early 1950s, to the projects of Alison and Peter Smithson, with their strong stress on horizontality; yet those were exactly the years when the very first high blocks were being enthusiastically constructed. By 1970, the enthusiasm had almost completely evaporated, but precisely during that year the very highest blocks in Birmingham and Leeds were still being completed – although to minimal public acclaim. By the years around 1980, a further paradoxical twist had emerged: although the tower block remained the most universally acknowledged object of public and professional vilification, it was in reality the 1960s conglomerate blocks, built partly in reaction against the towers, which had become the most 'difficult to manage' estates, and were accordingly targeted for the earliest large-scale demolitions; on the 'last in, first out' principle, some of the major deck-access complexes lasted less than two decades, and by now almost all of them have disappeared.

The account in this book ends strictly with the moment of a block's completion, just before the first tenants were to move in. This means that the second great narrative of the British Welfare State tower block lies entirely outside its scope. The study in this book is focused on the fabric itself, on how it was planned and constructed, and on all those principally involved in this process: the public authorities, the professional designers and the builders. The second narrative, which, all in all, has received far more public attention than the first, is concerned with the experience of inhabiting, and managing, the completed blocks. This is a story that frequently includes significant material changes to the buildings, including decay and destruction on the one hand, and renovation and revitalisation on the other. The people at the centre of this second narrative are not, however, the designers or 'providers' but the inhabitants themselves. Their dissatisfactions have sometimes been expressed directly, but also often have been appropriated by the professional commentators who have voiced the most articulate condemnations of multi-storey public housing –

STOP SLUM
CLEARANCE-NOW

By ALAN STONES

Above: Unidentified urban view, published in 1972 – it is Liverpool, some streets adjacent to The Braddocks and Creswell Mount (cf. p. 199).
Right: The same view in the *Liverpool Daily Post*, 1957.

a process in which many historians eagerly participated. In 2001, for example, Alison Ravetz, a longstanding adversary of high blocks, summed it up: The post-war building of mass housing, she argued, could only have been perpetrated because council tenants had been 'desperate to escape bad housing conditions and ready to be seduced by the fittings and spaciousness of their new homes'.[2] At any rate, during the 1970s and 80s we witness an astonishing period in which almost all Modernist domestic architecture, was condemned absolutely. Much more recently, however, Elain Harwood concluded her magisterial book on English post-war architecture, Space, Hope and Brutalism, with the words 'it seems unlikely

that a similar period of optimism and endeavour will return for a long time'.[3] An underlying issue here is the longstanding preoccupation of the British housing discourse with the dichotomy of modernity and 'tradition'. That back-and-forth debate constantly interacted with another entrenched aspect of housing discussions in Britain: The uniquely sharp divergences of opinion and constant changes of mind as to which kind of dwelling makes the best kind of home. Taken as a whole, all these controversies and passions about mass housing and tower blocks point to a broader cultural phenomenon: in Britain, more strongly than elsewhere, all buildings speak.

ABBREVIATIONS

ACRONYMS

BC	Borough Council	GLC	Greater London Council (from 1965)	MBC	(London) Metropolitan Borough Council
CDA	Comprehensive Development Area	HMSO	Her Majesty's Stationery Office	MHLG	Ministry of Housing and Local Government
CLP	County of London Plan, see also below	HWD	Housing and Works Department	RDA	Redevelopment Area
CB	County Borough	ILP	Independent Labour Party	RIBA	Royal Institute of British Architects
DLO	Direct Labour Organisation	LA	Local Authority	SSHA	Scottish Special Housing Association
		LBC	London Borough Council		
		LCC	London County Council (to 1965)		

JOURNALS

AAJ	*Architectural Association Journal (Arena)*	*HR*	*Housing Review* (publ. by the Housing Centre)	*MJ*	*Municipal Journal (1966: Municipal and Public Services Journal)*
AB	*Architecture and Building*		*Housing and Planning Review* see *JNHTPC*	*MR*	*Municipal Review*
ABN	*Architecture and Building News*			*MYB*	*Municipal Yearbook*
AD	*Architectural Design*	*IB*	*Interbuild (1953–1958 Prefabrication)*	*OAP*	*Official Architecture and Planning (Built Environment)*
AJ	*Architects' Journal*				
AR	*Architectural Review*	*IBSC*	*Industrial Building Systems and Components*		*Prefabrication* (see *Interbuild*)
AY	*Architectural Yearbook*			*S*	*Surveyor and Municipal (and County) Engineer*
B	*The Builder (Building)*	*JNHTPC*	*Journal of the National Housing and Town Planning Council;* also carries the title: *The British Housing and Planning Review*		
	British Housing and Town Planning Review see *JNHTPC*			*T*	*The Times*
	Built Environment see *OAP*			*TCP*	*Town and County Planning*
CQ	*Concrete Quarterly*	*JTPI*	*Journal of the Town Planning Institute*	*TPR*	*Town Planning Review*
HJIHM	*Housing. Journal of the Institute of Housing Managers*			*WN*	*Wimpey News*

BOOKS

Allan	John Allan, *Berthold Lubetkin. Architecture and the Tradition of Progress* (London: RIBA Publications, 1992)		*Design of Dwellings*, ['Dudley Report'] (London: HMSO, 1944).	*LiF*	*Living in Flats, Report of the Flats Sub-Committee of the Central Housing Advisory Committee* (Brooke Report) (London: HMSO, 1952)
Allerton	R.J. Allerton, *London County Council Housing Service Handbook* (publ. LCC, 1962)	Dunleavy	Patrick Dunleavy, *The Politics of Mass Housing in Britain 1945–1975* (Oxford: Clarendon Press, 1981)		
		FH	MHLG, *Flats and Houses 1958. Design and Economy* (London: HMSO, 1958)	Powers	Alan Powers, *Britain* (Series Modern Architecture in History) (London: Reaktion, 2002)
Bruckmann	Hansmartin Bruckmann and David L. Lewis *New Housing in Great Britain* (London: Tiranti, 1960)	Finnimore	Brian Finnimore. *Houses from the Factory. System Building and the Welfare State 1942–1974* (London: Rivers Oram Press, 1989)	*PM*	'Parker Morris Report', so-called: *Homes for Today and Tomorrow* (publ. MHLG 1961; later editions publ. by Department for the Environment)
Bullock	Nicholas Bullock, *Building the Post-war World. Modern Architecture and the Reconstruction of Britain* (London: Routledge, 2002)	GAZ	Gazetteers in *TB*		
		Glendinning / *Matthew*	Miles Glendinning, *Modern Architect. The Life and Times of Robert Matthew* (London: RIBA Publications, 2008)	Ravetz	Alison Ravetz, *Council Housing and Culture. The History of a Social Experiment* (London: Routledge, 2001)
Calder	Barnabas Calder, *Raw Concrete. The Beauty of Brutalism* (London: Heinemann, 2016)				
CB	A.W. Cleeve Barr, *Public Authority Housing* (London: Batsford, 1958)	Harwood	Elain Harwood, *Space, Hope and Brutalism. English Architecture 1945–1975* (New Haven and London: Yale University Press, 2015)	*TB*	Miles Glendinning and Stefan Muthesius, *Tower Block. Modern Public Housing in England, Scotland, Wales and Northern Ireland* (New Haven and London: Yale University Press, 1994)
CLB	London County Council, *County of London Plan* (London: Macmillan, 1943)	*HfF*	*Housing from the Factory. Proceedings of the Conference London,* (publ. Cement and Concrete Association, 1962)		
Crawford	David Crawford, *A Decade of British Housing 1963–1973* (London: Architectural Press, 1975)			*TB* GAZ	Gazetteers in *TB*
		Jensen	Rolf Jensen, *High Density Living* (London: Leonard Hill, 1966)	YG	F.S.R. Yorke and Frederick Gibberd, *Modern Flats* [2nd ed.] (London: Architectural Press, 1958)
Dudley Report	Design of Dwellings Sub-committee ... Minister of Health,				

259

GENERAL BIBLIOGRAPHY

See above: Allan, Cleeve Barr, Bruckmann, Bullock, Dunleavy, Glendinning and Muthesius, Jensen, Powers, Ravetz, Sutcliffe, Yorke and Gibberd

For more works prior to 1993/94 see *TB,* pp. 408–09. Additional works from 1993/94:

Indispensable: Alan Cox, *Public Housing. A London Archive Guide* (publ. Guildhall Library and The London Archive Users' Forum, 1993)

Kate Ascher, *The Heights, Anatomy of a Skyscraper* (New York: Penguin Press, 2011)

P Balchin (ed), *Housing Policy in Europe* (London: Routledge, 1996)

Tom Begg, *Fifty Special Years – a Study in Scottish Housing,* (London: Henry Melland, 1987)

Barnabas Calder, *The Beauty of Brutalism. Raw Concrete* (London: Heinemann, 2016)

Beatrix Campbell, *Goliath – Britain's Dangerous Places* (London: Methuen, 1993)

Louise Campbell, Miles Glendinning, and Jane Thomas (eds), *Basil Spence – Buildings and Projects,* (London: RIBA, 2012)

Ian Cole and Robert Furbey, *The Eclipse of Council Housing* (London: Routledge, 1994)

Ian Colquhoun, *RIBA Book of 20th Century British Housing* (Oxford: Butterworth Heinemann, 1999)

Danny Dorking, *All that is Solid: the Great Housing Disaster* (London: Allen Lane, 2014)

Robert Elwall, *Building a better Tomorrow. Architecture in Britain in the 1950s* (Chichester: Wiley 2000)

Paul Evans, *The 1960s Home* (Botley: Shire, 2010)

Miles Glendinning and Diane Watters (eds), *Home Builders* (Edinburgh: RCAHMS, 1999)

John Gold, *The Experience of Modernism,* (London: Spon, 1997)

John Grindrod, *Concretopia. A Journey around the Rebuilding of Postwar Britain* (Brecon: Old Street Books, 2013)

Lynsey Hanley, *Estates – an Intimate History* (London: Granta, 2007)

Michael Harloe, *The People's Home* (Oxford: Blackwell, 1995)

Elain Harwood and Alan Powers (eds.), *The Sixties. Life. Style. Architecture* (publ. London: The Twentieth Century Architecture Society, 2002)

Elain Harwood and Alan Powers (eds.), *Housing the Twentieth Century Nation* (Series *Architecture 9*); the Journal of the Twentieth Century Society (publ. London: Twentieth Century Society, 2008)

Elain Harwood, *Space, Hope and Brutalism. English Architecture 1945-1975* (London and New Have: Yale University Press, 2015)

Elain Harwood, *A Guide to England's Post-war Listed Buildings* (London: Batsford, 2003)

Owen Hatherley, *Militant Modernism,* (Winchester: Zero Books, 2008)

Owen Hatherley, *A Guide to the New Ruins of Great Britain* (London and New York: Verso, 2011)

Simon Henley, *Redefining Brutalism* (London: RIBA Publications, 2017)

Peter Hennessy, *Never Again. Britain 1945–51* (London: Jonathan Cape, 1992)

Owen Hopkins, *Futures Found. The Real and Imaginary Cityscapes of Post-War Britain* (publ. London: Royal Academy, 2017) https://en.wikipedia.org/wiki/List of large_council_estates_in_the_UK (consulted August 2017) www.towerblock.eca.ed.ac.uk/

David Jeremiah, *Architecture and Design for the Family in Britain 1900–1970* (Manchester University Press, 2000)

Sophie Leighton, *The 1950s Home* (Botley: Shire, 2010)

Jamileh Manoochehri, *The Politics of Social Housing in Britain* (Oxford: P.Lang, 2012)

Anna Minton, *Big Capital. Who is London for?* (Penguin, 2017)

Kiel Moe and Ryan E. Smith (eds.), *Building Systems. Design Technology and Society* (London: Routledge, 2012)

Philip Nobel and others, *The Future of the Skyscraper* (SOM 2015)

Simon Phipps, *Finding Brutalism. A Photographic Survey of post-war British Architecture* (Zurich: Park Books, 2017)

Anne Power, *Estates on the Edge, The Social Consequences of Mass Housing in Northern Europe* (Basingstoke: Macmillan, 1997)

Anne Power, *Hovels to High Rise, State Housing in Europe since 1950* (London: Routledge, 1993)

Alison Ravetz, *The Place of Home. English Domestic Environments 1914–2000* (London: Spon, 1995)

Jane Rendell, *The Architecture of Psychoanalysis. Spaces of Transition* (London: I.B.Tauris, 2017)

Laurent Stalder, ' "New Brutalism", "Topology" and image: some remarks on the architectural debates in England around 1950', *Journal of Architecture,* vol., 13, June, pp. 263–281

Philip Steadman, *Building Types and Building Forms* (Kibworth: Beauchamp Matador, 2014)

Deyan Sudjic, *The Edifice Complex. The Architecture of Power* (London: Allan Lane, 2005)

Mark Swenarton, Tom Avermaete and Dirk van den Heuvel (eds.) *Architecture and the Welfare State* (London: Routledge, 2015)

Graham Towers, *Shelter is not enough. Transforming Multi-storey Housing* (Bristol: Policy Press, 1999)

Florian Urban, *Tower and Slab* (London: Routledge, 2012)

Special bibliographical sections: see Notes.

NOTES

CHAPTER 1 – 'POWER SYMBOLS'

1. *AJ,* 1-11-1961, pp. 825–42 (p. 826).
2. 'High London', *AR,* 7–1958, pp. 5–8.
3. Rodney Lowe, *The Welfare State in Britain since 1945*, 3rd ed. (Basingstoke: Palgrave, 2005), pp. 18, 262, 263, 270, 253, 265.
4. Cf. Ravetz.
5. Margaret Willis, 'Sociology and the Architect', *AAJ,* 2–1957, pp. 203–04.
6. John P. Macey and C.V. Baker, *Housing Management* (London: Estates Gazette, 1965), pp. 203-17, 303-16.
7. Allerton, p. 24; cf. Chapter 11.

CHAPTER 2 – STANDARDS, NUMBERS, COSTS

1. CB, p. 56; Dudley Report.
2. CB, pp. 56–57.
3. *MR,* 8-1960, p. 529.
4. Relates to a 21-storey Wimpey block in Queen Street Sarah Robinson House (1964), *Portsmouth Evening News,* 15-7-1966. Cf. Ladywood House, p. 167.
5. *AJ,* 5–8/15-3-1956, p. 261.
6. Ministry of Health, *Housing Manual 1949* (London: HMSO, 1949), p. 83; Ian Cole and Robert Furbey, *The Eclipse of Council Housing* (London and New York: Routledge, 1994), p. 98.
7. *AJ,* 7-12-1950, pp. 493–97.
8. CB, pp. 54–55.
9. *AJ,* 22-11-1956, p. 724.
10. Bullock, pp. 42–43, 212.
11. J.B. Cullingworth, *Housing and Local Government in England and Wales* (London: Allen & Unwin, 1966), pp. 142–43.
12. *TB,* pp. 1–2, 331.
13. MHLG, *Residential Areas Higher Densities* (London: HMSO 1962), Foreword.
14. *IBSC,* 9-1968, p. 21.
15. *AR,* 9-1970, p. 197.

16. GAZ; MHLG, *Housing Returns for England and Wales,* 1966 etc.
17. Sir Frederick Osborn, 'The Englishman's Home – a two-storey house and garden', *S,* 1-12-1956, p. 965; cf. *Family Life in High Density Housing... Report of a Symposium* (publ. London: RIBA 1957); *S,* 26-2-1955, p. 196.
18. John P. Macey, 'Problems of Flat Life', *OAP,* 1-1959, pp. 35–38.
19. *HJIHM,* vol. 4, no. 2, 7-1968, pp. 13–16.
20. CB, chapter 6.
21. *AJ,* 18-2-1960, p. 278; cf. *JRIBA,* 4-1956, pp. 240–49.
22. CB; p. 132ff; cf. P.A. Stone, *Housing Town Development Land and Costs* (publ. Estates Gazette, 1963).
23. Brandon: cf., p. viii; *Birmingham Post,* 22-12-1967; Trellick: *AJ,* 10-1-1973, p. 94.
24. Civic Trust, *Urban Redevelopment* (publ. London: Civic Trust, 1963), pp. 12–13; *TPR,* 4-1955, p. 32.
25. *FH,* p. 61.
26. City of Portsmouth, Health and Housing Committee, 21-2-1962.

CHAPTER 3 – WELFARE STATE PROVIDERS

1. M.F.P. Bouverie, *Daily Mail Book of Post War Homes* (publ. London Associated Newspapers, 1944); *TB,* p. 15.
2. Harold Macmillan, *Tides of Fortune 1945–55* (London: Macmillan, 1969), p. 403.
3. 'Better Housing Standards', *T,* 29-1-1949, p. 3.
4. Powers, p. 132; *AJ,* 15-1-1959, p. 87–8; *Building Design,* No. 362, 9-9-1977, p. 15 .
5. *AJ,* 4-7-1946, p. 3.
6. *JRIBA,* 5-1955, pp. 356–68.
7. *Daily Mail Book of Post-war Homes,* 1944; *TB,* p. 15.
8. *AR,* 7-1958, p. 6; Gordon E. Cherry, *Town Planning in Britain since 1900* (Oxford: Blackwell, 1996).
9. Peter J. Larkham, 'The Imagery of UK Post-war Reconstruction Plans', *Working Paper* Faculty of Built Environment, Series No. 88 (publ. UCE Birmingham, 2004).
10. *JTPI,* 5-1953, p. 126.
11. *JRIBA,* 7-1948, p. 386.
12. Interview Lubetkin, 3-7-1990.
13. *JRIBA,* 7-1946, p. 394.
14. Margaret Willis, 'Sociology and the Architect', *AAJ,* 2-1957, pp. 203–04.
15. Interview Percival 1986, see Miles Horsey and Stefan Muthesius, *Provincial Mixed Development. Norwich Council Housing 1955-1973* (publ. Norwich, 1986), p. 14.
16. Richard H. Sheppard,' Sociology and Architecture', *JRIBA,* 7-1946, pp. 386–94.
17. *LiF,* p. 1.
18. *TB,* Chapters 12 etc.

CHAPTER 4 – COUNCIL POWERS

1. Michael Harloe, *The People's Home* (Oxford: Blackwell, 1995), pp. 106–12; Anne Power, *Hovels to High Rise, State Housing in Europe since 1850* (London: Routledge 1993), pp. 165–241; J. S. Fuerst, *Public Housing in Europe and America* (London: Croom Helm, 1974), p. 31; Eve Blau, *The Architecture of Red Vienna 1919–1934* (Cambridge: MA and London MIT Press, 1999); Matthew Hollow, *Housing Needs. Power, Subjectivity and Public Housing in England 1920–1970,* PhD, Oxford University, 2012.
2. Power, *op. cit.*, p. 213.
3. Chris Matthews, *Homes and Places, a History of Nottingham's Council Housing,* (publ. Nottingham City Homes, 2015), p. 56; Nick Hayes, *Consensus and Controversy – City Politics in Nottingham 1945–1966* (Liverpool: Liverpool University Press, 1996), pp. 90, 135.
4. Finnimore, p. 371; Ministry of Public Building and Works, *A National Building Agency* (London, 1963).
5. United Nations, *The Housing Situation in European Countries* (New York, 1968); Interview by M Glendinning with R E Nicoll, 1987; Tom Begg, *Fifty Special Years – A Study in Scottish Housing* (London: Henry Melland, 1987).
6. J N Tarn, *Working-Class Housing in 19th Century Britain* (London: Lund Humphries, 1971).
7. *IBSC,* 4-1967, pp. 68.
8. M. Glendinning, 'The Ballantyne Report', in Deborah Mays (ed), *The Architecture of Scottish Cities* (East Linton: Tuckwell, 1997).
9. M. Horsey, *Tenements and Towers* (Edinburgh: RCAHMS, 1990), pp. 39–43.
10. CLP; P. Abercrombie and R. H. Matthew, *The Clyde Valley Regional Plan 1946* (Edinburgh HMSO, 1949).
11. G. Cherry (ed), *Pioneers in British Planning* (London: London Architectural Press, 1981), pp. 179–183.
12. *TB,* pp. 160–61, 170–73.
13. Interviews by J. Beddoe and E. Smythe with M. Glendinning, 1987.
14. *TB,* p. 265.
15. Finnimore, p. 81; R. Crossman, *The Diaries of a Cabinet Minister* (London: Hamish Hamilton, 1975), vol. 1, pp.108, 154.
16. *TB,* pp. 196; Interview with R. Mellish by M. Glendinning, 1987.
17. Central Housing Advisory Committee, Minutes, 11 October 1965 and 12 June 1967; Gosport Borough Council, Housing Committee Minutes, 28 April 1966.
18. Interview with A. G. Sheppard Fidler by M. Glendinning and S. Muthesius, 1987; J. Forshaw in Symposium on High Flats, *JRIBA,* 4-1955; *TB, p.* 179.
19. Interviews with J. Beddoe and J. Milefanti by M. Glendinning, 1987; *TB, pp.* 198–99.
20. Interview with G. Bowie by M. Glendinning, 1987.

CHAPTER 5 – ARCHITECTS ETC.

1. Glendinning, *Matthew*; Peter Carolin and Trevor Dannatt (eds.), *Architecture, Education and Research. The Work of Leslie Martin* (London: Academy Editions, 1996).
2. *AJ,* 4-7-1946, p. 3; Elizabeth Layton, *Building by Local Authorities* (London: Allen & Unwin, 1961); Peter Malpass, 'Professionalism and the role of the Architect in Local Authority Housing ', *JRIBA,* 6-1975, pp. 6–29; Nicholas Merthyr Day, *The Role of the Architect in Post-War State Housing. A Case Study if the Housing Work of the LCC 1919–1956,* PhD, Warwick University, 1988; Andrew Saint, *Politics and People in London. The LCC 1889–1965* (London: Hambledon Press, 1989).
3. Nicholas Taylor, 'The Failure of 'Housing', *AR,* 11-1967, pp. 341–59.
4. Richards, *AJ,* 10-3-1949, p. 228; Lubetkin, *AJ,* 2-6-1949, p. 495; *AJ* pictures: *AJ,* 17-3-1949, pp. 251–53; Gibson: *AJ,* 9-6-1949, p. 528; aesthetic: *A,J* 5-5-1949, p:402; amenities: *AD,* 1-1949, p. 2; *T,* 17-12-1949; Cf. also *ABN,* 11-2-1949, pp. 122-124; *OAP,* 4-1949, pp. 191–94; LCC, Housing. A Survey of the Post War Housing Work of the London County Council 1945–1949 (publ. LCC 14149); Bullock, p. 215.
5. *JRIBA,* 1-1946, pp. 88–89.
6. *JRIBA,* 7-1948, p. 382.
7. Glendinning, *Matthew,* pp. 110–12.
8. JRIBA, 10-1955, pp. 471–8; Andrew Saint, *Towards a Social Architecture. The Role of School Building in Post-War England* (New Haven and London: Yale University Press, 1987).
9. Eric Hollamby and David Gregory-Jones, 'The Structure and Personality of the LCC Architects' Department', *AB,* 5-1957, pp. 171–79.
10. R. Furneaux Jordan, 'LCC. New Standards in official Architecture', *AR,* 11-1956, pp. 303–24.
11. *JRIBA,* 11-1955, p. 5.
12. Sarah Menin and Stephen Kite, *An Architecture of Invitation. Colin St. John Wilson* (Aldershot: Ashgate, 2005), p. 31.
13. *JRIBA,* 3-1960, pp. 160–63.
14. Cf. Christine Wall, *An Architecture of Parts. Architects, Building Workers and Industrialisation in Britain 1940–1970* (London: Routledge, 2013).
15. *AJ,* 5-6-1952, pp. 703–09; *AJ,* 28-1-1954, pp. 137–41; *AJ,* 30-12-1954, pp. 815–17; *JRIBA,*4-1956, pp. 240–49.
16. Allan, p. 383.
17. *Engineering the World. Ove Arup and the Philosophy of Total Design,* exhibition cat., London, Victoria and Albert Museum, 2016.
18. *JRIBA,* 3-1962, pp. 91.
19. Andrew Saint, *Towards a Social Architecture,* op. cit.
20. *ABN,* 28-2-1957, p. 284; *B,* 11-11-1955, pp. 804–06.

21. *AJ*, 3-2-1955, p. 173; *AJ*, 29-11-1956, pp. 795–802; *JRIBA*, 4-1955, pp. 254–55.

22. *ABN*, 15-4-1954, p. 423; *B*, 17-9-1954, pp. 467–69.

23. *AJ*, 23-2-1956, p. 225.

24. *B*, 21-6-1963, p. 1249–50.

25. *B*, 25-1-1957, p. 200.

26. Exceptions: e.g. Bison, *B*, 24-5-1963, p. 1031; cf. p. 167).

27. *B*, 25-1-1957, p. 198.

28. *ABN*, 28-2-1957, p. 284.

29. *AJ*, 24-4-1958, p. 603.

30. Finnimore, pp. 67 etc.

31. Dunleavy, pp. 67, 107.

32. BILIOGRAPHICAL NOTE INDUSTRIALISED BUILDING: *IB*, 10-1962; *ABN*, 1965; *HfF*; A.F.L. Deeson (ed.), *The Comprehensive Industrialised Building Systems Annual* (London House Publications, vols. for 1965, 1966, 1967). R.M.E. Diamant, *Industrialised Building. 50 International Methods* (London: Iliffe, 1964); R.M.E. Diamant, *Industrialised Building 2 ...* (London: Iliffe, 1965); R.M.E. Diamant, *Industrialised Building 3 ...* (London: Iliffe, 1968); Thomas Schmid and Carlo Testa, *Systems Building. An International Survey* (London: Pall Mall Press, 1979); Barry Russell, *Building Systems, Industrialisation and Architecture* (Chichester: Wiley, 1981); B.R. Reves and British Research Establishment, *Large Panel System Dwellings: Preliminary Ownership and Condition* (publ. Department of the Environment, Watford 1986 [mimeo-graphed, RIBA Library]).

33. *HfF*, p. vi.

34. *MHLG Circular 76 /65*, 1965, quoted in Finnimore, p. 86.

35. Peter Guillery, ed. *Woolwich* (vol. 48 of Andrew Saint (ed.), *The Survey of London* (English Heritage, 2012), pp. 320–24.

36. Cf. p. 92.

37. *T*, 5-11-1963, p. 5.

38. Cf. Chapter 10.

39. Cf. p. 26.

40. Cf. p. 91.

41. *B*, 10-1-1964, p. 83.

42. Tom Dalyell, *Dick Crossman. A Portrait* (London: Weidenfeld and Nicolson, 1989), 116; *TB* 209.

43. *B*, 25 -2 -1966, pp. 402–08.

44. *AJ*, 8-4-1964, p. 787; *B*, 20-3-1964, p. 628.

CHAPTER 6 – *EXISTENZMUNIMUM*

1. See e.g. Karel Teige, *Nejmenšl byt* (Prague Vaclav Petr, 1932; also as *The Minimum Dwelling* Cambridge MA, MIT Press, 2002).

2. Paul Overy, *Light, Air and Openness. Modern Architecture between the Wars* (London: Thames and Hudson, 2000), p. 9.

3. *AJ*, 21-3-1935, pp. 438 ff.; *B*, 5-4-1935, pp. 628-9.

4. *Slum Clearance and Rehousing. The First Report of the Council for Research on Housing Construction* (publ. by Council ..., London: P.S. King, 1934), p. 73.

5. *Report*, p. 119.

6. See for example Y. M. Yeung and T. K. Y. Wong (eds.), *Fifty Years of Public Housing in Hong Kong* (publ. Hong Kong Housing Authority, Hong Kong, 2003), pp. 1–62.

7. Cf. *JRIBA*, 7-1946, pp. 389–90; CB, pp. 53.

CHAPTER 7 – HIGH RISE STORIES

1. F.R.S. Yorke and Frederick Gibberd, *Modern Flats* (London: Architectural Press, 1937).

2. *CLP*, p. 83.

3. Cf. p. 104.

4. *MJ*, 16-11-1956, p. 2739.

5. AJ, 23-7-1969, p. 151; cf. *B*, 17-5-1956, pp. 1544-45.

6. *JRIBA*, 3-1955, p. 195.

7. *B*, 18-3-1955, p. 483.

8. *JRIBA*, 4-1955, p. 252.

9. CB, p. 114.

10. *OAP*, 7-1959, pp. 304–05.

11. *FH*, pp. 137–139.

12. *JRIBA*, 3-1955, pp. 209–10.

13. CB, p. 114.

14. *MJ*, 16-11-1956, pp. 2739.

15. *TB*, 62; *AD*, 7-1961, p. 289.

16. Dunleavy, p. 39; GAZ.

17. Finnimore, p. 261.

18. *AJ*, 21-11-1961, p. 979.

19. *AJ*, 29-6-1961.

20. *AJ*, 22-11-1961, p 979.

21. *HfF, p.* VI.

22. *MJ*, 21-7-1967, p. 1903.

23. *MJ*, 31-7-1959, pp. 2093.

24. 'The Development of High Flats', *MJ*, 16-11-1956, pp. 2739–80.

25. Civic Trust, *Urban Redevelopment*, Conference (publ. London: Civic Trust, 1962), p. 13.

26. Jensen, pp. 1–3, 14, 29.

27. Allerton, p. 11.

28. *AJ*, 29-6-1961, p. 935; *TB*, p. 34.

29. *MJ*, 5-10-1962, p. 3025.

30. Dunleavy, p. 43.

31. Birmingham City Council, *Developing Birmingham 1889–1989. 100 years of City Planning* (publ. Birmingham, 1989), p. 76.

32. *Liverpool Daily Post*, 20-9-1957.

CHAPTER 8 – AESTHETICS

1. *JRIBA*, 3-1955, p. 195.

2. *AJ*, 22-11-1945, p. 386.

3. *WN*, 1-1963.

4. *AJ*, 24-1-1952, pp. 118–24.

5. *JRIBA*, 3-1955, p. 201.

6. Nikolaus Pevsner, 'Roehampton LCC Housing and the Picturesque Tradition', *AR*, 7-1959 , pp. 21–35.

7. Nikolaus Pevsner, *The Englishness of English Art* [the 1955 Reith Lectures]

(London: Architectural Press, 1956), p. 176.

8. Among recent discussions of these issues see Glendinning, *Matthew*, Harwood, Calder.

9. CB, pp. 97, 104.

10. A.G. Sheppard Fidler, 'The Building and Development of Flats', *National Housing and Town Planning Council Yearbook*, 1953, pp. 87–91.

11. *JRIBA*, 3-1955, p.195.

12. *AJ*, 18-2-1960, p. 283.

13. W. Eric Jackson, *Achievement. A short History of the London County Council* (London: Longmans, 1965), p. 105.

14. *MJ*, 24-1-1958, p.193 (F.–J. is cited here in an article on the New Towns.

15. BIBIOGRAPHICAL NOTE: THE HIGH BUILDINGS DISCUSSION: Osbert Sitwell, 'Towers', in O. Sitwell, *The Four Continents ...* (London Macmillan, 1954), pp. 108-33; *AR*, 5-1954, pp. 341–42; 'Symposium on High Flats' at the RIBA: *JRIBA*, 3-1955, pp. 195–212; *JRIBA*, 4-1955, pp. 251–259; *ABN*, 24-2-1955, p. 223; *B*, 18-3-1955, pp. 481-3; *AJ*, 7-4-1955, pp. 459–60; see also: *ABN*, 17-5-1956, pp. 521–22; *JRIBA*, 6-1956, pp. 350–53; *B*, 1-6-1956, pp. 621–22; *S*, 19-5-1956, pp. 258–59; *B*, 14-6-1957, p 1065; *AR*, 7-1958, pp. 5–8; JTPI, 3-1959 78-86; IB, 9-1959, p. 9; *ABN* 2-12-1959, p. 544; *AB*, 3-1959; *AJ*, 18-2-1960, pp. 271–72, 283–84; *B*, 19-2-1960, pp. 371–74; *B*, 22-4-1960, p. 787; *B*, 16-12-1960 , pp. 1103, 1121–23; *JRIBA*, 2-1961, pp. 137–39; *MJ*, 22-2-1961, p. 479; *AR*, 3-1961, pp. 194–200; *S*, 4-5-1963, pp. 589–90; *AR*, 3-1963, pp. 175–79; *TPR*, 4-1963, pp. 7–18; *TPR*, 4-1963, pp. 61–72; *JNHTPC*, 1/ 2 -1963, pp. 5–10; *AJ*, 26-2-1964, p. 455; *B[uilding]*, 31-5-1968, pp. 79–80; *AJ*, 22-10-1969, pp. 899; *AJ*, 23-7-1969, p. 141.

16. J.M. Richards, 'High London', *AR*, 7-1958 5–8.

17. *TB*, p. 119.

18. *AB*, 1954, pp. 441–42; cf. p. 79.

19. JTPI, 3-1959, pp. 78–86.

20. *AR*, 7-1958, p. 8.

21. *JRIBA*, 6-1956, p. 350.

22. *AB*, 3-1960, p. 87.

23. JTPI, 3-1959, p. 81.

24. *AB*, 3-1960, p. 97; *B*, 19-2-1960, p. 372.

25. *AJ*, 18-2-1960, pp. 283-4; *AJ*, 29-8-1957, p. 313.

26. *AJ*, 18-2-1960, p. 277.

27. Note by the Minister (MHLG), 'High Buildings in London', 30-12-1957 (M.O. 5489/57).

28. *JRIBA*, 3-1955, pp. 201–02.

29. *JRIBA*, 3-1955, p. 208.

30. *JRIBA*, 6-1956, p. 351.

31. For new developments in architectural photography see CF. Robert Elwall, *Photography takes Command. The Camera and British Architecture 1890–1939*.

CHAPTER 9 – TYPES OF FLATS

1. Anthony Sutcliffe (ed.), *Multi-Storey Living. The British Working Class Experience* (London: Croom Helm, 1974), p. ix.
2. *Flats Municipal and Private Enterprise* (publ. by Ascot Gas Water Heaters London, 1938), p. 5; cf. Dudley Report.
3. Thomas Sharp, *Town Planning* (Harmondsworth: Penguin, 1940), pp. 121–22; cf. *AJ*, 26-2-1953, pp. 287–88; cf. p. 113; *Planning Perspectives*, vol. 24, no. 1, 1-2009: issue on Thomas Sharp, pp. 1–98.
4. See Allan, Powers, Ravetz, Pepper (see Note 14 below); Elizabeth Darling, *Re-forming Britain. Narratives of Modernity before Reconstruction* (London: Routledge, 2009).
5. BIBLIOGRAPHICAL NOTE INTERNATIONAL STYLE HOUSING AND PLANNING: Florian Urban, *Tower and Slab* (London: Routledge, 2012); Mark Crinson and Clare Zimmerman (eds.), *Neo-Avantgarde and Postmodern Post-War Architecture in Britain and Beyond* (New Haven and London: Yale University Press, 2010); Michael Peterek, *Wohnung, Siedlung, Stadt. Paradigmen der Moderne* (Berlin: Mann, 2000); see General Bibliography in *TB; see* Note 14 below. Cf. Hamburg's Grindelberg 15-storey slab blocks, initiated 1945-6 by Royal Engineers (*AJ*, 17-4-1952, p. 477).
6. See e.g. Sydney Perks, *Residential Flats for all Classes including Artisan Dwellings* (London: Batsford, 1905).
7. See *TB*, Ch. 6.
8. *CLP, p.* 108; MHLG, *The Density of Residential Areas* (London: HMSO, 1952); *AJ*, 8-9-1960, p. 362; P.A. Stone, *Housing, Town Development, Land and Costs* (publ. London Estates Gazette, 1963).
9. MHLG, *The Density of Residential Areas* (London: HMSO, 1952), pp. ii, 63.
10. *The Density... op. cit.,* pp. 66.
11. *CLP,* p. 171.
12. See *op. cit.* in chapter 6, p. 75.
13. Tom Harrison 'Houses or Flats', *TCP*, vol. ix, no. 36 Winter 1941/2, pp. 117–18; Dudley Report.
14. BIBLIOGRAPHICAL NOTE MODERNIST HOUSING IN BRITAIN IN THE 1930s: Elizabeth Denby, *Europe Rehoused* (London: Allen & Unwin, 1938; reprint, intr. By Elizabeth Darling, London: Routledge, 2015), p. 264; Elizabeth Darling, 'The Star in the Profession she invented herself'; a brief biography of Elizabeth Denby, housing consultant', *Planning Perspectives,* no. 20, 7-2005*;* pp. 271–300*;* cf. Simon Pepper, 'The Beginnings of High-Rise Housing in the Long 1940s: The case of the LCC and the Woodberry Down Estate', in: Mark Swenarton & oth., *Architecture of the Welfare State* (London and New York: Routledge, 2015*)* pp. 69–92; S. Pepper,

'Early Tenement Houses', *Construction History,* vol. 23, 2008, pp. 98–117; Stefan Muthesius, 'It is as though we started a new life. Council Housing in Shoreditch 1945–1950', *Hackney History*, vol. 13, 2007, pp. 41–47; the *AJ* shows numerous projects of high slabs early on, e.g. *AJ*, 9-8-1945, pp. 1105; AJ, 19-4-1945, p. xiii.
15. Dudley Report; Marianne Walter, 'Flats', *AJ*, 6-2-1947, pp. 145–49; Nicholas Bullock, 'Plans for Post-war Housing in the UK. The case for mixed development and the flat', *Planning Perspectives,* no. 2 1987, pp. 71–98; G.R. Owens, *Mixed Development in Local Authority Housing in England and Wales 1943–1970*, PhD, London University, 1987; see also CB; *TB,* chapter 5; Bullock, pp. 151ff; Harwood.
16. *MJ*, 6-8-1954, pp. 1804–09.
17. Owens, *op. cit.*, p. 291.
18. *FH, p.* 16.
19. 1934 *Report* op. cit. Chapter 6, p. 53.
20. A.A. Bellamy, 'High Flats in the USA', *Housing Review*, 1/2-1958, pp. 12–18; A.A. Bellamy 'Housing in large cities in the USA', *TPR*, vol. 29, 10-1958/9, pp. 179–87; R. Bradbury in *JRIBA*, 3-1955, pp. 199–201.
21. *FH*, page v.
22. *FH*, p. 123.
23. *HfF*, p. v.
24. See *TB*, pp. 146–50.
25. *OAP*, 2-1952, p. 70.
26. *OAP*, 4-1950, p. 200.
27. Cf. Eduard F. Seckler, *Das Punkthaus im europäischen Wohnungsbau* (Vienna, 1962, as Heft 16 of *Abhandlungen des Dokumentationszentrums für Technik und Wissenschaft*); N. Pevsner; LCC Housing and the Picturesque Tradition, *AR*, 7-1959, pp. 31–45; Christina Engford (ed.), *Folkshemmets Bostäder 1940–1960* (Arkitektur Museet Stockholm, 1987); *AJ*, 4-7-1946, p. 2; *AJ*, 15-8-1946, p. 124; Bertil Hultén, *Building Modern Sweden (*Harmondsworth: Penguin, 1951).
28. *AJ*, 4-7-1946, p. 2.
29. LCC Housing Committee, Minutes 8-11-1950, p. 667; cf. 8-11-1950, pp. 667–68.
30. LCC 1951 Council Minutes, Report of the Housing Committee 7-3 -1951 and 11-4-1951.
31. *AJ*, 28-2-1952, p. 264; *The Observer,* 24-2-1952, p. 8; *TB*, p. 54.
32. Margaret Willis, 'Living in High Blocks of Flats', *HR,* 1-1954, pp. 13–15; *JRIBA,* 3-1955, pp. 203–05.
33. J. Eastwick Field and J. Stillman, 'Flats in Berlin', *AJ*, 30-10-958, pp. 630-637; Gabi Dolff-Bonekämper and Franziska Schmidt, *Das Hansaviertel. Internationale Nachkriegsmoderne in Berlin* (Berlin: Verlag Bauwesen, 1999). Cf. Roehampton *AR*, 1-1954, p. 52.
34. *MJ*, 8-8-1952, pp. 1477–78.
35. Margaret Willis, 'Living in a House over a House', *HR,* 1-1954, pp. 5–7; Dudley Report, p. 185.

36. *MJ*, 9-7-1954, p. 1554; *AD*, 9-1953, p. 3, pp. 258–59; Sarah Menin and Stephen Kite, *An Architecture of Invitation. Colin St. John Wilson* (Aldershot: Ashgate, 2005).
37. Picton see pp. 23, 68, 83.
38. Irena Murray and Julian Osley (eds.), *Le Corbusier and Britain. An Anthology* (Abingdon and New York: Routledge, 2009).
39. *AJ*, 27-11-1958, p. 799.
40. *B*, 7-2-1962, pp. 1121–23; *B*, 4-9-1964, p. 485.
41. *AJ*, 28-2-1962, pp. 453–60.
42. *AJ*, 29-11-1951, p. 660.
43. St. Peter's Hospital Site, Vallance Road, *JRIBA*, 8-1956, pp. 407–11.
44. *AJ*, 7-1-1960, pp. 25–27.
45. *AJ*, 28-2-1962, p. 453.
46. *LCC Housing Type Plans* (publ. by LCC, 1956); new ed. 1960.
47. *AR*, 1-1969, p. 22.
48. *B*, 27-12-1963, p. 1311.
49. *TB,* Chs. 12–19; cf. Max Risselada and Dirk van den Heuvel (eds.), *Team 10 1953-81. In Search of a Utopia for the Present* (Rotterdam: NAI Publishers, n.d. c.2005). Mark Swenarton, *Cook's Camden. The Making of Modern Housing* (London: Lund Humphries, 2017).

CHAPTER 10 – CONSTRUCTION

1. CB, p. 114.
2. *AJ*, 16-2-1956, p. 205; *AJ*, 17-4-1958, pp. 583–8.
3. *National Housing and Town Planning Council Yearbook* 1953, p. 89.
4. Marian Bowley, *Innovations in Building Materials: an Economic Study* (London: Duckworth, 1960), p. 42; Adrian Forty, *Concrete and Culture. A Material History* (London: Reaktion, 2012); Calder.
5. *National Housing and Town planning Council Yearbook,* 1953, p. 89.
6. CB, pp. 104, 107.
7. CB, pp. 106–8.
8. Jane Rendell, *The Architecture of Psychoanalysis. Spaces of Transition* (London: I.B. Tauris, 2017).
9. Allan, pp. 381–83.
10. *AJ*, 17-3-1955, pp. 357–368.
11. *TB*, chapter 10.
12. *AJ*, 30-12-1954, 815-7; *ABN*, 30–12, pp. 815-17; *ABN*, 5-4-1956, pp. 344–50; *AB*, 6-1958; *AJ*, 9-1960; A.E.J. Morris, *Precast-Concrete Cladding* (London: Fountain Press, 1964).
13. *T*, 5-3-1964, p.17; *TB*, p. 87.
14. Calder.
15. J. Gilchrist Wilson, *Concrete Facing Slabs* (publ. by Cement and Concrete Association London), 1st ed. 1954, 4th ed. no date [1960s].
16. CB, p. 96.
17. E.g. blocks by the Camus system, *TB*, p. 84.

18. *TB*, p. 92; *JRIBA*, 1-1952, pp. 79–87; *AJ* 24-2-1952, pp. 118–24.
19. *AR*, 3-1951, pp. 138–40; see Allan, p. 399.
20. R. Banham, 'Facade', *AR*, 11-1954, pp. 303-8.
21. *AJ*, 10-1-1962, p. 64; Unité: *OAP*, 11-1967, pp. 1606-7.
22. Except, e.g. Portsmouth, cf. p. 167; *MJ*, 8-1-1967.
23. *AR*, 5-1950, pp. 331–42.
24. *B*, 25-1-1957, p. 200.
25. 'Architecture and System Building', *B*, 29-3-1963, pp. 651–57 (653); see *B*, 21-6-1963, pp. 1249-51; *MJ*, 25-1-1963 pp. 224–43; *OAP*, 5-1963, pp. 439–40; *HfF*, pp. 129–41.
26. *HfF*, pp. 140–41.
27. *S*, 13-10-1962, pp. 1249–50.
28. 'After Ronan Point: Designing for stability. *IBSC*, 7-1969 51-54 (54); *Report of the enquiry into the collapse of flats at Ronan Point ..., presented to the Minister of Housing and Local Government* by Hugh Griffiths, Alfred Pugsley, Owen Saunders (London: H.M.S.O.,1968); see recently John Grindrod, *Concretopia. A Journey around the Rebuilding of Post-war Britain (*Brecon: Old Street Publishing, 2013); Owen Hopkins, *Lost Futures. The Disappearing Architecture of Post-War Britain* (London: Royal Academy of Arts, 2017).
29. 'Six Storeys and higher', in: [Wimpey], *Redevelopment in Wimpey No-Fines Concrete* [publ. Wimpey 1967], p. 38.
30. *OAP*, 7-1957, pp. 327–30.
31. *T*, 5-11-1963, p. 5.
32. *HfF*, p. 89; Concrete Ltd., *Introduction to the Bison Wall Frame System for High Flats* (publ. Concrete Ltd. October 1962); cf. 'Variety in high flats' [Bison advertise-ment feature], *MJ*, 23-8-1963, pp. 2459.

CHAPTER 11 – ENVIRONMENT

1. *JNHTPC*, 5/6-1962, p. 8.
2. *OAP*, 1-1959, p. 39; *MR*, 1-1961, 67.
3. John P. Macey, 'Problems of Flat Life', *OAP*, 1-1959, pp. 35-8; cf.'Housing', *AJ*, 4-9-1968; *Family Life in High Density Housing. With particular reference to the Design of Space about Buildings. A Symposium ...* (publ. London: RIBA, 1957).
4. CB, pp. 89–90.
5. CB, pp. 195.
6. E.g. Bentham Road Hackney, *B*, 24-9-1954, p. 494.
7. *AAJ*, 2-1957, p. 203.
8. *OAP*, 1-1959, p. 37; *AJ*, 14-2-1962, p. 361.
9. *ABN*, 25-2-1959, pp.190–92.
10. *OAP*, 1-1959, p. 38.
11. *JNHTPC*, 5/6-1962, p. 11.
12. *FH*, p. 119.
13. CB, p. 91.
14. *FH*, p. 120; CB, p. 64.
15. Cf. LCC Housing Committee Minutes, 14-11-1950.

16. *JRIBA*, 3-1962, p. 90.
17. *AJ*, 28-3-1957, p. 452.
18. *JTPI*, 3-1959, p. 80.
19. CB, p. 83; *AJ*, p. 14-1-1962, p. 361–68.
20. Jensen, p. 56.
21. *Government Housing Act 1946*, part III of First Schedule; see *JRIBA*, 3-1947, p. 248.
22. *FH*, p. 117.
23. Jensen, p. 55–56.
24. *AJ*, p. 17-10-1957, p. 700.
25. B.S. Townroe, *Britain Rebuilding: The Slum and overcrowding Campaign* (London: Muller, 1936), p. 119 ; *B*, 5-4-1935, p. 628–29.
26. CB, p. 65.
27. CB, p. 65.
28. D. Sheppard, 'Access Arrangement in High Blocks of Flats', publ. by Department of Scientific Research, Central Office of Information, December 1962, p. 8; *LiF*, pp. 54–67; Dudley Report.
29. CB, p. 65.
30. Alison and Peter Smithson, *Urban Theories 1952–1960 and their Application in a building project 1963–1970,* (London: Faber and Faber, 1970).
31. Vere Hole, *Children's play on Housing Estates* (London: HMSO, 1966), p. 1.
32. *LiF*, p. 24–25.
33. CB, p. 41; one car: *JNHTPC*, 5/6-1962, p. 11; *OAP*, 1-1959, p. 38.
34. *AJ*, 30-10-1958, p. 635.
35. ABN, 24-6-1954, p. 754.
36. CB, p. 48; Vere Hole, *Children's play on Housing Estates* (London HMSO, 1966).
37. *AJ*, 8/15-3-1956, p. 261; G.E. Kidder Smith, *Sweden Builds* (London: Architectural Press, 1950).
38. Jensen, p. 34.
39. CB, p. 50.
40. *FH*, p. 46; *Landscaping for Flats* (MHLG *Design Bulletin*, no. 4, 2nd edition (London: HMSO, 1967).
41. *AJ*, 8-9-1960, p. 349; 'space': *AB*, 8-1958, pp. 295-300.
42. Jensen, p. 36.
43. CB, p. 44.
44. Nikolaus Pevsner, *The Englishness of English Art* (London: Architectural Press, 1956), p. 180 .
45. Four acres, *CLP*, p. 45; relaxation: Ministry of Health, *Housing Manual 1949*, p. 35; freedom: *Family Life in High Density Housing with particular Reference to the Design of Space around Buildings. Report of a Symposium* (publ. RIBA 1957), p. 10.
46. LCC Housing Committee Minutes 9-12-1959.
47. Michael Brown, 'Landscape and Housing', *OAP*, 6-1967, p. 791; *OAP*, 6-1967, p. 800–01.
48. *S*, 11-12-1970, pp. 25–29; Matthew Aitchison (ed.), *Visual Planning and the Picturesque* [on Pevsner] (Los Angeles: Getty, 2010).
49. '31 town centre plans ...' *AJ*, 14-6-1967, p. 1395; John Holiday, *A Study in British City Centre Planning* (London: Knights, 1973); John Larkham,' The Rise of the

"Civic Centre" in English Urban Form', *Urban Design*, vol. 9, 2004, pp. 3–15.
50. Hugh Wilson 'Civic Design and the Shopping Centre', *OAP*, 6-1958, pp. 271–73.
51. *AJ*, 14-6-1967, p. 1395.
52. *AJ*, 13-2-1963, p. 328.
53. *JRIBA*, 6-1956, p. 351.
54. Coventry: *ABN*, 23-10-1963, p. 29; Nottingham: Alan Simpson, *Stacking the Decks. A Study in Race, Inequality and Council Housing in Nottingham* (publ. Nottingham CRC, 1981), p. 22; Birmingham: *Birmingham Sunday Mercury*, 23-7-1967; Salford: *OAP*, 8-1963, p. 753.
55. LCC Housing Committee Minutes 19-1-1963, page 7 cf. Birmingham House Building Committee 2-6-1966.
56. [J.P. Macey], *Alphabetical List of Blocks and Streets ... Pt. III of Housing Services Handbook* (publ. LCC, 1964).
57. *MJ*, 15-8-1969, p. 2067.

CHAPTER 12 – LONDON VARIANTS

1. BILIOGRAPHICAL NOTE LONDON POST-WAR PUBLIC HOUSING. See Cox; *Annual Reports* Greater London Council Housing Department, e.g. *Annual Report* 1971–2; Greater London Council, *Housing and the GLC* (publ. London GLC, 1967); Kenneth Campbell (Foreword,) *Home Sweet Home. Housing designed by the London County Council and Greater London Council 1888–1975* (London: Academy Editions, 1976); Ken Young and John Kramer, *Strategy and Conflict in Metropolitan Housing* (London: Heineman, 1978); Herbet Wright, *London High* (London: Frances Lincoln, 2013); Simon Phipps, *Brutal London*, (Tewkesbury: September, 2016); See recent volumes of the *Survey of London* (gen. ed. Andrew Saint etc.). See also above, ch. 11, note 56. Peter Guillery and David Kroll, *Mobilising Housing Histories: Learning from London's Past* (London: RIBA Publications, 2017).

CHAPTER 13 – ENGLISH REGIONS AND WALES

1. *MJ*, 21-4-1961, p. 1297.
2. *AB*, 3-1960, p. 90; Fredrick Gibberd and others, *Harlow. The Story of a New Town* (Stevenage: Publications for Companies, 1980), p. 107.
3. Jeremy and Caroline Gould, *Coventry. The Making of a Modern City 1939–73* (London: Historic England, 2016); L. Carter and J. L. Holliday, *Post-War Council Housing in Coventry* (publ. Coventry, 1970); *MJ*, 24-10-1969, pp. 2686–94.
4. *B*, 10-5-1957, p. 871.

5. Finnimore, pp. 51, 54.
6. *B,* 18-11-1960, p. 924.
7. *B,* 6-7-1962, pp. 13–15; cf. *ABN,* 11-7-1962.
8. *S,* 20-2-1965, p. 23.
9. *S,* 27-8-1963, p. 1022; *The Master Builders' Journal* 9-1963 32.
10. *ABN,* 23-10-1965, pp. 29; *AJ,* 14-4-1981, p. 525.
11. *AJ,* 10-7-1963, p. 53.
12. *MJ,* 1-4-1960, p. 1077; cf. *ABN,* 25-7-1962, pp. 113–20.
13. Andrew Saint [ed.], *Park Hill. What next?* (publ. London Architectural Association, 1996).
14. On Womersley, see Andrew Saint, *The Image of the Architect* (London and New Haven: Yale University Press, 1983), p. 148.
15. *Ten Years of Housing in Sheffield 1953–63. The Housing Development of the City of Sheffield* (publ. Sheffield April, 1962), p. 2; cf. *B,* 27-4-1962, p. 957; *AD,* 9-1961.
16. *TB, p.* 262.
17. *MJ,* 1-4-1960, p. 1081.
18. *Ten Years,* op.cit., p. 40.
19. *Ten Years,* op.cit., p. 3.
20. *Ten Years,* op.cit., p. 4.
21. *MJ,* 7 11 1969, pp. 2793–98.
22. *MJ* 7 11 1969, pp. 2793–98.
23. David W. Lloyd, *Buildings of Portsmouth and Environments* (publ. Portsmouth, 1974); Barry Russell, *Building Systems. Industrialisation and Architecture* (London: Wiley, 1981), p. 652.
24. *TB,* 166.
25. Housing Committee Minutes 1/7-1963 (Report City Architect to Housing Committee).
26. Lyons: Barbara Simms (ed.) *Eric Lyons and Spam* (London: RIBA Publications, 2006).
27. *HJIHM* vol. III, No. 3, 9-1967, p. 15.
28. *JNHTPC,* vol. 17, 10-1962, p. 5.
29. *MJ,* 30-1-1970, pp. 211–13.
30. Brian Little, 'The impact of multi-storey housing in Bristol', *CQ* 4/6-1960), pp. 35–42.
31. *City and County of Bristol, Housing 1959–1964* (publ. Bristol, 1964), p. 14.
32. *Bristol Civic News,* no. 122, 7/8-1968.
33. *MJ,* 6-6-1969 p. 1433.
34. A.G. Sheppard Fidler, 'Post-war Housing in Birmingham', *TPR,* 4-1955, pp. 25–47 (27); Anthony Sutcliffe, 'A Century of Flats in Birmingham 1873–1973', in: Anthony Sutcliffe and Roger Smith, *Birmingham 1939–1970* (vol. 3 of *History of Birmingham*) (Oxford: OUP, 1970), pp. 181–206; *When we build again. A Study based on Research into Conditions of Living and Working in Birmingham. A Bourneville Trust Research Publication* (London: Allen & Unwin, 1941); Dunleavy.
35. Kenneth Newton, *Second City Politics, Democratic Processes and Decision-Making in Birmingham* (Oxford: Clarendon Press, 1976), p. 194.
36. *MYB,* 1971, p. 912–13.
37. Lynsey Hanley, *Estates. An Intimate History* (London: Granta, 2013).
38. *Ideal Home,* 2-1944; Herbert Manzoni, [no title page], *Duddesdon and Nechells Redevelopment Area. 44 Report* [publ. by] Council House, 27-5-1943 (British Library 8289g18).
39. *OAP,* 3-1954, pp. 118–20.
40. CB, p. 224.
41. Birmingham HCM Report 7-9-1950 'Housing Type and Associated Matters' p. 5; ABN, 15-4-1959, pp. 476–79.
42. *MJ,* 13-2-1953, pp. 329–35; Bullock, 234–37.
43. *OAP,* 1-1959, 33–38.
44. *TB,* p. 167.
45. *B,* 21-6-1957, pp. 1136–37.
46. *TB,* 251-2.
47. Dunleavy, p. 288.
48. Finnimore, p.77ff.
49. *TB,* p. 247.
50. J .A. Maudsley, 'A housing record – by system building', MJ, 24-5-1968, pp. 1289–90; AJ, 15-7-1970, p. 125; *TB, p.* 205.
51. *MJ,* 24-5-1968, pp. 1289–90.
52. *MR* 3-1964, 157–8; B. House Building Committee Civic Centre Site, B. Planning Dept. Micro 26 208.
53. *Birmingham Mail* 12-11-1965.
54. See *Sunday Mercury* 23-7-1967 (B. Library Press Cuttings).
55. Tentative manner, B. House Building Committee 18-2-1965; 32 storeys, *Birmingham Post,* 22-12-1967; glazed elevations: *Birmingham Mail,* 19-2-1965 [?]; standards: B. House Building Committee 17-3-1966; unaffordable: *Birmingham Mail,* 11-1-1971; city centre, from, *Architecture West Midlands* 6-1971 9-11.
56. *Birmingham Post,* 16-11-1972.
57. *Birmingham Mail,* 19-4-1969.
58. *MJ,* 30-8-1964, p. 3502.
59. *AD,* 8-1967, p. 453.
60. Nick Hayes, *Consensus and Controversy, City Politics in Nottingham* (Liverpool: Liverpool University Press, 1996); Chris Matthews, *Homes and Places – a History of Nottingham's Council Houses* (Nottingham: City Homes, 2015).
61. *TB,* p. 263.
62. MHLG, *Housing for single people* (*Design Bulletin 24*) (London: HMSO, 1974).
63. [Ronald Bradbury] *Liverpool Builds* (publ. Liverpool Corporation, 1967); Deirdre Morley (ed.), Margaret Cormack, *Liverpool. Housing Facts and Figures* (publ. Liverpool Council for Voluntary Service, 1981); Matthew Whitfield, *Multi-storey Housing in Liverpool during the Interwar Years*, PhD, Manchester Metropolitan University, 2010; AJ, 1-9-1965, pp. 461-9; F.T. Chen, *High Rise in Liverpool*, BA Architectural Thesis, University of Liverpool, 1988
64. City of Liverpool Housing, *Multi-storey Housing in the USA – Report of the City of Liverpool Housing Delegation* (Publ. Liverpool, 1954), pp. 40–41.
65. *JRIBA,* 3-1955.
66. *Liverpool Daily Post,* 16-9-1959.
67. *The Braddocks, John and Bessie Braddock* (London: Macmillan, 1963).
68. *JRIBA,* 6-1953, pp. 151–60.
69. *Liverpool Daily Post,* 20-9-1957.
70. *Liverpool Post,* 1-10-1957.
71. [Thomas Alker, Town Clerk]*, Liverpool Builds 1945–1965* (publ. Liverpool, 1967), p. 45.
72. B, 3-4-1963, pp. 677; *B,* 26-2-1964, p. 456; Otto Saumarez Smith, 'Central Government and Town-Centre Redevelopment in Britain', *Historical Journal,* vol. 58, no 1, 2015, pp. 217–44.
73. John J. Parkinson-Bailey, *Manchester. An Architectural History* (Manchester: Manchester University Press, 2000); Peter Shapely, Duncan Tanner, Andrew Walling, 'Civic Culture and Housing Policy in Manchester 1945–79', *Twentieth Century British History,* vol. XV, no. 4 2004, pp. 410–34; *S,* 7-7-1956; *B,* 24-6-1960, pp.1181–83; *MJ,* 10-10-1969, pp. 2576–80.
74. *S,* 30-3-1963, p. 371.
75. *TB,* p. 256; Peter Shapely, 'The Press and the System -Built Developments of Inner City Manchester 1960s–1980s', *Manchester Region History Review,* vol. XVI, 2002–03, pp. 30–39.
76. *TB,* p. 258.
77. *TB,* p. 189. Department of the Environment plan store (accessed October 1989), file HLG 131–19, note of 8-12-1960 from Cleeve Barr to Clayton.
78. Good standard *JNHTPC,* 5-1969, pp. 12–13; Wimpey: *WN,* 6-1966, p. 6.
79. *S,* 7-8-1965, p. 35; Nikolaus Pevsner, *The Buildings of England. North Lancashire* (Harmondsworth: Penguin, 1969), p.198; cf. Mark Crinson, 'The Uses of Nostalgia. Stirling and Gowan's Preston Housing', *Journal of the Society of Architectural Historians,* vol. 65, no. 2, 2006, pp. 217–37.
80. *S,* 7-8-1965, p. 35
81. Alison Ravetz, *Model Estate. Planned Housing at Quarry Hill Leeds* (Abingdon: Routledge, 2013, 1st ed. 1974*);* City of Leeds, *A Short History of Civic Housing* (publ. Leeds, 1954).
82. *MJ,* 22-1-1960, p. 257; *B,* 1-2-1957, p. 227.
83. *S,* 24-9-1960.
84. *B,* 5-5-1961, p. 843.
85. *WN,* 8-1969, p. 10.
86. Cf. pp. 28, 29.
87. *S,* 14-5-1960, p. 576.
88. *Northern Architect,* no. 18 9/10 -1964, p. 403.

CHAPTER 14 – SCOTLAND

1. *TB,* pp. 220–24.
2. Miles Horsey, *Tenements and Towers* (Edinburgh: HMSO, 1990), pp. 28–38.
3. Horsey, op. cit., p. 30–42; *B,* 12-6-1953, pp. 910–11; Glasgow Corporation, *First Quinquennial Review,* 1960, 124–32;

Glasgow Corporation, *Report on the Clearance of Slum Houses* (publ. Glasgow, 1957).

4. *Surveyor*, 6-3-1954, p. 571.
5. Scottish Record Office (SRO) file DD6-1326, note of 10-5-1957 meeting; J, 23-4-1954, 899–902; *OAP*, 10-1958, pp. 469–72; *AR, 11*-1967, pp. 348–49; interviews with I. Arnott, H. Buteux and C. Robertson, 1987. Miles Glendinning (ed.), *Rebuilding Scotland* (East Linton: Tuckwell Press, 1997), p. 20.
6. TB, 368. SRO, file DD6-2201, notes of 10-7-1961, 20-7-1961, 21-7-1961; *OAP*, 3-1958, pp.126–29.
7. E. Farmer and R. Smith, *Urban Studies*, vol.12, 1975, p. 163.
8. *Glasgow Herald*, 1-9-1963, p. 3; *Scottish Daily Express*, 28-3-1964, p. 9; interview with Sir R. Grieve, 1987.
9. Horsey, op. cit., p. 43.
10. *TB,* 222. Interview with R. Smyth, 1987. SRO, file DD6-2362, notes of 6-6-1961, 21-7-1961; DD6-2357, note of 9-6-1961.
11. Interviews with R.E. Nicoll and R. Smyth, 1987; TB, pp. 224–27.
12. *TB*, pp. 230–2.
13. Horsey, op cit., pp. 54–8; TB, pp. 170–71, 232–34.
14. *TB*, pp. 235.
15. *TB*, pp. 235–36.
16. Horsey, op. cit., pp. 56–57.
17. Interview with H. Sneddon, 1987; *TB*, p. 236.
18. J. D. Mabon, cited in Glendinning, *Rebuilding Scotland*, op. cit. pp. 50–61; Interview with J. D. Mabon, 1987.
19. Interviews with H. Sneddon, H. Brannan, J. D. Mabon, 1987; Horsey, op. cit, p. 58; *TB*, p. 246.
20. Glendinning, *Rebuilding Scotland*, op. cit. pp. 58–59; interview with H Brannan, 1987;

21. M. Glendinning, 'Cluster Homes, Planning and Housing in Cumbernauld New Town', in E. Harwood and A. Powers (eds), *Housing the 20th Century Nation* (*Twentieth Century Architecture 9*) (publ. London; 20th Century Society, 2008), pp. 132–46.
22. Interview with P. Rogan, 1987.
23. Edinburgh Central Library, City Housing Committee Minutes, 28-1-1958, 315; B, 31-1-1958, pp. 214-23; *AJ*, 6-2-1958, pp. 205–16, AJ, 7-4-1965, pp. 837–48; *TB*, pp. 237–38.
24. P. Rogan, 'Rehousing the Capital', in Glendinning, *Rebuilding Scotland*, op. cit. 66–75. Interviews with P. Rogan and G. A. Theurer, 1987; P. Rogan, *OAP* 1965, p. 1078; Edinburgh Central Library, City Housing Committee Minutes, 24-11-1959, 15-12-1959, 29-3-1960.
25. Interview with T. Watson, 1987. F. Magee, *Aberdeen Evening Express*, 13-2-1978. M. Glendinning, G. Ritchie, J. Thomas, *Aberdeen on Record, Images of the Past* (*Edinburgh*: HMSO, Edinburgh, 1997), pp. 50-2. Aberdeen City Library, City Housing Committee Minutes, 2-3-1959.
26. Glendinning, Ritchie and Thomas, op. cit., pp. 51–53.
27. Interview with J. Fleming. *Dundee Courier*, 7-2-1980, 9-2-1980, 14-3-1980, 20-6-1980; Dundee City Library, City Housing Committee Minutes, 26-4-1966.
28. M. Horsey and G. Stell, *Dundee on Record, Images of the Past* (Edinburgh: HMSO, 1992), pp. 55 and 61.
29. Horsey and Stell, *Dundee on Record*, op. cit. p. 62; *TB*, pp. 240–43.

30. SRO, file DD6-6362, memo of 24-12-1964. *TB*, pp. 315–16.
31. Interview with Nori Toffolo, 1987.
32. Glendinning, Ritchie and Thomas, op. cit., pp. 53–54.

CHAPTER 15 – GLOBAL

1. The material in this chapter derives from a personal research programme by Miles Glendinning, provisionally entitled *'The Hundred years' War: A Global History of Mass Housing'* – a project to document the global history of public social housing, especially in multi-storey blocks, during the 'long 20th century'. This multi-strand research initiative includes both broad-brush overview research into mass housing 'hotspots' across the world, combined with in-depth research into the special cases of Hong Kong and Singapore. The programme will eventually generate two major monographs, a global survey (provisional title *Mass Housing*) to be published by Bloomsbury Academic in 2020, and a Hong Kong housing history to be published by Routledge in 2022. For an interim summary of the overall research theme, see for example the following e-proceedings of a 2013 lecture in Vilnius: www.archfondas.lt/leidiniu/en/alf-03/lectures/miles-glendining

CHAPTER 16 – AFTERWORD

1. *AR*, 2-1971, pp. 69–72.
2. Ravetz, p. 106.
3. Harwood, p. xxxi.

ILLUSTRATION DETAILS

PRELIMS

C O V E R – Glasgow, Townhead Comprehensive Development, Area B, cf. p 240.
F R O N T I S P I E C E – London Swedenborg Gardens / Swedenborg Square, part of St. George's Estate, GLC Architects, contractor TMI (Thomas McInerney): [Foreword by Kenneth Campbell], *Home Sweet Home. Housing designed by the London County Council and Greater London Council Architects 1888–1975* (London: Academy Editions, 1976), p. 69, cf. p 47.vi. Courtesy London Metropolitan Archives.
vi. Birmingham, Ladywood RDA, City Architect / DLO, cf. p.188.

CHAPTER 1 – POWER SYMBOLS

page viii. Brandon, view: Allerton, Courtesy London Metropolitan Archives.; Vision 1957: *ABN*, 3-1-1957, p 8; distant view: 1961: *Architects' Journal*, 1-11-1961, p 826; 'economical fusion': *OAP*, 1-1961, p 11.
2. Lambeth: *HJIHM*, vol. VI, 5-1970.
3. Margaret Willis, 'Designing for Privacy', *Architects' Journal*, 29-5-1963, pp 1137–40.

CHAPTER 2 – STANDARDS

page 4. Sink: *MJ*, 7-2-1969, p 329.
5. Kitchen: City of Leeds, *Annual Report of the Housing Committee... to 31 March 1964* (publ. Leeds 1964).

CHAPTER 3 – WELFARE STATE PROVIDERS

page 8. The Queen: July 18 1962: Allerton. Courtesy London Metropolitan Archives.

CHAPTER 4 – COUNCIL POWERS

page 11. Stafford Cripps: *AB, 2-1954,* p 53, cf. p 114.
12. Shoreditch, Fairchild House, Pitfield Estate, 1950, with Shoreditch Housing Committee Chairman J. Samuels: *Hackney Gazette*, 27-9-1950, front page, Courtesy Archant; cf. p 106. Crossman (with Development Corporation Architect Hugh Wilson, on the right): *S*, 20-2-1965,

p 65. E. Sharp: Photo 1950 by Elliott & Fry, courtesy National Portrait Gallery.

13. Bradford: *WN*, 8-1957, p 7. E.E. Woods: *JNHTPC*, 3 / 4-1968.

14. Nottingham: *Architects' Journal*, 20-9-1956, p 415. *MR*, 10-1970, cover.

15. St. Anne's: *Architects' Journal*, 22-12-1955, p 836.

16. LLC Finance: *Housing and the GLC* (publ. by The Greater London Council, 1967), p 22, Courtesy London Metropolitan Archives.

17. Enfield: far right Eric Smythe, Housing Committee Chairman; in this case the flat was not one in a high block. *Courtesy* London Borough of Enfield Local Studies and Archive.

CHAPTER 5 – ARCHITECTS

page 20. Hilldrop: *Architects' Journal*, 17-3-1949, p 251.

21. W. Lewis: *Architects' Journal*, 19-1-1956, p. 78.

22. Preparations for a series of articles on 'Architect-Builder Co-operation' in *the Architects' Journal.* Left to right; 'N. Stanley Farrow, the builder; Ivan Tomlin, the estimator; A.W. Cleeve Barr, the architect; James Niblett, the quantity surveyor; E.F.L. Brech, the management consultant': *Architects' Journal*, 10-11-1955, p 622; also *Architects' Journal*, 23-2-1956, p 225. Cf. pp 46, 83.

23. Picton: LCC Architects, among them A.W. Cleeve Barr; engineers: Ove Arup; Building Research Station of the Central Government; contractors: Laing; *B*, 11-11-1955, p 804.

25. Bison: *OAP*, 1-1965, p 1166. *MJ* 30-12-1966, cover.

26. Wimpey: *MJ*, 18-10-1963. '5½ hrs: Manchester 9, 12-storey blocks. 8 hrs: Elizabeth Street Preston. 3½ hrs: Leeds'.

27. Wates: *IB*, 4-1963.

28. Reema: *MJ*, 18-10-1963, p 3137.

29. List: GAZ.

30, 31. 'Progress': *JNHTPC*, 1 / 2 - 1964.

CHAPTER 6 – *EXISTENZMINIMUM*

page 33. Evelyn Court: *Flats Municipal and Private Enterprise* (publ. by Ascot Gas Water Heaters Ltd, London, 1938), pp 126–31.

34. 'CRHC': *Slum Clearance and Rehousing. The First Report of the Council for Research on Housing Construction* (publ. London ,1934), pp 87–111. Breuer: *Die Form*, vol. 5, 1930, pp 115–17.

CHAPTER 8 – AESTHETICS

page 40. 1939 vignette: from S.P.B. Mais, *Fifty Years of the L.C.C.* (Cambridge: Univ. Press, 1939), p 52

41. Frederick Gibberd, *The Design of Harlow* (publ. Harlow Council, n.d., c. 1980).

42. RA: *B*, 13-5-1960, p 902.

43. Lansdowne Green, Wandsworth Road, Hartington Street, Allen Edwards Drive: *B*, 14-5-1954, pp 844–45; cf. Edmund Bird and Fiona Price, *Lambeth Architecture. A Brave New World 1945–65* (publ. Borough of Lambeth, 2014), p 97.

44. K. Browne, 'A Study of Tower Buildings in relation to Landscape', *The Architectural Review*, 3-1960, pp *175–79*.

45. Street: *OAP*, 4-1972, p 56.

46. Regent's Park Dev., with G.S. Bainbridge, Borough Engineer and Surveyor: *JRIBA*, 7-1948, p 396.

CHAPTER 9 – TYPES OF FLATS

page 48. Pimlico: YG, p 29.

50. F.R.S. Yorke and Frederick Gibberd, *Modern Flats* [1st ed.] (London: Architectural Press, 1937) pp 14–15. Thomas Sharp, p 121.

51. From the Left: Karel Teige, *Nejmenši Byt* (Prague: V. Petr, 1932, also as *The Minimum Dwelling* (Cambridge MA: MIT Press, 2002), p 305. Walter Gropius, *The New Architecture and the Bauhaus* (London: Faber & Faber, 1935), pp 104–205; also in his *The Scope of Total Architecture* (New York: Harper & Row, 1955). Below: Johannes Göderitz & oth., *Die gegliederte und aufgelockerte Stadt* (Tübingen: Wasmuth: 1957), p 28.

52. Minerva: *Architects' Journal*, 27-3-1947, p 1255. Woodberry Down: *OAP*, 4-1949, p 193. Dombey Street *The Architectural Review*, 11-1949, p 337.

53. Golden Lane: *MJ*, 7-3-1952, p 488. Golden Lane: *B*, 30-7-1954, p 164; plan: *AB*, 8-1957.

54. CLP, pp 81, 83.

55. Dolphin Square, Gordon Jones for the Costain Group, 1250 flats. Birmingham: Herbert H. Humphries City Engineer and Surveyor: Stanley Gale, *Modern Housing Estate* (London: Batsford, 1949), p 229.

57. FH, pp 22, 18, 8.

58. Loughborough Road: C.G. Weald, C. St. J Wilson, *FH*, p 20. Harlow: YG, p 32.

59. Halesowen, Remo and Mary Grenelli in association with Miall Rhys Davies: *Architects' Journal*, 22-12-1964, p 1540.

60. Willis: *HR*, 5-1954, p 5.

61. Stockholm, Sven Backström and Leif Reinius, *Architects' Journal*, 15-8-1946, p 24. Drancy, Marcel Lods and Eugène Beaudoin: Thomas Sharp, *Town Planning* (Harmondsworth: Penguin, 1940). Roehampton / Alton West: *The Architectural Review*, 1-1954, p 52. Berlin:

Gabi Dolff-Bonekämper, *Das Hansaviertel* (Berlin: Verlag Bauwesen, 1999), p 34.

62. Reigate: *Architects' Journal*, 29-8-1957, p 313. Leeds, Wellington Hill: City of Leeds, *Annual Report of the Housing Committee... to 31 March 1964* (publ. Leeds 1964).

63. Harlow Mark Hall, by Frederick Gibberd, View: Bruckmann, p 94; plan: *JRIBA*, 3-1955, p 203, cf. p.58. East Ham, Woodgrange Road, E7, Thomas E North, Borough Architect and Planning Officer: *Architects' Journal* ,17-10-1957, p 596, cf. p 104. Perkins Heights, Paddington, by Major Rolf Jensen: *MJ*, 29-1-1954, pp 201–04. Fitzhugh, Trinity Road, SW18, 1953–56, LCC Architects Rosemary Stjernstedt, Oliver Cox, Kenneth Grieb: *Architects' Journal*, 20-11-1956, p 795. Bath, Snow Hill: 1955–58, by Snailum and LeFevre for Bath Corporation: ABN, 19-11-1958, p 673; plan: *JRIBA*, 3-1955, p 203. Coventry, Tile Hill, Donald Gibson City Architect: *MJ*, 25-9-1953, p 2089, cf. p 157.

64. Ackroydon: Profile: *OAP*, 1-1951, pp 30–33; estate plan: *Architects' Journal*, 7-12-1950, p 476. Presentation:. Courtesy London Metropolitan Archives.

65. Ackroydon, Oatlands: *MJ*, 6-8-1954, pp 1807; plans: *Architects' Journal*, 7-12-1950, p 476; *MJ*, 6-8 1954, p 1806; interior 'of a typical flat': *B*, 16-7-1954, p 93.

66. Alton East: Model: *Architects' Journal*, 8-11-1951, p 548. Air: *B*, 18-12-1959, p 887.

67. Alton West, Point blocks: *JRIBA*, 7-1960, p 327. Air: Frederick Gibberd, *Town Design* (London: Architectural Press, 1962), p 296.

68. Picton: *ABN*, 20-11-1957.

69. Maisonette, built on the initiative of Leslie Martin at Purley, LCC Architects' Department, P.J. Carter, A.H. Colquhoun and Colin St. John Wilson; engineer F. J. Samuels, contractor Rush &Tompkins: *MJ*, 9-7-1954, p 1554. Mock-up, section, Interior: Living Room *B*, 24-9-1954, p 494. Cf. Sarah Menin and Stephen Kite, *An Architecture of Invitation. Colin St. John Wilson* (Aldershot: Ashgate, 2005). Interior Alton West: Bruckmann, p 87.

70. Bentham Road Estate, model, plan: *MJ*, 9-7-1954, pp 1554–55; cf. also Loughborough Road blocks, p. 113.

71. Hillgrove: cf. LCC Housing Committee Minutes 14-5-1952. Yates House, the upstairs passages serve as escape routes.

72. Craig Court, ABC Cinema Site, Area B.

73. Stifford: *ABN*, 31-1-1962, p 166. Plan: *Architects' Journal*, 28-3-1957, p 452.

75. Draper Street *New Sights of London* (publ. by LCC, n.d., c. 1960), p 75.

76. Tidey Street, later Sleaford House, Blackthorn Street, Devons Road, E3, 1962. LCC Architect A.J.M.Tolhurst: *MJ*, 16-11-1956, p 2739. Diagram scissors: *200,000 County Council Homes* (publ.

LCC 1962), p 24. Marseille: sketch
drawing Nicholas Warr.

77. Section, plans, interior: *Architects'
Journal*, 28-2-1962, pp 444, 453, 455. Royal
Victoria Yard Grove Street Bowditch,
LCC Architects' Dept., David Gregory
Jones & oth. View: *GLC Architecture
1965/70. The Work of the GLC's
Development of Architecture and Civic
Design* (publ. GLC, 1968), 24, Courtesy
London Metropolitan Archives...

78. Abbeyfield: *The Architectural Review*,
1-1965, p 56.

79. Broadwater, Gloucester Road, C.E.
Jacob and A. Weizel , LA Architects
Haringey LBC. Barbican: *New Sights
of London* (publ. by LCC, n.d., c. 1960),
p 75. Cf. Jane Alison and Anna Ferrari,
Barbican. Life, History, Architecture...
(publ. London Barbican, 2014).

CHAPTER 10 – CONSTRUCTION

page 80. Rathcoole: *MJ*, 6-5-1966, p 1447.

82. *Slum Clearance and Rehousing*..., see.
p 32. Wates: *MJ*, 23-4-1954, p 919. Box
frame: *Architects' Journal*, 14-6-1945,
p 440

83. Crosswall: *ABN*, 10-11-1955, p 580.
Brandon: *Architects' Journal*, 1-11-1961,
p 837. Roehampton: *Architects Journal*,
1-11-1959, p 1837'.

84. Woolwich: *B*, 16-12-1960, p 1122.
Liverpool, Cranmer Street, Boundary
Street, Latimer Street: [Thomas Alker,
Town Clerk], *Liverpool Builds 1945–1965*
(publ. Liverpool, 1967), p 45. Courtesy
Liverpool Record Office and Liverpool
Libraries. Lubetkin: *CB*, p 107.

85. Stramit: *MJ*, 26-4-1963.

86. Cementone: *Architects' Journal*, 5-7-1956.
Hide Tower: *Architects' Journal*, 20-10-
1960, p 58.

87. Gibberd: *JRIBA*, 1-1952, pp 79–87;
Architects' Journal, 24-2-1952, pp 118–24.

88. Aegis Grove: LCC Architects: *Ib*, 10-1962,
p 40. Aegis Grove Screen: R.J. Allerton
(ed.) / London County Council, *Housing
Service Handbook* (publ. by LCC, 1964),
Courtesy London Metropolitan Archives;
cf. p 69.

90. Sketch: *B*, 15-5-1964, p 1028.

91. Model: *Ib*, 10-1962, p 37.

92. Sectra block, construction: *B*, 22-3-1963,
pp 603. Newham Clever Road
Redevelopment, Butchers Road: *IBSC*,
12-1967, p 125. Ronan damage: Internet.

93. Top: Reema: *MJ*, 13-8-1965. Bottom:
Reema Concrete: *MJ*, 20-5-1960, p 1638.

94. Wimpey, *Rationalised Planning in
No-Fines Construction* (publ. by Wimpey,
n.d. [c. 1963]). Ramsgate: *WN*, 4-1964.

95. Finishes: Wimpey, *Redevelopment
in Wimpey No-Fines Concrete* (publ.
by Wimpey, n.d. [c. 1963]).

96. Bison Concrete Limited, *Introduction
to the Bison Wall Frame system for high

flats*, (publ. by Bison, n. d. [c. 1963]).
Cf. p 25.

97. Kidderminster (blocks now clad in brick):
MJ, 18-10-1968, p 1134. Bison Concrete
Limited, *Introduction,* op. cit.

CHAPTER 11 – ENVIRONMENT

page 99. *PM*, p 36.

100. CB, p 72.

101. 'Sociology; Windows in tall blocks,
tenants' opinions,' *Architects' Journal*,
10-7-1958, pp 64–65.

102. Birmingham: *ABN*, 18-10-1961, p 585.

103. Golden Lane: *ABN*, 6-6-1957.

104. West Ham, Thomas E. North, Borough
Architect: *Architects' Journal*,
17-10-1957, p 605.

106. Blocks in London, Fanshaw Street, N1.

107. Peter Dunham Widdup and Harrison for
Oldham CB, Royal Academy Summer
exhibition: *Architects' Journal,* 11-5-1966,
p 1180. Ballymena, £1m scheme by Munce
& Kennedy: *S*, 31-8-1963, p 1099.

111. Barnwood, North Woolwich Road,
Eastwick Field for Newham Borough
Council 1967: *MJ*, 12-5-1967, p 1279.
Norwich: design City Architect.

112. St. Pancras, *ABN*, 24-6-1954, pp 753–57.
Untitled: *Housing and the GLC* (publ.
GLC 1967), p 12, Courtesy London
Metropolitan Archives.

113. Loughborough Road: *OAP*, 9-1952,
cover, cf. p 70.

114. Stafford Cripps: *AB*, 2-1954, p 53. Cf. p 11.
Winstanley, by George, Trew,
Dunn for Battersea BC: Crawford,
p 97, cf. p.135.

115. R.P.A. Edwards, *The Tower Block* (Series:
The Changing Scene, London: Burke, 1969).

116. Lambeth: *Architects' Journal*,
14-6-1967, p 1396.

CHAPTER 12 – LONDON

page 124. Keeling: *B*, 29-11-1957, 949.
Cf. William Curtis, *Denys Lasdun.
Architecture, City, Landscape* (London:
Phaidon, 1994).

125. Grayson: *ABN* 31-12-1958; cf. *OAP*,
11-1967, pp 1623–28. Cf. 'High Flats in
Finsbury', a chapter in D.V. Donnison and
Valerie Chapman (eds.), *Social Policy
and Administration* (London: Allen and
Unwin, 1965).

126. Workmen: *Architects' Journal*, 18-8-1960,
p 246.

127. Plan: *JRIBA*, 3-1962, p 87; view: Gustav
Hassenpflug and Paulhans Peters, *Neue
Wohnhochhäuser (*Munich: Callwey,1966),
p 156; construction: *Architects' Journal*,
5-1-1961, p 20; Holford: *JRIBA*, 3-1962, p 86.

128. Avondale construction: *ABN* 27-9-1961,
p 31.

129. Avondale: drawing: *Ib*, 11-1959, p 22;
plan: p 24.

130. Sivill: Allan, pp 540–43.

131. Woolwich: *B*, 16-12-1960, p 1122.

134. The Combe, Munster Square, St. Pancras
Borough Council. A large mixed develop-
ment, with its 19 storeys the tower was,
while building, the highest in the country:
The Architectural Review, 8-1960, p 144.
Kensal Golborne Gardens, Kensington
Borough Council, designs 1958. 'Modular
Planned Flats': all measurements are
multiples of a 4-inch module. Hazelwood
Tower, Adair Tower, building from 1959:
Architects' Journal, 26-2-1959. Block
at Stockwell for the LCC at Lambeth;
Royal Academy Exhibition, 1962: *ABN*,
9-5-1962, p 673; *B*, 11-5-1962, p 964. Fifty
Roman Road, Globe Road, Bacton Street,
Bethnal Green; builders Wates, 1965–67
for Bethnal Green Borough Council *ABN*,
17-1-1968, pp 90–94.

135. Winstanley Estate, Sporle Court, Darien
Road, for Battersea LBC 1963–66,
engineer W.V. Zinn of Arup; contractors,
Wates, *IBSC*, 3-1967. Compton House,
Surrey Lane Estate, Parkham Street,
Battersea, SW11, 1969, for Wandsworth
LBC; see *Survey of London.* Kelson
House, Samuda Estate, Manchester
Road, Isle of Dogs, E 14 for LCC. Cross-
over / 'scissor' – type maisonettes,
1964. Agar Grove, for Camden Council:
Architects' Journal, 24-5-1967, p 1229.
Cf. also Basil Spence as consultant
architect for Basildon Town Centre Tower,
at RA Exhibition 1960, *B*, 13-5-1960, p 902;
see p 42.

136. Plans: *ABN*, 25-10-1967, p 890; *Architects'
Journal*, 20-8-1969, p 463; Crawford
pp 79–87. Further estates: Somerset
Estate, Westbridge Road, Battersea,
SW11, 1962;. Westbury Estate,
Wandsworth Road, SW8, 1963.

139. Lambeth: *The Architectural Review,*
1-1966, p 38.

140. *The Architectural Review,* 1-1966, p 39;
presentation: 'Tomorrow's Lambeth' at
the Royal Festival Hall; 3rd from the left
R. Crossman, Housing Minister, first from
the right: E. Hollamby, courtesy Lambeth
Borough Council. Cf. also Lambeth
Towers, 76 Kennington Road SE11, 1966.

142. Barbot Estate: Courtesy Enfield Local
Studies and Archive.

143. Plan: *S*, 20-4-1968, p 30.

144. SF 1, view in c. 1990; *S*, 11-5-1963, p 613.

146. Misleadingly also named De Beauvoir
Town; plan: Courtesy Hackney Borough
Archives.

150. Balfron:, *MJ*, 8-3-1966; side elevation:
The Architectural Review, 1-1964, p 20.

151. Trellick, view, plan, section: *Architects'
Journal,* 10-1-1973. Cf. Nigel Warburton,
Ernö Goldfinger (London Routledge,
2003); Calder.

152. Robin Hood: Alan Powers (ed.), *Robin
Hood Gardens Revisions* (publ. Twentieth
Century Society, n.d.), pp 63, 31; cf.
Alison and Peter Smithson, *Ordinariness*

and Light. Urban Theories and their application in a Building Project 1963–1970 (London: Faber & Faber, 1970).

153. World's End. Cf. Barbara Simms (ed.), *Eric Lyons and Span* (London RIBA, 2006); Internet: Municipal Dreams in Housing London.

154. Thamesmead, Woolwich / Erith Site, Stages I, II, III, (LCC 1962) GLC 1967–73; comprises 29 thirteen-storey towers. Cf. Valerie G. Wigfall, *Thamesmead. A Social History* (The History Press, 2008).

155. Cranbrook: Allan, pp 553, 549.

CHAPTER 13 – ENGLISH REGIONS

page 156. HARLOW NEW TOWN Section: Frederick Gibberd, *The Design of Harlow* (publ. Harlow Council, n.d. [c. 1970]). Map: *AB*, 3-1960, pp 90–95, cf. p. 41. Portrait: *Architects' Journal*,19-1-1956; cf. Frederick Gibberd & oth., *Harlow. The Story of a New Town* (Stevenage: Publications for Companies, 1980).

157. COVENTRY: Tile Hill: [Wimpey], *Redevelopment in Wimpey No-Fines Concrete* (publ. Wimpey n.d. [1957], p 71). Arcon: *Architects' Journal*, 1-1-1948, p 115.

158. Plans: Phoenix House: *B*, 18-11-1960, p 935. Model: *The Architectural Review*, 1-1959, p 62.

159. Hillfields: *B*, 6-7-1962, p 15. Arthur Ling City Architect with British Lift Slab [Company]: *AJ*, 28-12-1966, p 1588.

160. Jackblock: section: *B*, 2-2-1962, pp 250–51; Plan, close-up view: *B*, 20-9-1963, pp 557–58; works: *The Master Builders'* Journal, 9-1963, p 32.

161. Early design, view: *Architects' Journal*, 13-4-1961, p 527. Lady Godiva: *Architecture West Midlands, no 1 7/8-1970*, p 11.

162 SHEFFIELD: MJ, 7-11-1969, p 2793. Park Hill only: *Architects' Journal*, 31-3-1955, p 428.

163. J. Piper (copyright Architectural Press), in: *Ten Years of Housing in Sheffield 1953–1963. The Housing Development of the Corporation of Sheffield* (publ. Sheffield, 1962;), p 2. Map: *MJ*, 7-11-1969, p 2794.

164. Hyde Park: *The Architectural Review*, 11-1967, p 351. Plan: *B*, 27-4-1962, p 857.

165. Model: *Ten Years*, op. cit. p.74. Norfolk Park: *Sheffield Emerging City, prepared for the Town planning Committee* (publ. Sheffield, 1969), p.78.

166. Portsmouth, Portsdown, building from 1968: *Architects' Journal*, 6-10 1965, p 773.

167. Somerstown, maisonettes left and right by Kelsey, Hunter and Ptrs.

168. Southampton: Weston: *Southampton Echo*, 23-7-1966.

171. WALES: Cardiff: *WN*, 1-1967. Cwmbran: *Architects' Journal*, 13-2-1963, p 328. Tower: Internet.

172. BRISTOL: Redcliffe RDA: City and County of Bristol, *Housing Report of the Housing Manager...* 1-4-1956 to 31-3-1958. Canynge, St. Mary Redcliffe RDA, Block E.

175. Glendare / Brandon, City Architect Albert H Clarke and T.S. Singer, Deputy City Architects: *CQ*, 4/6-1960, pp 35–43. Plan: *B*, 29-7-1960, p 185.

176. Barton Hill, builder Holland Hannen & Cubitt: *MJ*, 5-3-1954, p 487.Hotwells: *ABN*, 2-3-1960, pp 279-80.

177. Easton Way: City and Country of Bristol, *Housing Report of the Housing Manager... from 1-4-1966 to 32-3-1968.*

178. Kingsdown: colour advertisement for Electricaire, 1969 e.g. in *MJ*, 6-6-1969. Kingsdown: *Bristol Civic News, no 122, 7/8-1969.*

179. BIRMINGHAM: Reproduced with the permission of the Library of Birmingham.

180. Manzoni: Getty Archives. Macey: *MJ*, 28-9-196, p 2924.

181. Nechells: H. J Manzoni, 'Birmingham's Post-war Homes', *Ideal Home*, 2-1944, pp 84–85. Lyon: *Flats Municipal and Private Enterprise* (publ. by Ascot Gas Water Heaters London, 1938), p 48.

182. Duddeston: Reproduced with the permission of the Library of Birmingham; see also A.G. Sheppard Fidler,' Post-war Housing in Birmingham', *TPR*, 4-1955, pp 25–47.

183. Duddeston construction: *MJ*, 2-4-1953 741; plan: *OAP*, 5-1953, p 245. Tile Cross: *OAP*, 5-1953, p 245. Aston: *CB*, p 229.

184. Millpool, Whitlock Grove, J.R. Sheridan Shedden, Deputy City Architect, J.W.Boddy, principal architect (housing); View, plan: *Architects' Journal*, 16-2-1956, p 207. Truscon: *Architects' Journal*, 18-7-1957.

185. 16-storey flats: *Architects' Journal*, 18-9-1958, p 404. Primrose Hill: *S*, 29-12-1962, p 1570.

186. Castle Vale: Photo M. Glendinning c. 1990. *Birmingham Post*, 3-6-1969. Unett Street: *Birmingham Mail*, 21-10-1966.

188. Ladywood RDA Spring Hill, Summer Hill Street. Lee Bank: *MJ*, 7-8-1964. Wilson: *WN*, 3-1966. Maudsley: *Birmingham Post and Mail* / Reproduced with the permission of the Library of Birmingham.

189. Civic Centre: *MR*, 3-1964, p 157.

190. Sentinels, early: *Birmingham Mail*, 19-2-1968. Air view: *Birmingham Mail*, 29-1-1971.

191. Plan: Courtesy Family Optima Birmingham; City of Birmingham Planning Dept.

192. Nottingham: Victoria Centre: *[Nottingham] Civic News*, 11-1968, p 1967.

193. Lenton: *Architects' Journal,* 1-10-1969, p 810.

194. Leicester: Southgate: *S*, 3-9-1966, p 15. Rowlatts Hill: *MR*, 24-6-1966.

195. L. J. Simonds, Wolverhampton Borough Architects Dept.. Drawing: *The Architectural Review*, 1-1969, p 22.

197. LIVERPOOL: Coronation Ct. first design: *MJ*, 30-5-1952, p 1060. *The Architectural Review*, 1-1955, pp 126–27.

198. Braddocks opening and slum visit: Jack Braddock, *The Braddocks* (London: Macdonald, 1963). Cresswell Mount, Anthony Street RDA, Boyd Street RDA, Northumberland Terrace, Netherfield Road: *Redevelopment in Wimpey No-Fines Concrete* (publ. Wimpey, 1957), p 36. 21 Storeys: *Liverpool Echo*, 7-10-1957.

199. Cresswell Mount: *ABN*, 23-5-1957, pp 663–67. The Braddocks: Anthony Street RDA, Arkwright Street, Ronald Bradbury City Architect with Wimpey; *WN*, 11-1957; cf. caption in *Liverpool Daily Post*, 20-9-1957.

200. RA: *B*, 20-5-1960, p 1629. Entwistle Heights: [Thomas Alker, Town Clerk], *Liverpool Builds 1945–1965* (publ. Liverpool, 1967), p 47.

202. Hartsbourne: *WN*, 3-1965. Sefton Park, Croxteth Drive: *Liverpool Builds, op. cit. 1945–1965*, p 47.

203. View 146, formerly The Landmark and Milburn Heights, Conway Street / Rose Vale RDA, Everton, 1963; builders: Unit. Kirkby: *Liverpool Builds*, op. cit., p 50. *Liverpool Builds*: Courtesy Liverpool Record Office and Liverpool Libraries.

204. Birkenhead: *B*, 7-9-1956, p 409.

205. THE MANCHESTER REGION: Heywood: *ISBC*, 4-1966, p 110.

206. Walter Greenwood Court, Albany Street: *HJIHM*, 1-1966.

207. City Engineer G. Alexander McWilliam and Surveyor, and City Architect J.H. Earle: *Architects' Journal*, 12-5-1960, p 722. Street: *The Architectural Review*, 1-1965, p 57. Air view: Salford City Libraries.

209. Experiment: 1964 *WN*, 2-1964. View: *HJIHM*, vol.5 no 1, 5-1969, pp 12–13.

210. Sandown Court, Brunswick Scheme, BDP Principal (Sir) Grenfell Baines, in charge N. Keith Scott, 1963. Oxford Street: *The Architectural Review*, 11-1967, p 346.

211. LEEDS: Saxton Gardens, Marsh Lane: City of Leeds, *A short History of Civic Housing* (publ. Leeds, 1954), p 66.

212. Ordnance Survey 1962. Point Block design: *S* ,19-1-1957, p 62; plan: *B*, 1-2-1957, p 227. Sims, Reema, Shepherd, Wimpey: *MJ*, 22-1-1960, p 256.

213. Granville Road, Lincoln Road, Lincoln Towers, Lindsey Mount Towers, Ferriby Towers, from 1958. 23-storey flats: *B*, 27-1-1961, p 176.

216. *Yorkshire Evening Post*, 20-4-1972.

219. Hull: Orchard Park, later names were Vernon and Drake Houses: *WN*, 4-1970.

220. Sunderland: Gilley Law: Neil T. Sinclair, *Sunderland City and People since 1945*

(Sunderland Echo, Breedon Books Publishing, n.d.), p 76.
221. Teams RDA, Derwentwater Road, Leslie Berry, Borough Architect. Stanley Miller, Contractor, Architect to contractor: Douglass Wise & Partners. Thornaby, Airfield Housing Dev. Site B: builder Shepherd. From *Tower Block – UK Database* University of Edinburgh www.towerblock.eca.ed.ac.uk.
222. Ravensworth Road RDA, for Whickham UDC, contractor G.M. Pearson: *Northern Perspective* 1 / 2 -1972, pp 4–5; plans: *The Architectural Review*, 1-1967, pp 30–31.
223. NEWCASTLE UPON TYNE: Cruddas Park, Scotswood Development: *MR*, 4-1963, p 236.
224. Scotswood Road Development, Westmoreland Road, with Shopping Centre.

226. Vale House, Fore Street, Springbank Road, Lansdowne Gardens: also with D. Cunningham City Housing Architect. Vale House insert: Bruce Alsop (ed.) *Modern Architecture of Northern England* (Newcastle Oriel Press 1969, p 92).
227. Byker: Internet. See Michael Drage, 'Byker...', in: Elain Harwood and Alan Powers (eds.), *Housing the Twentieth Century Nation (Twentieth Century Architecture 9;* publ. The Twentieth Century Society 2008), pp 147–74.

CHAPTER 14 – SCOTLAND

page 229. Bottom: Courtesy of City of Glasgow District Council.
230. Top: *MJ*, 23-4-1954, p 899. Bottom: Planair Ltd.

231. Spence: *The Architectural Review,* 11-1967, p 848.
232. Top: *ABN*, 20-12-1967, p 1006. Bottom: *MJ*, 5-8-1966, front cover.
235. Top: Courtesy of George Wimpey Ltd. Bottom: Courtesy of City of Glasgow District Council
237. *IB*, 2-1967, p 18.
246. Courtesy Crudens.

CHAPTER 16 – AFTERWORD

page 258. *OAP*, 2-1972, pp 107: Introduction: 'Alan Jones makes a plea for the end of what he calls Liverpool Corporation's "blitzkrieg against the inner city", and his charges answered by J.C. Amos, Liverpool's City Planning Officer'. Below: *Liverpool Daily Post,* 18-10-1957.

INDEX